Christina Latham-Koenig
Clive Oxenden
Jerry Lambert

# ENGLISH FILE

## Advanced   Student's Book A

Paul Seligson and Clive Oxenden are the original co-authors of
*English File 1* and *English File 2*

# Contents

**G** have: auxiliary or main verb?
**V** personality
**P** using a dictionary

**1A** Self-portrait

> People are pretty forgiving when it comes to other people's families. The only family that ever horrifies you is your own.
>
> *Douglas Coupland,*
> *Canadian author*

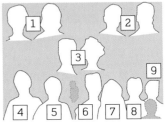

## 1 LISTENING

**a** Look at a painting by Frida Kahlo and answer the questions with a partner, giving your reasons.

1 Do you know anything about Frida Kahlo? Which person do you think is her in the painting?
2 Do you think the painting is finished? Why (not)?
3 Who do you think the people in the 'cloud' are, and why do you think they are arranged in that way?
4 What do you think the unborn child in the middle represents?
5 Who do you think the three people with blank faces in the bottom right-hand corner might be?

**b** **1 2))** Listen to an audio guide about the painting and check your answers to **a**. Then match the people below to numbers 1–9 in the diagram.

- [ ] Frida
- [ ] her maternal grandparents Antonio and Isabel
- [ ] her parents Matilde and Guillermo
- [1] her paternal grandparents
- [ ] her niece Isolda
- [ ] her nephew Antonio
- [ ] her sister Matilde
- [ ] her sister Adriana
- [ ] her sister Cristina

**c** **1 3))** Listen to **Part 1** again, about Frida. Complete Frida's biography.

### Frida Kahlo

She was born in ¹_____ in ²_____ . She was the ³_____ of ⁴_____ daughters. She caught ⁵_____ as a child, and when she was ⁶_____ years old, she was in a terrible accident when a ⁷_____ crashed into a ⁸_____ . She had previously wanted to study ⁹_____ , but after the accident she decided to ¹⁰_____ instead. Frida started work on this painting in ¹¹_____ , but never ¹²_____ it. She died in ¹³_____ at the age of ¹⁴_____ .

**d** **1 4))** Listen to **Part 2** again, about the painting. Answer the questions.

1 What is the significance of the position of the unborn child?
2 Where were her father's family from?
3 Where were her mother's family from?
4 What do we learn from the painting about her parents' marriage?
5 What was Frida's relationship like with her sister Cristina?

**e** Talk to a partner.

1 What do you think of the painting?

2 Do you have any photos of your family that you particularly like or dislike? Why?

3 Imagine that your family has been painted in the same way. Draw a quick sketch and tell your partner about the people.

## 2 SPEAKING

**a** Work in small groups. Choose one of the sets of questions below and answer them.

- Do you have any ancestors from a different country? Who were they? Where did they come from? When did they come to live in your country?

- Who are you closest to in your family? Why do you get on well? Is there anyone you don't get on with?

- Who are you most like in your family? Are there any family traits (appearance or personality) that members of your family share?

**b** You are going to discuss the statements below. First decide individually if you agree (**A**), half-agree (**HA**), or disagree (**D**) with the statements. Think of reasons and examples to support your opinion.

" You have to love your family, but you don't have to like them.

Your 'family' are the people who care about you, not necessarily your blood relatives.

It's better to be an only child than to have brothers and sisters.

Your parents brought you up, so it's your responsibility to take care of them when they're old.

When children are young it's better for one parent not to work and to look after them.

The only person who should be allowed to criticize your family is you.

You should always defend members of your family against the police, even if they have done something wrong. "

**c** (1 5)) Listen to the expressions in the box. Which words carry extra stress for emphasis? Listen again and repeat the phrases, copying the rhythm and intonation.

> **Expressions for agreeing and disagreeing**
>
> **agreeing**
> 1 I totally agree.
> 2 That's just what I think, too.
> 3 Absolutely!
>
> **half-agreeing**
> 4 I see your point, but...
> 5 I see what you mean, but...
> 6 I agree up to a point, but...
>
> **disagreeing**
> 7 I'm not sure I agree with you.
> 8 I'm afraid I don't really agree.
> 9 I don't really think you're right.
>
> British people tend not to use strong expressions of disagreement, e.g. I completely disagree, but try to soften the fact that they disagree by half-agreeing, or by using expressions like 7–9 above.

**d** Have a short discussion about the topics in **b**. Use language from **c** to agree, half-agree, or disagree with the other people in your group, and say why.

## 3 GRAMMAR *have*: auxiliary or main verb?

**a** With a partner, look at the groups of sentences 1–4. Answer the three questions for each group.

- Are all the options possible?
- Is there any difference in meaning or register?
- Is *have* a main verb or an auxiliary verb?

1 I **haven't got** time
I **don't have** time     to see my family often.
I **haven't** time

2 I**'ve been making** loads of food.  | We're having a family
I**'ve made** loads of food.           | dinner tonight.

3 **Have** we **got to**
**Do** we **have to**     dress up for the party, or is it just family?

4 I**'ve had** a portrait **painted**
I**'ve painted** a portrait     of our children.

**b** ➤ p.140 Grammar Bank 1A. Learn more about *have*, and practise it.

**c** With a partner, for each of the sentences below say if it's true for you or not, and why.

- I can't stand having my photo taken, and I'd hate to have my portrait painted.
- I've got lots of friends online, but I only have a few close friends that I see regularly face-to-face.
- I've never wanted to leave home. I really like living with my family.
- I'm the most competitive person in my family. Whenever I play a sport or game, I always have to win.
- I've got to try to get out more. I think I spend too much time at home.
- I have a few possessions that are really important to me and that I would hate to lose.
- I've been arguing a lot with my family recently.

## 4 VOCABULARY personality

**a** Look at the adjectives that describe personality below. With a partner, say if you consider them to be positive or negative qualities, and why. Would you use any of them to describe yourself?

affectionate   assertive   bossy   curious   easy-going
loyal   moody   outgoing   rebellious   reliable   sensible
sensitive   stubborn

**b** ➤ **p.160 Vocabulary Bank** *Personality.*

## 5 PRONUNCIATION using a dictionary

**a** Underline the stressed syllable in the words below.

1 con|sci|en|tious
2 de|ter|mined
3 tho|rough
4 ea|sy|-go|ing
5 stea|dy
6 spon|ta|ne|ous

**b** Look at the pink letters in each word. Match them to the sound pictures below.

  □    □    □

  □    □   □

**c** (**1 9**)) Listen and check your answers to **a** and **b**.

---

🔍 **Checking pronunciation in a dictionary**
All good dictionaries, whether paper or online, give the pronunciation of a word in phonetics, with a stress mark (') to show the stressed syllable. Online dictionaries also have an icon you can click on to hear the words, many giving both British and American pronunciation.

**needy** *adjective*

/'niːdi/ (🔊) BrE   ;   /'niːdi/ (🔊) NAmE

---

(of people) not confident, and needing a lot of love and emotional support from other people

◆ *She is shy and needy.*

---

**d** Look at the phonetics for some more adjectives of personality. With a partner, work out how they are pronounced and spelt, and say what they mean if you know. Check with a dictionary.

1 /'æŋkʃəs/   2 /'laɪvli/   3 /'nəʊzi/   4 /'səʊʃəbl/   5 /'stɪndʒi/

**e** Do you normally use a paper dictionary or an online one? What do you think are its main advantages?

## 6 READING

**a** To what extent do you think the following are good ways of predicting personality types?

- online quizzes
- personality tests
- your handwriting
- your star sign

**b** You are going to do a well-known personality test. Before you start, look at the following painting for 30 seconds. Write down what you see. You will need this when you do the test.

### LEXIS IN CONTEXT

---

🔍 **Looking up phrasal verbs and idioms in a dictionary**
**Phrasal verbs** **PHR V**
Phrasal verbs are listed in alphabetical order after the entry for the verbs.
If the object (sb or sth) is shown **between** the two parts, e.g. *put* **sth** *off*, this means the phrasal verb is separable, and the object can go between the verb and the particle **or** after the particle. If the object is shown **after** the particle, e.g. *look for* **sth**, it means the verb and the particle cannot be separated.

**Idioms** **IDM**
You can usually find the definition of an idiom under one of its 'main' words (nouns, verbs, adverbs, or adjectives, but NOT prepositions and articles), e.g. the definition of *catch your eye* will be given under *catch* or *eye*.

After some very common verbs, e.g. *be, get*, and adjectives, e.g. *good, bad*, the idioms are usually under the entries for the next 'main' word, e.g. *be a good sport* comes under *sport*.

---

**c** With a partner, look at the test *What's your personality?* Read the questions and possible answers. Try to work out the meaning of the highlighted phrasal verbs and idioms, but don't look them up yet.

**d** Use a dictionary to check the meaning of the highlighted phrases.

**e** Now do the test. For each question, decide which answer best describes you and circle it.

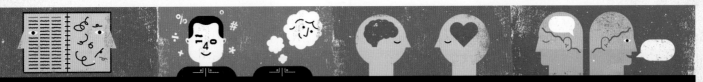

# WHAT'S YOUR PERSONALITY?

## A PLANNER OR SPONTANEOUS

**1 Are you…?**
a a perfectionist who hates leaving things unfinished
b someone who hates being under pressure and tends to over-prepare
c a bit disorganized and forgetful
d someone who puts things off until the last minute

**2 Imagine you have bought a piece of furniture that requires assembly (e.g. a wardrobe or a cupboard). Which of these are you more likely to do?**
a Check that you have all the items and the tools you need before you start.
b Carefully read the instructions and follow them to the letter.
c Quickly read through the instructions to get the basic idea of what you have to do.
d Start assembling it right away. Check the instructions only if you get stuck.

**3 Before you go on holiday, which of these do you do?**
a Plan every detail of your holiday.
b Put together a rough itinerary, but make sure you leave yourself plenty of free time.
c Get an idea of what kinds of things you can do, but not make a decision until you get there.
d Book the holiday at the last minute and plan hardly anything in advance.

## B FACTS OR IDEAS

**4 Which option best describes what you wrote about the painting in b on page 6?**
a It's basically a list of what appears in the painting.
b It tells the story of what's happening in the painting.
c It tries to explain what the painting means.
d It's a lot of ideas that the painting made you think of.

**5 You need to give a friend directions to your house in the country. Do you…?**
a write down a list of detailed directions
b give them the postcode and expect them to use a satnav
c give rough directions
d draw a simple map showing only the basic directions

**6 When you go shopping at the supermarket, do you…?**
a always go down the same aisles in the same order
b carefully check prices and compare products
c buy whatever catches your eye
d go round a different way each time, according to what you want to buy

## C HEAD OR HEART

**7 If an argument starts when you are with friends, do you…?**
a face it head-on and say what you think
b try to find a solution yourself
c try to keep everyone happy
d do anything to avoid hurting people's feelings

**8 Imagine you had the choice between two flats to rent. Would you…?**
a write down what your ideal flat would be like and then see which one was the most similar
b make a list of the pros and cons of each one
c just go with your gut feeling
d consider carefully how each flat would suit the other people living with you

**9 Imagine a friend of yours started going out with someone new, and they asked you for your opinion. If you really didn't like the person, would you…?**
a tell them exactly what you thought
b be honest, but as tactful as possible
c try to avoid answering the question directly
d tell a white lie

## D INTROVERT OR EXTROVERT

**10 You are out with a group of friends. Do you…?**
a say hardly anything
b say a little less than most people
c talk a lot
d do nearly all the talking

**11 When you meet a new group of people, do you…?**
a try to stay with people you already know
b have to think hard about how to keep the conversation going
c try to get to know as many people as possible
d just enjoy yourself

**12 If your phone rings while you are in the middle of something, do you…?**
a ignore it and continue with what you're doing
b answer it quickly, but say you'll call back
c have a conversation, but make sure you keep it short
d welcome the interruption and enjoy a nice long chat

*From* www.bbc.co.uk/science

Now find out which type you are for each section.

**A** more a and b = **PLANNER**
more c and d = **SPONTANEOUS**

**B** more a and b = **FACTS**
more c and d = **IDEAS**

**C** more a and b = **HEAD**
more c and d = **HEART**

**D** more a and b = **INTROVERT**
more c and d = **EXTROVERT**

g ➤ **Communication** *What's your personality? p.104.*
Find out which category you fit into and read the description of your personality. Compare with your partner. How accurate were the descriptions of your personalities?

**G** discourse markers (1): linkers
**V** work
**P** the rhythm of spoken English

"
Whenever you are asked if you can do a job, tell 'em
'Certainly I can'. Then get busy and find out how to do it

*Theodore Roosevelt,*
*US President 1901–1909*
"

# 1B Nice work!

## 1 READING & SPEAKING

**a** Think about people you know who either absolutely hate or really love their jobs. What do they do? Why do they feel that way? How do you know how they feel?

**b** *The Guardian* runs a weekly series called *What I'm really thinking*, where people in different jobs or situations reveal their true feelings. Look at the three jobs in the articles. With a partner, say which person you think said the following, and why.

1   Although it is not my place to judge, I get frustrated sometimes.

2   People assume you're an idiot.

3   Your expressions and bodies reveal far more than you know.

**c** Read the articles and check. Reading between the lines, do you think on the whole they like or dislike their jobs?

**d** Read the articles again and answer **A**, **B**, or **C**. Who…?

1 ☐ implies that he / she sometimes finds the job boring
2 ☐ says people seem to think he / she can't see them
3 ☐ feels misjudged by the people he / she comes in contact with
4 ☐ has to ask one particular question, to which it is not always easy to get the answer
5 ☐ would like the opportunity to give feedback on the people he / she works with
6 ☐ notices a physical change in him / herself when he / she is working
7 ☐ describes a moment when he / she really loves the job
8 ☐ suggests he / she won't be doing the job for much longer
9 ☐ tries to empathize with the people he / she speaks to

### LEXIS IN CONTEXT

**e** Look at the highlighted phrasal verbs and idioms and guess the meaning of the ones you don't know from the context. Then match them to the definitions 1–8.

1 _____ **PHR V** think they are better than sb / sth
2 _____ **IDM** makes me very upset
3 _____ **PHR V** move or make progress at the same rate as sb / sth
4 _____ **IDM** (*informal*) makes me annoyed
5 _____ **IDM** becomes exhausting
6 _____ **IDM** vitally important
7 _____ **PHR V** get bigger
8 _____ **IDM** can't think what to do or say

# What I'm really thinking

**A | THE CHECKOUT GIRL**

Of course I judge you by your shopping. It's the only diversion I have. The work isn't that intellectually demanding – the till does all the maths – and it does become robotic. Having identical conversations every day quickly gets wearing.

You get to know types of customers. The stressed-out mum, feeding her kids on the way round and thrusting the empty packet at me to scan. The sweet older couple, carefully packing cat food and biscuits into a trolley. The woman in a suit who buys a bottle of own-brand vodka, then puts it in her handbag. Sometimes I like to channel my inner Sherlock. Dark circles, nappies and aspirin? New baby. Rice cakes and spinach? The diet starts tomorrow.

Older women are very polite and chatty, but watching a queue build up as they count out pennies does my head in. Usually I take a deep breath and try to treat them as I would my own grandma. And I don't mind when people have to stay on their phone, but it is rude.

People assume you're an idiot. The fact is, I'm studying for a history degree. But that's irrelevant; neither I nor my colleagues are stupid, and people have no right to look down on us.

**B | THE UNIVERSITY LECTURER**

I look at the 23 of you in the room – a small group this year – and wonder if you're even aware of me as I teach. Might it be that because you're not talking directly to me, you forget to adjust the expressions on your faces? Or is it that you imagine, in a crowd, you are somehow invisible? Your expressions and bodies reveal far more than you know – sneering, eye-rolling, yawning, you can barely stay awake sometimes.

Your indifference bears no relation to my hours of preparation. The university asks you to comment, anonymously, on the quality of my teaching. I would like the chance to comment on the quality of your listening. When you are really disengaged and disconnected, I see hands reach for phones in bags. You connect, but it's usually to someone outside this room. Sometimes you even pass notes, giggle, and whisper.

Yet I also see you when you laugh at my jokes. When you are concentrating hard, I can almost hear your minds working. Some of you take notes so intensively, fighting to keep up with my words, as if it's life or death if you miss something. I see your faces light up when you want to say something, the eagerness to comment, to take part. You are relaxed, smiling, enjoying the moment of understanding. We connect. Now I see you and you see me.

## THE 999 OPERATOR

The hardest part of my job is also the simplest – getting the address. Often when someone calls, they go blank. Or in the case of a road accident, they don't know exactly where they are. But the most important element is the address, because that's what brings the ambulance. I have to ask for it twice, which infuriates people.

It still surprises me to hear my voice during a call. It changes, becoming deeper, almost authoritative. I have to take control of the situation. I suppose that's why I wear a uniform. I have a script, but I refuse to be a robot; hearing people at their most vulnerable makes me add to it. When the caller is hysterical, telling them, 'I'm going to help you' and 'I know you're frightened' calms them down. But it breaks my heart when they're in pain or their loved one is dying; I have to take a 'stress break' after harrowing calls.

Although it is not my place to judge, I get frustrated sometimes. The man who rang because his toothpaste was burning his mouth; the mother whose baby was afraid of a fly. Don't they realize they're taking up precious time when a life-or-death situation may be needing help? But the moment I call them time-wasters is the moment I should quit my job.

**f** Look at some extracts from other *What I'm really thinking* articles. Match them to the jobs in the list. What do they imply that the people (sometimes) feel about their jobs?

beauty counter manager ☐   dentist ☐   driving instructor ☐
IT support worker ☐   pizza delivery man ☐   taxi driver ☐

1   Sometimes what I do is painful, and I'm not a sadist.

2   I don't expect to chat, but sometimes my cab becomes a mobile confessional.

3   Men are risk-takers. They go too fast and don't like being told what to do.

4   I'd like some respect – people who answer the door while they're on the phone really bug me, as do the ones who take ages to find the money.

5   It's a cliché, but 'Have you turned it on and off again?' is the first thing that comes to my mind every single time someone calls.

6   I work in an industry that convinces people to part with their cash in pursuit of a perfection that does not exist. I am betraying my sisterhood.

**g** Of all the jobs mentioned in the articles and extracts, which one(s)…?
   • would you never do under any circumstances
   • might you consider doing if you desperately needed the money
   • would you actually quite like to do

## 2   VOCABULARY work

**a** Look at three sentences from the articles and complete the missing words.
   1   The work isn't that intellectually **d**_____.
   2   …neither I nor my **c**_____ are stupid, and people have no right to look down on us.
   3   But the moment I call them time-wasters is the moment I should **qu**_____ my job.

**b** ➤ p.161 Vocabulary Bank *Work*.

**c** Complete sentences 1–5 with words or phrases from the list. Then write five sentences for your partner to complete with the other five words.

apply for   be fired   be laid off   clock off
perks   quit   rewarding   skills   tedious   unpaid

1   Can we leave whenever we like or do we have to _____ at a certain time?
2   Nursing is often described as a _____ job, even though it may be badly paid.
3   The company has decided that around 20% of its workforce will have to _____ until the economic situation improves.
4   The only _____ required for this post are a good level of English and the ability to drive.
5   If you are prepared to do _____ work, there are several voluntary organizations that are looking for people.

## 3 SPEAKING & LISTENING

**a** Since 2001, the *Sunday Times* has been running an annual survey to find the 100 best companies in the UK to work for. Look at the criteria which they use to assess the companies and complete them with the headings.

**Fair deal**
**Giving something back**
**Leadership**
~~**My company**~~
**My manager**
**My team**
**Personal growth**
**Well-being**

1   *My company*   : how staff feel about the organization they work for as opposed to the people they work with

2 _____ : how staff feel about the pressures of work and the balance between their work and home duties

3 _____ : how much companies are thought by their staff to contribute to the local community and society

4 _____ : to what extent staff feel they are stretched and challenged by their job

5 _____ : how staff feel towards their immediate boss

6 _____ : how employees feel about the head of the company and its senior managers

7 _____ : how staff feel about their immediate colleagues

8 _____ : how happy the workforce is with their pay and benefits

**b** Which three criteria do you think are the most important when judging a company you are thinking of working for?

**c** Now look at the photos and read about Skyscanner, a travel comparison website, one of the top-rated companies in last year's survey. Does it sound like a company you would like to work for? Why (not)?

skyscanner

English (EN) GBP £ Change ▼

## Who are they?

AS A KEEN SKIER who regularly escaped to the slopes, maths graduate Gareth Williams became frustrated with the tedious process of searching through a multitude of airline and travel-agency websites to find the cheapest flights. So he and two university friends set about creating a single website that could collect, collate, and compare prices for every commercial flight in the world. Launched in Edinburgh in 2001, Skyscanner, which also provides instant online comparisons for hotels and car hire, gets more than 60 million visitors a month and now operates worldwide – it also has offices in Singapore, Beijing, Miami, and Barcelona. No organization offers as many opportunities to learn and grow as this one does, say its employees. Skyscanner perks include a paid day off to do a social activity, and home-country working, where people who aren't native to the UK can spend up to three weeks a year working in their country of origin. As the staff represent more than 35 different nationalities, this is a particularly popular benefit.

| Skyscanner statistics: | |
| --- | --- |
| Male / female ratio | 70:30 |
| Average age | 32 |
| Earning £35,000+ | 36% |

**d** (1 13)» Listen to an interview with Lisa Imlach, who works for Skyscanner. What is her position in the company? How positive is she about the company and her job on a scale of 1–5 (5 = very positive)? What makes you think so?

> **Glossary**
> **PR** Public Relations

**e** Now listen again and answer the questions.

1 How long has Lisa been at Skyscanner?
2 Why did she apply for a job there?
3 Where did she go the day after the interview, and where was she when she heard she'd got the job?
4 What three benefits does she mention about working for Skyscanner?
5 Which benefit does she value most highly and why?
6 What challenge does she say that the company faces?

**LEXIS IN CONTEXT**

**f** (1 14)» Listen to the phrases in context. What do you think the highlighted words and phrases mean?

1 …somewhere that was kind of travel-focused…
2 …it very quickly becomes the norm for someone who works here…
3 …maybe that's the plan, maybe that's the ploy that they've gone with!
4 …it's quite a casual thing…you're in charge, you're the, you're the one who knows your workload…
5 …so I think at some point that will be something that becomes more of an issue…I'm pretty confident that Skyscanner will be able to tackle that…

**g** What do you think of Skyscanner after listening to Lisa's interview? Are you more or less attracted to working there?

## 4 GRAMMAR discourse markers (1): linkers

> …it very quickly becomes the norm for someone who works here, all these amazing benefits we have, _____ when you talk to someone else in another company, you suddenly think 'Wow, we're so lucky'.

**a** Look at the extract from Lisa's interview. What do you think the missing word is? What kind of clause does it introduce?

**b** With a partner, put two linkers from the list into each column.

> as consequently despite due to even though in order to so as to therefore

| a result | a reason | a purpose | a contrast |
|----------|----------|-----------|------------|
| so | because | to | but |

**c** ▶ p.141 Grammar Bank 1B. Learn more about linkers, and practise them.

## 5 PRONUNCIATION the rhythm of spoken English

> 🔍 **Fine-tuning your pronunciation: the rhythm of English**
> In spoken English, words with two or more syllables have one main stressed syllable. In sentences, some words have stronger stress and other words are weaker. This pattern of strong and weak stress gives English its rhythm. Stressed words in a sentence are usually **content words**, e.g. nouns, verbs, adjectives, and adverbs. Unstressed words tend to be **function words** and include auxiliary verbs, prepositions, conjunctions, determiners, and possessive adjectives.

**a** (1 15)» Listen and repeat the sentences. Try to copy the rhythm as exactly as possible.

> London Underground workers were on strike yesterday. As a result, it took people twice as long to get to work.

**b** (1 16)» Listen and write down the beginnings of eight sentences. Compare with a partner, and then decide how you think the sentences might continue.

**c** (1 17)» Now listen and complete the sentences. Are they similar to what you predicted? Practise saying them with a natural rhythm.

## 6 WRITING

▶ p.112 Writing *A job application*. Analyse a model email and write a covering email applying for a job at a festival.

## 7 (1 MP3)» SONG *We Work The Black Seam* ♬

# 1 Colloquial English    Talking about...

## 1 ▶ THE INTERVIEW Part 1
VIDEO

**a** Read the biographical information about Eliza Carthy. Have you ever heard any English, Scottish, or Irish folk music?

> **Eliza Carthy** is an English folk musician known both for singing and playing the violin. She is the daughter of singer / guitarist Martin Carthy and singer Norma Waterson, who are also English folk musicians. In addition to her solo work, she has played and sung with several groups, including as lead vocalist with Blue Murder. She has been nominated twice for the Mercury Music Prize for UK album of the year and has won seven BBC Folk Awards. In 2010 she released an album of collaborations with her mother, entitled *Gift*. A BBC reviewer wrote: 'The gift in question here...is a handing of talent from generation to generation'.

**b** (1 19)) Watch or listen to **Part 1** of the interview. What is her overwhelming memory of her childhood?

**c** Now listen again. What does she say about…?

1 her father in the 50s and 60s
2 The Watersons
3 her mother's grandmother
4 her mother's uncle and father
5 *The Spinning Wheel*
6 the farm where she was brought up
7 her parents' friends

> **Glossary**
> **Bob Dylan** (b.1941) an American singer-songwriter, who has influenced popular music and culture for more than five decades
> **Paul Simon** (b.1941) an American singer-songwriter, at one time half of the duo Simon and Garfunkel
> **Hull** /hʌl/ a city in Yorkshire, England
> **travellers / gypsies** people who traditionally travel around and live in caravans
> **banjo** a musical instrument like a guitar, with a long neck, a round body, and four or more strings
> ***The Spinning Wheel*** an Irish ballad written in the mid-1800s

## ▶ Part 2
VIDEO

**a** (1 20)) Now watch or listen to **Part 2**. What do you think Eliza Carthy was like as a child? What do you find out about her as a mother?

**b** Listen again and answer the questions.

1 Did Eliza Carthy originally want to become a musician?
2 Why did her mother retire?
3 How old was she at her first public performance?
4 How much did she sing during the concert?
5 How has she reorganized her life because of having her own children?
6 What does she feel she's lacking at the moment?

> **Glossary**
> **the Fylde** /faɪld/ an area in western Lancashire, England
> **Fleetwood** a town in the Fylde
> **the Marine Hall** a venue in Fleetwood

## ▶ Part 3
VIDEO

**a** (1 21)) Now watch or listen to **Part 3**. How has Eliza Carthy's family influenced her approach to music?

**b** Listen again. Mark the sentences **T** (true) or **F** (false). Correct the false sentences.

1 Eliza Carthy thinks the reason she doesn't like working alone is because of being brought up surrounded by people.
2 At the moment she has a 30-piece band.
3 Her father understands that working with family members is different.
4 Her father was a blood relation in the group The Watersons.
5 Eliza Carthy's daughter Florence plays three musical instruments and also sings well.
6 She thinks there's a close link between foreign languages and singing.
7 Her younger daughter Isabella is not yet interested in music.
8 She would rather her children didn't become touring musicians.

> **Glossary**
> **Twinkle, Twinkle** a well-known children's song (*Twinkle, twinkle little star, How I wonder what you are…*)

12

# ork and family

## LOOKING AT LANGUAGE

**Discourse markers**
Eliza Carthy uses several discourse markers when she speaks, that is, adverbs (e.g. *so*, *anyway*) or adverbial expressions (e.g. *in fact*, *after all*) which connect and organize language, and help you to follow what she is saying.

**1 22 ))** Watch or listen to some extracts from the interview and complete the gaps with one or two words.

1 'and they were also instrumental in the beginning of the 60s folk revival, the formation of the folk clubs, and the, the beginning of, _____, the professional music scene that I work on now.

2 **Interviewer:** 'And were your parents both from musical families?'
   **Eliza:** 'Um, _____, both sides of my family are musical...'

3 'My mum retired in 1966 – 65 / 66 from professional touring to raise me. _____ _____, the road is a difficult place...'

4 'But yes, _____ I just – the first song they started up singing, tugged on his leg...'

5 **Interviewer:** 'Has having children yourself changed your approach to your career?'
   **Eliza:** 'Er, yes, _____ a _____, yes, _____ a _____, it has.'

6 'The Watersons was a brother and two sisters, and he joined that, and _____ _____ he was married to my mum, but he wasn't related to her.'

7 'And Isabella, my youngest as well, she's really, she's really showing interest in it, I love it when they do that. _____ _____ whether or not I'd want them to be touring musicians...'

8 'But, you know, I think the – I think the world is changing _____, I don't know how many touring musicians there are going to be in the world in 20 years...'

b How do the discourse markers affect the meaning of what Eliza says in each extract?

## 3 ◀ IN THE STREET
VIDEO

a **1 23 ))** Watch or listen to five people talking about their family trees. Who mentions foreign ancestors? Where were they from?

Tom, *English*   Kent, *American*   Alison, *English*   Marylin, *American*   Hannah, *American*

b Watch or listen again. Who (**T, K, A, M,** or **H**)...?

☐ has an ancestor who died in a famous disaster
☐ has traced their family tree back almost 1,000 years
☐ has tried unsuccessfully to contact some distant relatives
☐ has used www.ancestry.com to research their family tree
☐ thinks their ancestors worked on the land

c **1 24 ))** Watch or listen and complete the Colloquial English phrases. What do you think they mean?

1 'Er, my dad's _____ _____ genealogy and the family tree...'
2 'Um, 'cause I think they were farmers, I'm not _____ _____...'
3 'Um, I know a _____ _____ because, um, my dad's done some research...'
4 'Um, well, _____ _____, it's precisely those relatives...'
5 '...but it doesn't _____ _____ _____ than that and that's only on my dad's side.'

**Glossary**
**Durham** /'dʌrəm/ a city in the north of England
**Cornwall** a county in the south-west of England
**Prohibition** in the USA, a national ban on alcohol in the 1920s and 30s

## 4 SPEAKING

Answer the questions with a partner or in small groups.

• How much do you know about your family tree? Have you ever researched it?
• Is there anyone in your family that you'd like to know more about?
• Do you know anyone who works in a family business? How well do the relationships work?
• Would you like to work with your parents or with your siblings? Why (not)?
• Do you think it's easier or more difficult for the children of successful parents to be successful themselves?

**G** pronouns
**V** learning languages
**P** sound–spelling relationships; understanding accents

> Americans who travel abroad for the first tim
> are often shocked to discover that many forei
> people still speak in foreign language
>
> *David Barry,*
> *US writer*

# 2A Changing language

## 1 SPELLING

**a** **①25》** A recent survey found the ten words most commonly misspelt by British people. Listen to sentences 1–10 and complete the missing words. How many did you spell correctly? What do many of the words have in common?

1  He always _____ to his father as 'my old man'.

2  I like all vegetables except _____ .

3  The food was _____ , but no more than that.

4  I think taking the dog with us is an _____ complication.

5  There was a _____ of opinion that the article should not be published.

6  It was a very strange _____ .

7  Please don't _____ me by wearing that hat!

8  In your driving test you will be asked to perform some standard _____ .

9  We'll _____ be there by seven.

10  They married in 2010, but _____ two years later.

**b** **①26》** Now listen to the following poem. Find nine spelling mistakes of a different kind. What is the message of the poem?

> I have a spelling checker
>
> It came with my PC
>
> It plainly marks for my revue
>
> Mistakes I cannot sea
>
> I've run this poem threw it
>
> I'm sure your pleased to no
>
> It's letter-perfect in it's weigh
>
> My checker tolled me sew

## 2 READING & SPEAKING

**a** With a partner, decide how to pronounce the following words. Do you know what they all mean?

**b** Read the review on p.15 of *Spell it out*, a book about the story of English spelling. What do you learn about the spelling and pronunciation of the words in **a**?

### LEXIS IN CONTEXT

**Making sense of whole phrases**
Even when you understand the individual words in a text, you may still have problems understanding the meaning. When you read, focus on whole phrases or sentences, and refer to the surrounding context to work out what the writer is saying.

**c** Read the review again and look at phrases 1–6 in context. In pairs, say what you think the reviewer means.

1  he was bewildered by the random nature of English spelling (lines 11–12

2  Fashion and snobbery have played as big a part in spelling as they hav in other parts of English life. (lines 26–27)

3  scribes looked to Latin for guidance (line 29)

4  For a long time, there was no stigma attached to variant spellings. (line 3

5  Even today, spelling is more fluid than we might think. (line 41)

6  the internet is the ultimate spelling democracy (line 43)

**d** Answer the questions in small groups.

1  How do you think the reviewer feels towards students of English? Do you agree?

2  What modern example does she give of the damaging effects of bad spelli

3  Are there any words in your language which people have particular problems spelling? Why (not)?

4  Do you think good spelling matters?

Have you ever wondered why *ghost* is spelt with an *h*? Why isn't it 'gost' or 'goast' to rhyme with 'most' or 'toast'? Other words that begin with a hard *g*, such as 'golf', don't have an *h*. The answer, according to David Crystal's entertaining *Spell it out*, is a result of the whim of a Flemish compositor, a man whose job it was in the late 15th century to arrange type for printing. His English wasn't good, and, like many non-native speakers, he was bewildered by the random nature of English spelling. So when he saw the word 'gost' (spelt 'gheest' in Flemish) he decided to spell it the Flemish way, with an *h*.

The Flemish *h* in *ghost* is one of Crystal's many examples that show that the development of English spelling has been both random and unsystematic. The original monks who tried to write down Anglo-Saxon English in a Latin alphabet, he says, did a pretty good job. Every word was pronounced phonetically – so the *g* in *gnome* would be pronounced, as would the *k* in *know*. But the alphabet they devised didn't have enough letters to represent all the sounds in spoken English and that was where the problems started. Scribes started to double vowels to represent different sounds, such as double *o* for the long /uː/ sound in *moon, food*, etc. But then in some words like *blood* and *flood* the pronunciation changed in the south of England, shortening the vowel, so that now, as Crystal puts it, 'these spellings represent the pronunciation of a thousand years ago.'

Fashion and snobbery have played as big a part in spelling as they have in other parts of English life. After the Norman invasion, Anglo-Saxon spellings were replaced by French ones: *servis* became *service*, *mys* became *mice*, for instance. During the Renaissance, scribes looked to Latin for guidance – take the word *debt*. In the 13th century this could be spelt *det*, *dett*, *dette* or *deytt*. But 16th-century writers looked to the Latin word *debitum*, and inserted a silent *b* – linking the word to its Latin counterpart but making it much harder to spell.

For a long time, there was no stigma attached to variant spellings. Shakespeare famously wrote his name several ways (Shaksper, Shakspere, Shakspeare), but, by the 18th century, an English aristocrat was writing to his son that 'orthography…is so absolutely necessary for a man of letters, or a gentleman, that one false spelling may fix a ridicule upon him for the rest of his life.' Dan Quayle, the former US vice-president, never recovered from spelling *potato* with an *e* on the end when he corrected a pupil's writing in front of the cameras at a junior school in 1992.

Even today, spelling is more fluid than we might think. *Moveable*, for example – *The Times* style guide keeps the *e*, *The Guardian* prefers *movable*. And online there are no guides – the internet is the ultimate spelling democracy. Take *rhubarb*, with its pesky silent *h*: in 2006 there were just a few hundred instances of *rubarb* in the Google database; they have now passed the million mark. 'If it carries on like this,' Crystal notes, '*rubarb* will overtake *rhubarb* as the commonest online spelling…And where the online orthographic world goes in one decade, I suspect the offline world will go in the next.'

Reading this book made me thankful that English is my native language; the spelling must make it so fiendishly hard to learn!

*By Daisy Goodwin in the Sunday Times*

**Glossary**
**Flemish** /ˈflemɪʃ/ from Flanders, the northern part of present-day Belgium
**monk** /mʌŋk/ a member of a religious group of men who often live apart from other people in a monastery
**scribe** /skraɪb/ a person who made copies of written documents before printing was invented
**the Norman Invasion** the occupation of England in 1066 by the Normans, who came from the north of France
**orthography** /ɔːˈθɒɡrəfi/ (*formal*) the system of spelling in a language

# 3 PRONUNCIATION
sound–spelling relationships

> 🔍 **Learning spelling rules or patterns**
> Although many people think that English pronunciation has no rules, especially regarding sounds and spelling, estimates suggest that around 80% of words are pronounced according to a rule or pattern, e.g. the letter *h* before a vowel is almost always pronounced /h/.

**a** With a partner, say each group of words aloud. How are the pink letters pronounced? Circle the different word if there is one.

1 /h/ hurt dishonest inherit heart himself
2 /əʊ/ throw elbow lower power grow
3 /aɪ/ compromise despite river write quite
4 /w/ whenever why whose where which
5 /dʒ/ jealous journalist reject job enjoy
6 /tʃ/ challenging achieve chorus catch charge
7 /s/ sense seem sympathetic synonym sure
8 /ɔː/ awful raw flaw drawback law
9 /ɜː/ work world worse worth reporter
10 /ɜː/ firm dirty third T-shirt birth

**b** ⏺ **1 27** ))) Listen and check. What's the pronunciation rule for each spelling? Can you think of any more exceptions?

**c** Think about the spelling patterns in **a**. How do you think these words are probably pronounced? Check their pronunciation and meaning with your teacher or with a dictionary.

chime   howl   jaw   whirl   worm

# 4 GRAMMAR pronouns

**a** ⏺ **1 28** ))) Look at the phonetics for a word which is often misspelt, but never corrected by spell checkers. How is it pronounced? Listen and check.

/ðeə/

**b** Now complete the gaps with three different spellings of the word in **a**.

1 _____ pronoun + contracted verb
2 _____ adverb
3 _____ possessive adjective

**c** ➤ **p.142 Grammar Bank 2A**. Learn more about pronouns, and practise them.

## 5 VOCABULARY learning languages

**a** Look at the section headings 1–4 in *Working with words*. With a partner, say what they mean.

**b** Do the exercises in *Working with words*. Then compare with a partner.

# Working With Words

## 1 Collocations

**Complete with *say*, *speak*, *talk*, or *tell*.**

1 I can _____ three languages fluently: English, French, and German.
2 _____ me the truth. Did you <u>really</u> do this yourself?
3 This situation can't go on. We need to _____ .
4 What did you _____? I couldn't hear you because of the noise.
5 Did you _____ Mark about the party next week?
6 Hi. Could I _____ to Gill, please? It's Jane here.
7 You could learn the basics in, let's _____ , six months.
8 Sorry, I can't _____ now. I'm in a meeting.

## 2 Phrasal verbs

**Match the phrasal verbs in 1–5 to their meanings A–E.**

1 ☐ I spent a month in Florence and I was able to **pick up** quite a bit of Italian.
2 ☐ I'll need to **brush up** my Spanish before we go to Mexico. I haven't spoken it since university!
3 ☐ **A** How will you manage in Germany if you don't speak the language?
   **B** I think I'll be able to **get by**. I can speak a bit of German and most people speak some English.
4 ☐ Your pronunciation is fantastic. You could almost **pass for** a local!
5 ☐ Even though my English is fluent, I found it hard to **take in** what my boss said in the meeting because he spoke so fast.

A be accepted as sb / sth
B to quickly improve a skill, especially when you haven't used it for a long time
C to absorb, understand
D to learn a new skill or language by practising it rather than being taught
E to manage to live or do a particular thing using the money, knowledge, equipment, etc. that you have

## 3 Synonyms and register

**a Match the words or expressions 1–5 to synonyms A–E.**

| | | | |
|---|---|---|---|
| 1 | error | A | respond to sb |
| 2 | answer sb | B | language |
| 3 | request sb to | C | vocabulary |
| 4 | tongue | D | mistake |
| 5 | lexis | E | ask sb to |

**b Which word is more formal in each pair?**

## 4 Idioms

Your father isn't well, is he?

How's your father?

**Match sentences 1–5 to A–E.**

1 ☐ I think we're talking at cross purposes.
2 ☐ The word's on the tip of my tongue.
3 ☐ I'm terribly sorry, I got the wrong end of the stick.
4 ☐ I just can't get my tongue round this word.
5 ☐ I can't get my head round this definition.

A I was asking you about your family, but you're telling me about mine!
B It's really hard for me to pronounce.
C It's too complicated and I can't understand it.
D I can't remember it at this moment, but I'm sure I will soon.
E When you said 'lunch on Sunday' I thought you meant this Sunday, not next Sunday.

## 6 PRONUNCIATION understanding accents

**a** **1 29 ))** Listen to six people talking with different native-speaker accents. Which one speaks with RP? Write the speaker's number in the 'England' box. Can you match any of the other accents?

1 Mairi

2 Diarmuid

3 Jerry

4 Andrea

5 Lily

6 Paul

- ☐ Australia
- ☐ Ireland
- ☐ England (RP)
- ☐ Scotland
- ☐ South Africa
- ☐ the USA

**b** **1 30 ))** Listen and check. Are you familiar with any of these accents? Which ones, and why?

## 7 LISTENING

**a** You're going to hear Joanna from Poland, who has lived in the UK for several years, answering some questions about her experiences of being a non-native speaker of English. Before you listen, answer questions 1–3 with a partner.

1 Are there any native speaker accents that you find especially difficult to understand?
2 How comfortable do you feel with your own accent?
3 Do you find it easier to understand native or non-native speakers of English?

Joanna and her son on the beach near Buckie

**b** **1 31 ))** Now listen to Joanna. How does she answer the questions? How easy do you find it to understand her accent?

**c** Listen again. What does she say about...?
- *No Country for Old Men*
- a Polish-English phonetics class
- sounding posh
- strong regional or foreign accents

**d** Answer questions 4–7 with a partner.
4 How do you feel about having your English corrected?
5 Is there anything you still find difficult about English?
6 Do you feel in any way a different person when you're speaking English compared to when you're speaking in your own language?
7 Do you have any stories about not understanding someone?

**e** **1 32 ))** Now listen to Joanna. How does she answer the questions?

**f** Listen again. What does she say about...?
- being corrected by a person who isn't friendly
- the word *intrepid*
- writing emails in Polish
- the expressions *bairn* and *doon the brae*

**g** Were any of Joanna's answers the same as yours? What else did she say that you identified with?

G the past: habitual events and specific incidents
V word building: abstract nouns
P word stress with suffixes

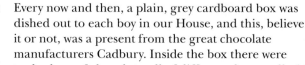

> Children begin by loving their parents;
> after a time they judge them; rarely,
> do they forgive them.
>
> *Oscar Wilde,*
> *Irish dramatist*

# 2B Do you remember...?

## 1 READING

a Imagine that you were going to write your autobiography. Where would you start? What periods of your childhood or specific incidents would you definitely include?

b **1 33 )))** You're going to read and listen to an extract from *Boy*, the autobiography of author Roald Dahl. Read and listen to **Part 1** and answer the questions with a partner.

1 Why did the chocolate bars have numbers stamped underneath them?
2 What do you think was the point of the control bar?
3 What exactly did the boys have to do?
4 Why was it clever of Cadbury's to use the boys?
5 How did they behave when they were sampling the products?

c **1 34 )))** Now do the same for **Part 2**.

1 How did Roald Dahl imagine the 'inventing room' to be?
2 What would he sometimes imagine himself doing?
3 How did he imagine Mr Cadbury reacting to his invention?
4 What effect did the testing of the chocolate bars have on Dahl in later life?

### LEXIS IN CONTEXT

> 🔍 **Understanding dramatic language**
> A good writer will often use dramatic verbs to make the action in a scene come alive. In this text, **Part 1** narrates a sequence of events, but in **Part 2** Roald Dahl achieves a more dramatic, imaginative effect, partly through his choice of vocabulary.

d Read **Part 2** again carefully. Find more dramatic synonyms for the following verbs.

1 _____ imagine
2 _____ cook
3 _____ create by mixing together
4 _____ take quickly (in one's hand)
5 _____ run quickly
6 _____ jump
7 _____ hit (with the hand)

e What kind of child do you get the impression that Roald Dahl was? When you were a child, what did you use to dream of doing?

## Part 1

1 Every now and then, a plain, grey cardboard box was dished out to each boy in our House, and this, believe it or not, was a present from the great chocolate manufacturers Cadbury. Inside the box there were
5 twelve bars of chocolate, all of different shapes, all with different fillings and all with numbers from one to twelve stamped underneath. Eleven of these bars were new inventions from the factory. The twelfth was the 'control' bar, one that we all knew well, usually a Cadbury's Coffee
10 Cream bar. Also in the box was a sheet of paper with the numbers one to twelve on it as well as two blank columns, one for giving marks to each chocolate from nought to ten, and the other for comments.

   All we were required to do in
15 return for this splendid gift was to taste very carefully each bar of chocolate, give it marks, and make an intelligent comment on why we liked or disliked it.
20 It was a clever stunt. Cadbury's were using some of the greatest chocolate-bar experts in the world to test out their new inventions. We were of a
25 sensible age, between thirteen and eighteen, and we knew intimately every chocolate bar in existence, from the Milk Flake to the Lemon Marshmallow. Quite obviously our opinions on anything new would be valuable. All of us entered into this game
30 with great gusto, sitting in our studies and nibbling each bar with the air of connoisseurs, giving our marks and making our comments. 'Too subtle for the common palate' was one note that I remember writing down.

> **Glossary**
> **House** many UK boarding schools are divided into 'Houses' and each student belongs to one; Houses may compete with one another in sports and other activities, thus providing a focus for group loyalty
> **with great gusto** (*old-fashioned*) with enthusiasm and energy

# Part 2

For me the importance of all this was that I began to realize that the large chocolate companies actually did possess inventing rooms and they took their inventing very seriously. I used to picture a long white room like a laboratory, with pots of chocolate and fudge and all sorts of other delicious fillings bubbling away on the stoves, while men and women in white coats moved between the bubbling pots, tasting and mixing and concocting their wonderful new inventions. I used to imagine myself working in one of these labs, and suddenly I would come up with something so unbearably delicious that I would grab it in my hand and go rushing out of the lab and along the corridor and right into the offices of the great Mr Cadbury himself. 'I've got it, Sir,' I would shout, putting the chocolate in front of him. 'It's fantastic! It's fabulous! It's marvellous! It's irresistible!' Slowly the great man would pick up my newly-invented chocolate and he would take a small bite. He would roll it round his mouth. Then all at once he would leap from his chair crying, 'You've got it! You've done it! It's a miracle!' He would slap me on the back and shout, 'We'll sell it by the million! We'll sweep the world with this one! How on earth did you do it? Your salary is doubled.'

  It was lovely dreaming those dreams, and I have no doubt at all that thirty-five years later, when I was looking for a plot for my second book for children, I remembered those little cardboard boxes and the newly-invented chocolates inside them, and I began to write a book called *Charlie and the Chocolate Factory*.

**Glossary**
**fudge** /fʌdʒ/ a type of soft, brown sweet made from sugar, butter, and milk

## 2 GRAMMAR the past: habitual events and specific incidents

**a** Look at the highlighted verbs in **Part 2** of the extract from *Boy*. Which ones describe…?

1 specific incidents in the past
2 repeated or habitual actions in the past

**b** What other verb forms could you use for 1 and 2?

**c** ➤ p.143 Grammar Bank 2B. Learn more about verb forms for describing habitual events and specific incidents in the past, and practise them.

## 3 SPEAKING & WRITING

**a** (1 35)) Listen to six people talking about their childhood. What are the different expressions they use to say (approximately) how old they were at the time?

**b** With a partner, choose two of the topics below and talk about things you habitually did or felt in your childhood.

### things I used to be afraid of
### my primary school
### places we would go to for family holidays

food and drink I used to love (or hate)

### Christmas
being ill
toys and games
I used to love
### birthdays
nightmares I used to have

*When I was little I used to be terrified of the dark, and I'd always sleep with the light on…*

**c** Now take turns to choose one of the topics and talk about a specific incident from your childhood.

*I remember the time when we went on our first family holiday abroad…*

**d** ➤ p.114 Writing *An article*. Analyse an online article and write an article about how life has changed over the last 30 years.

## 4 VOCABULARY & PRONUNCIATION

word building: abstract nouns; word stress
with suffixes

---

**🔍 Abstract nouns**

An abstract noun is one that is used to express an
idea, a concept, an experience, or a quality rather than
an object, e.g. *childhood* and *fear* are abstract nouns,
whereas *bed* and *trousers* are not.

Abstract nouns are formed:
1  by adding a suffix to nouns, verbs, or adjectives,
   e.g. *child – child**hood***.
   nouns can add *-hood*, *-ship*, or *-dom*
   verbs can add *-ment* or *-tion*
   adjectives can add *-ness*, *-ity*, or *-dom*
2  with a new word, e.g. *afraid – fear*.

---

**a**  Make abstract nouns by adding a suffix to the words
below and making any other changes necessary, and
write them in the correct columns.

achieve  adult  amaze  aware
bored  celebrate  curious  disappoint
excite  free  friend  frustrate
generous  happy  ill  imagine  improve
kind  member  neighbour  partner
possible  relation  sad  tempt  wise

| 1 + -hood | 2 + -ship | 3 + -dom | 4 + -ity |
|---|---|---|---|
|  |  |  |  |

| 5 + -ness | 6 + -(a)tion | 7 + -ment |
|---|---|---|
|  |  |  |

**b**  ( 1 36 )) Listen to each group and check.

**c**  ( 1 37 )) Underline the stressed syllable in these words.
Listen and check. Which endings often cause a change
in stress?

| | | |
|---|---|---|
| 1 | a\|dult | a\|dult\|hood |
| 2 | ce\|le\|brate | ce\|le\|bra\|tion |
| 3 | cu\|ri\|ous | cu\|ri\|o\|si\|ty |
| 4 | dis\|a\|ppoint | dis\|a\|ppoint\|ment |
| 5 | free | free\|dom |
| 6 | ha\|ppy | ha\|ppi\|ness |
| 7 | re\|la\|tion | re\|la\|tion\|ship |

**d**  Now look at the abstract nouns and complete the
adjective and verb column.

| abstract noun | adjective |
|---|---|
| 1  anger | *angry* |
| 2  shame | _____ |
| 3  death | _____ |
| 4  danger | _____ |

| abstract noun | verb |
|---|---|
| 5  belief | _____ |
| 6  hatred | _____ |
| 7  loss | _____ |
| 8  memory | _____ |

**e**  ( 1 38 )) Listen and check.

---

**🔍 Collocations**

Noticing and recording words that go together, e.g.
*a remote possibility*, not *a distant possibility*, will improve
the accuracy and fluency of your speaking and writing.

---

**f**  Complete the highlighted phrases below with an
abstract noun from **a** or **d** which collocates in the
phrase.

1  I'm writing to express my sympathy for your
   terrible _____. John's death was a shock to us all…
2  To my complete _____, I realized I'd won first
   prize.
3  I've been seeing my girlfriend for about six months
   now. It's quite a serious _____.
4  There's a strong _____ that I'll be offered the
   manager's job in the next few weeks.
5  I could smell gas in my kitchen, but the plumber
   decided there was no immediate _____.
6  When I heard I'd failed the exam, it was a
   huge _____. I'd been expecting to pass.
7  Contrary to popular _____, for many children,
   schooldays are not the happiest of times.
8  My eldest daughter has a very vivid _____ – I think
   she'll end up becoming a writer.

# 5 LISTENING

**a** **(1 39)))** Listen to three people talking about their earliest childhood memory and answer the questions for each speaker.

1 How old was he / she?
2 What event was his / her memory of?
3 What emotion(s) did he / she feel?

**b** What is your earliest memory? Answer questions 1–3 about it with a partner.

**c** You're going to listen to a radio programme about some research that has been done on first memories. Before you listen, discuss the following questions with a partner.

1 How far back in our lives can we usually remember things?
2 Why can't we remember things before that age?
3 What kinds of a) feelings and b) events might people be more likely to remember?
4 Are our first memories mostly visual or of sounds and smells?
5 Why might some people's first memories be unreliable?

**d** **(1 40)))** Listen to what the speaker says and compare your answers. Were you surprised by anything? How reliable do you think <u>your</u> first memory is?

**e** **(1 41)))** Now listen to the speaker talk about psychologist Jean Piaget's first memory. Write down what you think are the key words. Listen again and try to add more detail. Compare your words with a partner and then retell the story together.

# 6 SPEAKING

**a** Do you have any childhood memories of the feelings or events below? Do you know roughly how old you were at the time? Choose one feeling and one event to talk about.

boredom

disappointment

amazement

**feelings**

embarrassment

excitement

pain

shame

frustration

sadness

a festival or celebration

a day out

the birth of a brother or sister

**events**

getting a wonderful or disappointing present

managing to do something for the first time

the death of a pet

---

🔍 **Talking about memories**
When we're talking about a memory of the past, we use *remember* (*sb* or *sth*) + verb + *-ing*:
*...I remember standing in the back garden...*
*I remember arriving, and it was dark...*
*He remembered his nanny fighting the kidnapper.*

---

**b** In small groups, tell each other about your memories. Try to use the expressions in the box.

**7** **(1 MP3)))** **SONG** *The Best Day* 🎵

## GRAMMAR

**a** Complete the sentences with one word.

1 We need to _____ the central heating repaired soon, before it starts getting cold.

2 The Chinese economy is growing and _____ a result the standard of living is rising.

3 We were very late _____ of a traffic accident on the motorway.

4 Everybody seemed to enjoy the barbecue even _____ the weather wasn't very warm.

5 She wore a loose-fitting dress _____ people wouldn't notice that she'd put on weight.

6 Will the person who left _____ boarding pass at Security please go back and collect it?

7 If we lived closer to _____ another, we'd probably spend more time together.

8 Joe is quite reserved – he never talks about _____.

9 When I was young, my family _____ spend every summer holiday at the seaside.

10 This street looks different from when I was a child. Didn't _____ use to be a sweet shop on the corner?

**b** Rewrite the sentences using the **bold** word(s).

1 I need to pay someone to repair my glasses. **have**
I need _____ .

2 If we buy a dishwasher, it won't be necessary to do the washing-up. **have**
If we buy a dishwasher, _____ .

3 The last time I saw him was in 2010. **seen**
I _____ 2010.

4 They managed to get here even though the traffic was heavy. **despite**
They managed to get here _____ .

5 It was foggy, so the flight was cancelled. **due**
The flight _____ .

6 She wore dark glasses so that she wouldn't be recognized. **so as**
She wore dark glasses _____ .

7 If you learn a few phrases, the local people really appreciate it. **one**
_____ , the local people really appreciate it.

8 Jane sees Martha once a month. **each**
Jane and Martha _____ once a month.

9 The children wrapped the present on their own. **by**
The children wrapped the present _____ .

10 My aunt always used to bake biscuits for us. **would**
My aunt _____ for us.

## VOCABULARY

**a** Complete the missing words.

1 He's quite an unadventurous person – he doesn't like **ta**_____ **ri**_____ .

2 They suddenly got married on holiday in Las Vegas – they're very **sp**_____ .

3 She never asks for anyone's help. She's completely **se**_____-**su**_____ .

4 He won't listen to me, but he might **ch**_____ his **mi**_____ if you talk to him.

5 My brother wasn't very **sy**_____ when I failed my driving test – in fact, he just laughed!

6 He was **de**_____ to be a musician even as a boy.

7 He always finds a solution to problems – he's very **re**_____ .

8 He seems tough, but **de**_____ **do**_____ he's quite sensitive.

**b** Complete the idioms with one word.

1 My kids can be a real _____ **in the neck** when we eat out – they're so fussy!

2 My grandfather's always had **a quick** _____ . We were quite scared of him when we were young.

3 He can be a bit bad-tempered, but he's got **a** _____ **of gold**.

4 My boss is very **down to** _____ ; you can talk to him about anything.

5 I've read the instructions three times, but I still can't **get my** _____ **round** them.

6 What's that actor's name? It's **on the tip of my** _____ !

7 She got completely **the wrong end of the** _____ . I was offering her a promotion and she thought she was getting fired!

**c** Circle the right word or phrase.

1 She's been *off* | *out of* work for three days with the flu.

2 I won't get that job; I don't have the *qualifications* | *benefits*.

3 He resigned before they could *quit* | *sack* him.

4 I'm hoping to get *promoted* | *a rise* to a more senior post.

5 I must have applied *for* | *to* dozens of jobs.

6 *Job-searching* | *Job-hunting* can be really demoralizing.

7 Factory work is usually very *monotonous* | *motivating*.

8 The manager is in charge of 400 *staff* | *workforce*.

**d** Complete the sentences with the noun form of the **bold** word.

1 I wish there were more good restaurants in our _____. **neighbour**
2 There are training courses available for people who have a _____ of flying. **afraid**
3 Don't let this misunderstanding get in the way of our _____. **friend**
4 The _____ of his job affected him very badly. **lose**
5 _____ of speech is a basic human right. **free**
6 The news of their engagement caused great _____. **excite**
7 My _____ is getting worse as I get older. **remember**

# CAN YOU UNDERSTAND THIS TEXT?

**a** Read the article once. What main advantage of learning a second language does it describe?

**b** Read the article again and mark the sentences **T** (true) or **F** (false).

1 There had been other studies into bilingualism and the brain before Dr Bak's.
2 Not all the participants in the study spoke a second language when they were young.
3 People who speak more than one language become more confused as they get older.
4 Learning a second language as a child protects the brain more than learning it as an adult.
5 It isn't known whether speaking three languages would protect the brain more than speaking two.
6 The charity Age UK will start advising elderly people to learn a second language.

**c** Look at the highlighted words and phrases and work out their meaning. Check with your teacher or with a dictionary.

# ◼◀ CAN YOU UNDERSTAND THIS FILM?

VIDEO

**1 MP3 ))** Watch or listen to a short film on the history of English and mark the sentences **T** (true) or **F** (false).

1 English has been changing for more than a thousand years.
2 The Latin-speaking Romans conquered the native Celts in AD 43.
3 The Anglo-Saxons came to Britain from northern France after the Romans left.
4 The Anglo-Saxons rejected the monks who wanted to convert them to Christianity.
5 The arrival of the Vikings gave English about 2,000 new words.
6 King Harold defeated the Vikings and then the Normans in just three weeks.
7 The Normans didn't introduce many French words.
8 Shakespeare gave English as many new words as the Vikings.
9 In the 20th century British English 'borrowed words' from American, but not vice versa.
10 Today there are more native than non-native speakers of English.

## Learning a second language in adulthood can slow brain ageing

Learning a second language can slow cognitive ageing, that is, the speed at which the mental activity of the brain ages, even if it is learnt in adulthood, according to new research. Previous studies have shown that being bilingual could delay the onset of dementia by several years. The latest research sought to answer the question of whether people improve their brain function through learning new languages, or whether those with better brain function are more likely to become bilingual.

Dr Thomas Bak of the University of Edinburgh, who led the research, said that his study was the first to examine whether learning a second language affects the performance of the brain later in life. His team assessed data from 835 native English speakers. The participants had been given an intelligence test in 1947, at the age of 11, and were retested in their early seventies, between 2008 and 2010. Of the participants, 262 said they were able to communicate in at least one language other than English. Of those, 195 learnt the second language before the age of 18, while 67 learnt the language after this age.

Researchers found that those who spoke two or more languages had significantly better cognitive abilities in later life compared to what would be predicted from their performance in the intelligence tests at age 11. The strongest effects were seen in general intelligence and reading ability, though verbal fluency also improved. Researchers said the effects were present in those who acquired their second language later in life, as well as early. No negative effects of bilingualism were observed.

Dr Bak said the improvements in brain performance could not be explained by the participants' original levels of intelligence. He added: 'These findings are of considerable practical relevance. Millions of people around the world acquire their second language later in life. Our study shows that bilingualism, even when acquired in adulthood, may benefit the ageing brain.' But he admitted that the study also raised many questions, such as whether learning two or more additional languages could also have the same positive effect on cognitive ageing, and whether actively speaking a second language is better than just knowing how to speak it.

Caroline Abrahams, charity director at Age UK, which supported the research, said: 'Over one million people in the UK aged 65 and over are estimated to have some degree of cognitive impairment. We urgently need to understand what influences cognitive ageing so that we can give people better advice about protecting their cognitive health. This latest breakthrough is another stride forward in finding out how thinking skills can be preserved in later life.'

*By Lucy Kinder in* The Telegraph

**G** get
**V** phrases with *get*
**P** words and phrases of French origin

" When a woman says nothing's wrong, that means everything's wrong. And when a woman says everything's wrong, that means everything's wrong "

*Homer Simpson,
cartoon character*

# 3A Don't get mad, get even

## 1 READING & SPEAKING

**a** Read the ten top break-up lines from a website. Which one do you think is the least hurtful way of explaining to someone that you want to break up with them?

" It's not you, it's me.
I love you, but I'm not in love with you.
You are like a brother / sister to me.
I think we'd be better off as friends.
I don't love you any more.
I need some time to be on my own.
You're a fantastic person, but you're too good for me.
I think I'm just too young to settle down.
We're at very different points in our lives now.
I think we rushed into this relationship too fast. "

**b** Now read an article about how a French artist replied to the break-up email from her former partner. What do you think her motivation was?

1 She wanted to humiliate him.
2 She wanted them to get back together.
3 She wanted to help herself get over the break-up.
4 She wanted to make art.

**c** Choose the right word for gaps 1–10 in the article.

| | | | |
|---|---|---|---|
| 1 | a turned out | b turned off | c turned up |
| 2 | a fear | b pain | c joy |
| 3 | a getting | b sending | c writing |
| 4 | a included | b involved | c covered |
| 5 | a instead of | b according to | c because of |
| 6 | a praised | b blamed | c ridiculed |
| 7 | a married | b arrested | c avoided |
| 8 | a get back | b get over | c get rid of |
| 9 | a returned | b revived | c replaced |
| 10 | a Though | b Because | c Despite |

**d** Read the article again and answer in groups.

1 Why do you think the exhibition was so successful?
2 Do you think Sophie Calle was justified in making the man's email public?
3 How do you think he felt about the exhibition?
4 Do you think men enjoyed it as much as women?
5 What do you think the moral of the story is?

# Getting your own back

The exhibition *Prenez soin de vous* ('Take care of yourself') was first a huge success at the Venice Biennale and then at the Bibliothèque Nationale in Paris. It has since toured in Europe and the Americas, and has been published as a book with the same title.

One day, Sophie Calle's mobile beeped. It was an email from her boyfriend. He was dumping her electronically, adding that it hurt him more than it hurt her. Here is a short extract:

> Whatever happens, you must know that I will never stop loving you in my own way – the way I've loved you ever since I've known you, which will stay part of me, and never die…I wish things had
> 1 _____ differently. Take care of yourself…

Sophie was heartbroken. But she is one of France's best-known avant-garde artists, specializing in turning private 2 _____ into public art, and two days after 3 _____ the email she started a new project:

> I received an email telling me it was over.
> I didn't know how to respond.
> It was almost as if it hadn't been meant for me.
> It ended with the words, 'Take care of yourself'.
> And so I did.
> I asked 107 women, chosen for their profession or skills, to interpret this letter.
> To analyse it, comment on it, dance it, sing it.
> Dissect it. Exhaust it. Understand it for me.
> Answer for me.
> It was a way of taking the time to break up.
> A way of taking care of myself.

Sophie Calle in front of what the editor did.

The women Sophie sent the email to ⁴_____ an actress, an editor, an opera singer, a criminologist, a linguist, a lyricist, and her mother. She asked them to read the email and to analyse it or interpret it ⁵_____ their job, while she filmed or photographed the result. Sophie's mother, who clearly knows her well, wrote:

> You leave, you get left, that's the name of the game, and for you this break-up could be the wellspring of a new piece of art – am I wrong?

The editor ⁶_____ the boyfriend's grammar, the lyricist wrote a song, and the criminologist had this to say about the email writer:

> He is proud, narcissistic, and egotistical (he says 'I' more than 30 times in a letter with 23 sentences). It is possible that he studied literature. He probably prefers jazz to rock. I can imagine him wearing polo-neck sweaters rather than a suit and tie. He must have a small kitchen and cook up tasty little meals. He must have charm, but not be classically handsome. He is an authentic manipulator, perverse, psychologically dangerous, and / or a great writer. To be ⁷_____ at all costs.

It was therapy for Sophie, and she quickly began to _____ the end of her relationship. 'After a month I felt better. There was no suffering. It worked. The project had _____ the man.'

With hindsight, Sophie's ex almost certainly wishes that he had followed his first instinct (*It seems to me it would be better to say what I have to say to you face-to-face*). _____ he isn't named in the exhibition, it's a sure bet that when he dumps his partners in the future, he'll never again say, 'Take care of yourself.'

## 2 PRONUNCIATION
words and phrases of French origin

a ②2)) Look at the extract from the text. How do you pronounce the **bold** word? Listen and check.

Sophie was heartbroken. But she is one of France's best-known **avant-garde** artists…

> 🔍 **Fine-tuning your pronunciation: French words used in English**
> A number of French words and phrases are commonly used in English, e.g. *café* /ˈkæfeɪ/, *ballet* /ˈbæleɪ/, *coup* /kuː/. They are usually said in a way that is close to their French pronunciation, so they do not necessarily follow normal English pronunciation patterns.

b <u>Underline</u> a French word or expression in each sentence below. What do you think they mean? Do you use any of them in your language?

1 I made a real faux pas when I mentioned his ex-wife.
2 When we were introduced I had a sense of déjà vu, though I knew we'd never met before.
3 We used to have a secret rendezvous every Thursday in the National Gallery.
4 She's engaged to a well-known local entrepreneur.
5 I know it's a cliché, but it really was love at first sight.
6 On our anniversary, he always buys me a huge bouquet of flowers!
7 I met Jane's fiancé last night. They're getting married next year.
8 They knew their parents wouldn't want them to get married, so they did it anyway and presented them with a fait accompli.

c ②3)) Listen and focus on how the French expressions are pronounced. Then practise saying the sentences.

## 3 VOCABULARY phrases with *get*

a With a partner, try to remember these expressions with *get* from the article.

1 get _____ _____ _____ on someone (= take revenge on someone)
2 get _____ a break-up (= recover from a break-up with someone)
3 get _____ (*informal*) (= to cause somebody the same amount of trouble or harm as they have caused you)
4 get _____ _____ (= to start a romantic relationship with somebody again, after having finished a previous relationship with the person)

b ► p.162 **Vocabulary Bank** Phrases with *get*.

## 4 ②MP3)) SONG *50 Ways to Say Goodbye* ♫

## 5 SPEAKING & LISTENING

**a** Have you ever been on a blind date or a date set up by friends? If yes, how did it go? If no, would you consider going on one?

# Blind Date

*The Guardian* has a weekly feature called *Blind Date*, where two readers are matched and a date is organized at a restaurant. Stef and Graham met in London at Miss Q's, an American restaurant with pool tables and a dance floor.

**b** Read the introduction about Stef and Graham's date. Who do you think said the following – Stef about Graham, or Graham about Stef?

1 First impressions: 'Effortlessly beautiful and unforgivably late.'
2 Table manners: 'Impeccable even though it was burgers.'
3 Best thing about them: 'Really genuine and friendly.'

**c** ➤ **Communication** *Blind date* **A** *p.105* **B** *p.109*. Check your answers to **b** and find out what else they said about each other.

**d** You're going to listen to a radio programme about first dates. Before you listen, guess what the missing words are in tips 1–6.

## Dos

1 Choose the _____ carefully.
2 Make an effort with your _____.
3 Be _____, even if you think the date is going nowhere.

## Don'ts

4 Don't forget your _____.
5 Don't _____ to be anything you're not.
6 Don't make an instant _____.

**e** (2 8))) Listen to the programme and check. Were your answers exactly the same? If not, did they mean the same thing?

**f** Listen again. Answer questions 1–6 with a partner.

What do the tips say about…?
1 the best place for a first date
2 looking good
3 lying
4 politeness
5 exaggeration
6 first impressions

**g** Which do you think are the top two dating tips? Are there any you don't think are important?

### LEXIS IN CONTEXT

**h** (2 9))) Listen to some extracts and complete the phrasal verbs and idioms. What do you think they mean?

1 The advantage of keeping the first date _____ _____ _____ …is that if you don't like each other, you don't have to make it through a seven-course meal together.
2 …if you turn up with unwashed hair, wearing yesterday's clothes, you aren't likely to _____ anyone _____ .
3 Don't tell someone that you'll phone and that you can't wait to see them again if you have absolutely no intention of _____ _____ !
4 Turn off your phone, and if the other person is _____ the _____ , do remember to say 'thank you'.
5 It can be very tempting to exaggerate, or to _____ _____ the truth, or just to plain lie…
6 Many of us _____ _____ our _____ whether we like someone in the first few seconds or minutes of meeting them.
7 Try not to _____ someone _____ straightaway.
8 If you make a snap decision, you may risk _____ _____ on the love of your life.

## GRAMMAR *get*

Look at some sentences from the listening script which contain phrases with *get*. Answer the questions with a partner.

> A  By **getting your hair done**, say, or wearing something you know you look good in, those kinds of things show that you care.
>
> B  Try not to yawn even if you're **getting a bit tired**.
>
> C  It can be very tempting to exaggerate, or to dress up the truth, or just to plain lie to try to **get your date interested**.

In which phrase…?
1  ☐ does *get* mean *make*
2  ☐ does *get* mean *become*
3  ☐ could you replace *get* with *have* with no change in meaning

▶ **p.144 Grammar Bank 3A**. Learn more about *get*, and practise it.

Work in pairs. Read the *get* questionnaire and tick (✓) eight questions you'd like to ask your partner. Then ask and answer the questions. Explain your answers.

# *get* questionnaire

☐ Are you the kind of person who regularly gets rid of old clothes, or do you tend to keep things forever?

☐ Did you use to get into trouble a lot when you were a child?

☐ Do you consider yourself a person who usually gets their own way? Why (not)?

☐ Do you tend to keep up to date with your work or studies, or do you often get behind?

☐ Do you think young drivers get stopped by the police more than older drivers? Do you think this is fair?

☐ Have you ever got caught cheating in an exam? Have you ever cheated in an exam and got away with it?

☐ Do you think going on holiday together is a good way to really get to know people?

☐ How often and where do you usually get your hair cut?

☐ If an electrical appliance doesn't work, do you try to sort it out yourself or do you immediately get an expert to come and fix it?

☐ If you were able to get just one room in your house redecorated, which would it be and why?

☐ Do you think women are better than men at getting presents for people?

☐ If you were invited to a karaoke evening, would you try to get out of going?

☐ If you were supposed to get a flight the day after there had been a serious plane crash, would you cancel it?

☐ Is there anyone in your family or group of friends who really gets on your nerves?

☐ What kinds of things do / did your parents get you to do around the house?

**G** discourse markers (2): adverbs and adverbial expressions
**V** conflict and warfare
**P** stress in word families

" If you don't know history, then y
don't know anything. You are a le
that doesn't know it is part of a tre

*Michael Crichton, US author* "

# 3B History in the making

## 1 READING & VOCABULARY conflict and warfare

**a** Look at the stills from three films. Have you seen any of them? If yes, are there any scenes you particularly remember?

# The scenes you'll never forget
## Three film critics choose their most memorable moments

**A** *Gladiator* directed by Ridley Scott, 2000

**B** *The Great Escape* directed by John Sturges, 1963

**Gladiator**, which won five Oscars, tells the story of a Roman general, Maximus Decimus Meridius, a favourite of the Emperor, Marcus Aurelius. The Emperor wants Maximus (Russell Crowe at his best) to succeed him, but Commodus, the Emperor's weak and treacherous son (wonderfully played by Joaquin Phoenix), has other plans. Commodus kills his father and becomes Emperor himself, and arranges for Maximus and his wife and child to be executed. Maximus escapes, but cannot save his family. He is captured and sold as a gladiator, and eventually makes his way to the Colosseum in Rome, where he becomes a hero by engineering a spectacular victory against overwhelming odds. In this gripping scene Emperor Commodus descends to the arena to congratulate him – not knowing his true identity. Maximus removes his helmet and confronts the Emperor in one of the most stirring speeches in modern cinema: 'My name is Maximus Decimus Meridius, commander of the armies of the north, general of the Felix Legions, loyal servant to the true Emperor, Marcus Aurelius, father to a murdered son, husband to a murdered wife, and I will have my vengeance in this life or the next.' And somehow, we just know he's going to get it!

**The Great Escape** is set in a prisoner-of-war camp in German during the Second World War. The camp is supposedly 'escape-proof', but the British and American prisoners (played by an all-star cast) are determined to get out. They dig three tunnels and forge identity documents in preparation for a large-scale escape attempt. 76 prisoners manage to crawl through a tunne and get away. Most are quickly recaptured, but in this legendary scene, Captain Virgil Hilts (played by Steve McQueen) steals a motorbike and a German uniform and tries to get over the Swiss border. Coming to a roadblock, he breaks through and gets away, despite being shot at, but is immediately pursued by German troops. He rides across open countryside in a desperate bid to reach safety, and eventually gets to the border. But two high fences separate him from Switzerland and freedom. He jumps the first, but becomes hopelessly trapped in the second, and is forced to surrender. *The Great Escape* is always shown in the UK a Christmas, and however many times you've seen it before, you sti hope he might just make it over the second fence.

**b** Read some film critics' descriptions of three memorable scenes. What information does each extract give? Tick (✓) the boxes as you read each one.

1 prizes the film won A ☐ B ☐ C ☐
2 the book the film is based on A ☐ B ☐ C ☐
3 where and when the film is set A ☐ B ☐ C ☐
4 who the main characters are and who they are played by A ☐ B ☐ C ☐

5 what the film is about A ☐ B ☐ C ☐
6 one of the most memorable scenes A ☐ B ☐ C ☐
7 how the director's decisions affect the scene A ☐ B ☐ C ☐
8 how it makes you feel A ☐ B ☐ C ☐

*12 Years a Slave* directed by Steve McQueen, 2013

**12 Years a Slave**, which won the Oscar for Best Picture in 2014, is based on the memoir by Solomon Northup in which he describes how, despite being free-born, he was kidnapped in Washington D.C. in 1841 and sold as a slave. Northup worked on plantations in Louisiana for 12 years before his release. The book was written in 1853, eight years before the American Civil War began. It was this war that led to the abolition of slavery in the USA. One of the most famous scenes is the hanging scene. It comes after Solomon (Chiwetel Ejiofor) gets pushed too far by his slave master and attacks him. He is punished by being hanged from a tree in such a way that the rope around his neck is always choking him, but his toes can touch the ground just enough to keep him from being strangled. As it goes on, and director Steve McQueen refuses to let you look away, you start to realize that all the other slaves have gone back to their normal lives. Work starts up again, children go back to playing, and you realize how common excruciating experiences like this must have been for slaves, and how thoroughly they must have been separated from their own sense of humanity.

Which of the three descriptions created the most vivid image of the scene in your mind?

**LEXIS IN CONTEXT**

**d** Look at the highlighted words related to conflict and warfare. With a partner, say what you think they mean. Check their meaning and pronunciation with your teacher or a dictionary.

➤ **p.163 Vocabulary Bank** *Conflict and warfare.*

## 2 PRONUNCIATION stress in word families

> 🔍 **Fine-tuning your pronunciation: changing stress in word families**
> It is useful to learn words in 'families', e.g. *capture* (noun) – *a captive* (person), *revolutionary* (adjective) – *to revolt* (verb), etc. However, you should check whether the stressed syllable changes within the 'family'.

**a** Complete the chart. Under<u>line</u> the stressed syllable in all the multi-syllable words.

| noun | person | adjective | verb |
|------|--------|-----------|------|
| cap\|ture | cap\|tive / cap\|tor | cap\|tive | _____ |
| co\|mmand | _____ | com\|mand\|ing | co\|mmand |
| ex\|e\|cu\|tion | _____ | | _____ |
| _____ | his\|to\|ri\|an | his\|to\|ric / _____ | |
| loo\|ting | loo\|ter | | |
| _____ | _____ | re\|bel\|lious | |
| | | re\|vo\|lu\|tion\|ary | re\|volt |
| siege | | be\|sieged | _____ |
| sur\|vi\|val | _____ | sur\|vi\|ving | _____ |
| _____ | | vic\|to\|ri\|ous | |

**b** (2)13))) Listen and check.

**c** Practise saying the sentences.
1 The rebels were captured and executed.
2 All the captives survived the siege.
3 It was a historic victory.
4 In the end, the revolutionaries were victorious.
5 The troops rebelled against their commander.
6 Historians disagree on the causes of the rebellion.

## 3 SPEAKING & WRITING

> 🔍 **Describing a scene from a film or a book**
> *In this legendary scene, Steve McQueen **steals** a motorbike and a German uniform and **tries** to get over the Swiss border. Coming to a roadblock, he **breaks through** and **gets away**.*
> We normally use the simple present ('the dramatic present') when we describe a scene from a film, or the plot.

**a** Think of a film or TV series you really enjoyed that was set in a historical period or based on a real event. Look at prompts 1–8 in **1b**. Think about this information for your film or TV series.

**b** Work in groups of three or four. Describe the film or TV series and the scene to others in the group. Do those who have seen it agree with you? How does the description make you feel about the film or TV series?

**c** Now write a paragraph describing the film or TV series and the scene, using the prompts and the three texts in **1** as models.

## 4 SPEAKING

**a** Look at the images from *Braveheart* in the film blog below. Each has one historical inaccuracy. What do you think they might be?

**b** Answer the questions in pairs.

- Are there any films or TV series you've seen which you thought were historically accurate, and which you felt taught you something about the period or event?
- Are there any films or TV series you've seen which you were aware were historically inaccurate? Did it bother you? Why (not)?
- Have you ever checked whether a film or TV series was accurate either during or after seeing it?
- Do you think big studios care whether the historical films they make are accurate or not?

**c** Read the extract from a film blog and answer the questions with a partner.

1 Did the blog mention any of the films you talked about in **b**? Do you agree about the ones that are mentioned?
2 Do you think the professor's research affected the films' success?
3 Have you seen people 'two-screening' in the cinema? How did you feel about it?

## 5 LISTENING

**a** (2 14)) You're going to listen to an interview with Adrian Hodges, who has written screenplays for several historical films and TV series. Listen to **Part 1** of the interview and choose the best option.

1 Adrian thinks historical details don't matter as long as they're things that most people wouldn't notice.
2 Adrian thinks historical details don't matter as long as a drama is honest about whether it is history or fiction.
3 Adrian thinks historical details don't matter at all.

**Glossary**
**Macbeth** /məkˈbeθ/ a play by Shakespeare about a king of Scotland
**William the Conqueror, Charles II, Victoria** English monarchs from the 11th, 17th, and 19th centuries
**to play fast and loose with** IDM *(old-fashioned)* to treat sth in a way that shows you feel no responsibility or respect for it

# Did you know...?

Princess Isabella of France

One of the films that has been most criticized for historical inaccuracy is Braveheart. Some scenes actually had to be reshot because the extras were wearing watches and sunglasses! Other films frequently included in the top ten most historically inaccurate films are JFK, Pearl Harbor, Shakespeare in Love, and Pocahontas.

Historical films that have been voted both excellent and historically accurate on numerous websites include Downfall, the German film about Hitler's last days, Clint Eastwood's Letters from Iwo Jima, Chariots of Fire, and Saving Private Ryan.

Hollywood studios are recruiting academics as 'history assassins' to help them undermine rival studios' Oscar-contending films. A Harvard professor says he was paid a $10,000 fee by an Oscar marketing consultant to look for factual errors in the current wave of historical films that boast that they are 'based on a true story'.

The concept of doing something else while watching a film or TV only used to stretch to eating popcorn or having a TV dinner. But since the arrival of smartphones, we have become a society of 'two-screeners', that is, people who watch a film or TV while using their smartphone. Things people do with their phones include tweeting or posting comments about what they're watching, or checking the accuracy in historical or period dramas.

William Wallace

**d** Listen again and tick (✓) the points Adrian makes.

1 ☐ It isn't a problem that Shakespeare's plays are not historically accurate.
2 ☐ Writers can change historical details if the drama requires it.
3 ☐ Most people never notice historical inaccuracies.
4 ☐ Nobody is certain how people spoke in ancient Rome.
5 ☐ Historical inaccuracies with costume are worse than with dialogue.
6 ☐ It's easier to be accurate when you are writing about recent history.
7 ☐ If you make it clear that something is fiction, it doesn't matter if it's not historically accurate.
8 ☐ Julius Caesar is not a good subject for drama because we know so much about him.

**c** (2 15))) Now listen to **Part 2**. In general, is Adrian positive or negative about *Spartacus* and *Braveheart*?

**d** Work in pairs. Before you listen again, can you explain these phrases Adrian uses?

1 'it becomes the received version of the truth'
2 'grossly irresponsible'
3 'the notion of freedom of individual choice'
4 'a resonance in the modern era'
5 'pushing the limits of what history could stand'
6 'a matter of purely personal taste'

**e** Listen again and answer the questions.

1 What is the most famous scene in the film *Spartacus*?
2 Why is it an example of a film becoming the 'received version of the truth'?
3 What does he say about the portrayal of William Wallace's life in the film *Braveheart*?
4 What did some people think *Braveheart* was really about?

**f** Do you agree with Adrian's main points? Which event or period of history from your own country do you think would be most interesting as a film or TV series?

WINNER OF **4** ACADEMY AWARDS!
"A NEW KIND OF MOVIE...A SUPERSPECTACLE WITH SPIRITUAL VITALITY AND MORAL FORCE!" –TIME MAGAZINE
*SPARTACUS*
TECHNICOLOR®

Poster of *Spartacus*, about a gladiator who led a slave rebellion against the Romans in the 1st century BC.

MEL·GIBSON
*BRAVEHEART*
WINNER 5 ACADEMY AWARDS including BEST PICTURE 1995 BEST DIRECTOR Mel Gibson
*Every man dies, not every man really lives.*

Poster of *Braveheart*, about William Wallace, one of the main leaders in the 13th and 14th century Wars of Scottish Independence.

## 6 GRAMMAR discourse markers (2): adverbs and adverbial expressions

**a** Read four extracts from the interview with Adrian Hodges. Match the **bold** discourse markers to what they are used for (A–D).

1 ☐ If you change detail to the point where history is an absurdity, then **obviously** things become more difficult.

2 ☐ So *Spartacus*...has become, I think, for nearly everybody who knows anything about Spartacus, the only version of the truth. Now **in fact** we don't know if any of that is true, really.

3 ☐ ...his whole career was invented in the film, or **at least** built on to such a degree that some people felt that perhaps it was more about the notion of Scotland as an independent country than it was about history...

4 ☐ But you know, again, these things are a matter of purely personal taste, **I mean**, I enjoyed *Braveheart* immensely.

A To introduce surprising or contrasting information
B To give more details, or make things clearer
C To introduce a fact that is very clear to see or understand
D To qualify what you have just said or to make it less definite

**b** ➤ p.145 Grammar Bank 3B. Learn more about adverbs and adverbial expressions, and practise them.

**c** ➤ **Communication** *Guess the sentence* A *p.105* B *p.109*. Guess the missing phrases, then check with a partner.

## 1 ◼◄ THE INTERVIEW Part 1
VIDEO

**a** Read the biographical information about Mary Beard. What do you think 'Classics' and 'classicist' refer to?

> **Mary Beard** is Professor of Classics at the University of Cambridge and a fellow of Newnham College. She is author of many books about ancient history, and writes a popular blog called *A Don's Life*. In 2010, she presented the BBC historical documentary, *Pompeii: Life and Death in a Roman Town*, which showed a snapshot of the residents' lives before the eruption of Mount Vesuvius in AD 79. In 2012 she wrote and presented the three-part television series *Meet the Romans*, about 'the world's first global metropolis.' She also wrote and presented *Caligula with Mary Beard* in 2013, where she attempts to sort the truth from the myth. Her frequent media appearances and sometimes-controversial public statements have led to her being described as 'Britain's best-known classicist.'

**b** ②16)) Watch or listen to **Part 1** of the interview. What does she think is the right (and the wrong) way to get people interested in ancient history? What does she think we can learn from history?

**c** Now listen again. Complete sentences 1–5.

1 If a place name ends with *-chester* or *-caster*, it means that it…
2 London is the capital of Britain because…
3 In 63 BC there was a terrorist plot in Rome to…
4 When Cicero discovered the plot, he decided to…
5 Mary Beard compares this situation with…

> **Glossary**
> **(63) BC** Before Christ. These letters refer to the years before 1 AD (*Anno Domini – the year of our Lord*)
> **torch** *verb* set fire to
> **Marcus Tullius Cicero** /ˈsɪsərəʊ/ a Roman politician and lawyer, one of Rome's greatest orators
> **the Senate** a political institution in ancient Rome
> **be exiled** be sent to another country for political reasons or as a punishment
> **Guantanamo Bay** a US military prison, where many suspected terrorists have been held

## ◼◄ Part 2
VIDEO

**a** ②17)) Now watch or listen to **Part 2**. Mark the sentences **T** (true) or **F** (false).

1 Mary Beard would not like to go back in time to any historical period.
2 She thinks that women have a better life now than at any time in the past.
3 She doesn't think that men would suffer from going back in time.
4 In her programme *Meet the Romans*, she decided to focus on the celebrities of the ancient world.
5 She thinks that most history textbooks don't answer questions about how people dealt with practical issues in the past.
6 She thinks that questions about practical issues are just as interesting as why Julius Caesar was assassinated.
7 She doesn't think we can learn much from studying the assassination of Caesar.

**b** Listen again. Say why the **F** sentences are false.

> **Glossary**
> **Julius Caesar** /ˈdʒuːlɪəs ˈsiːzə/ a Roman general (100–44 BC) who played a critical role in the fall of the Roman Republic and the rise of the Roman Empire. He was assassinated by a group of senators led by his former friend Brutus

## ◼◄ Part 3
VIDEO

**a** ②18)) Now watch or listen to **Part 3**. Answer the questions.

1 How important does Mary Beard think accuracy is in historical films?
2 What historical film did she really enjoy and why?
3 How does she feel about the fact that there are so many historical films nowadays?

# history

**b** Listen again. What do you think the highlighted informal words and phrases mean?

1 'I think that, that, um, film and television, um, programme makers can be a bit, can be a bit sort of nerdish about accuracy.'

2 '…if we're going to have a dog in the film should it be an Alsatian or, you know, a Dachshund or whatever?'

3 '…look, these guys are getting the whole of Roman history…utterly wrong…'

4 '…never mind its horribly schmaltzy plot…'

5 '…there's no such good story as a true story – and that's what history's got going for it…'

6 '…non-fiction in a, in a kind of way is always a better yarn than fiction is.'

> **Glossary**
> **Alsatian, Dachshund** /æl'seɪʃn, 'dæksnd/ breeds of dog

## 2 LOOKING AT LANGUAGE

> 🔍 **Collocations**
> Many of the expressions Mary Beard uses are typical collocations, that is, where one word frequently goes with the other. Try to learn these expressions as phrases. Incorporating them into your active language will help you both to understand spoken English more easily and to sound more fluent in your own speech.

**(2 19))** Watch or listen to some extracts from the interview and complete the collocating words.

1 '…an _____ lot of our culture and our geography and our place names and so on are actually formed by the Romans…'

2 '…one _____ example of that is a famous incident in Roman history in 63 BC where there's a terrorist _____ in, in the city of Rome…'

3 'Now, in many ways that's the kind of problem we're still _____ …'

4 'I mean, what – how far does, how far should homeland security be more important than _____ rights…'

5 'And in part we've learnt from how they debated those rights and _____ …'

6 '…if it, if it was a small antidote to modern _____ culture, I'm extremely pleased.'

7 '…look, these guys are getting the whole of Roman history in, in the big _____ utterly wrong…'

8 'But I think also, I mean, it shows that you don't always have to be deadly _____ about history.'

## 3 🎥 IN THE STREET
VIDEO

**a** **(2 20))** Watch or listen to five people talking about history. Match the speakers (**D**, **He**, **Ha**, **A**, and **R**) with the people they admire. What reasons do they give?

| Daisy, *English* | Heather, *South African* | Harry, *English* | Adam, *American* | Richard, *English* |

☐ a sailor from one of Nelson's ships
☐ Bess of Hardwick
☐ Julius Caesar
☐ Nelson Mandela
☐ Queen Elizabeth I

**b** Watch or listen again. Who (**D**, **He**, **Ha**, **A**, or **R**)…?

☐ doesn't mention a specific time they would like to go back to
☐ would like to listen to some philosophers talking
☐ is studying the period they would like to go back to
☐ would like to have been able to walk on quiet, peaceful roads
☐ would like to go back to the most recent historical period

**c** **(2 21))** Watch or listen again and complete the Colloquial English phrases. What do you think they mean?

1 'She was a real _____ _____ …'

2 'I would have loved to _____ _____ in California…'

3 '…she actually stood up and was a person to _____ _____ .'

4 '…he was a _____ _____ person…'

5 'So not a, a big person, _____ _____ _____ , but one of the hundreds of men…'

> **Glossary**
> **Derbyshire** /'dɑːbɪʃ(ɪ)ə/ a county in the middle of England
> **the Agora** the main meeting place in ancient Athens

## 4 SPEAKING

Answer the questions with a partner.

1 What periods and places in history did you study at school? Did you enjoy it as a subject?

2 How do you think a teacher can get students interested in history?

3 Do you think you have learnt more about history from school or from books and films?

4 Why do you think historical films and novels are so popular?

5 Is there a person from history whom you admire or find especially fascinating?

6 Is there a period of history that you would like to go back to?

**G** speculation and deduction
**V** sounds and the human voice
**P** consonant clusters

> I have often regretted my speech, never my silence.
>
> *Publilius Syrus, Roman writer*

# 4A Sounds interesting

## 1 VOCABULARY & WRITING
sounds and the human voice

**a** Try to sit for one minute in complete silence, listening carefully. Write down everything you hear. Then compare with a partner. Did you hear the same things?

**b** ➤ p.164 Vocabulary Bank *Sounds and the human voice.*

**c** (2 25)) Listen to the sounds and make a note of what they are. Then write three paragraphs based on the sounds. Begin your paragraphs as follows:

1 It was 12.30 at night and Mike had just fallen asleep…
2 Amanda was walking down Park Street…
3 It was a cold winter night…

## 2 PRONUNCIATION consonant clusters

> **Fine-tuning your pronunciation: consonant clusters**
> Combinations of two or three consonant sounds, e.g. *clothes*, *spring*, can be difficult to pronounce, especially if the combination of sounds is not common in your language.
> Three-consonant clusters at the beginning of words always begin with s, e.g. *scream*.
> Three-consonant clusters at the end of words are often either plurals (*months*), third person singular verbs (*wants*), or regular past tenses (*asked*).

**a** (2 26)) Listen to the words below. Then practise saying them.

| At the beginning of a word | |
| --- | --- |
| **two sounds** | **three sounds** |
| click | screech |
| slam | scream |
| crash | splash |
| slurp | |
| drip | |
| snore | |
| stammer | |

| At the end of a word | |
| --- | --- |
| **two sounds** | **three sounds** |
| shouts | crunched |
| sniffs | mumble |
| yelled | crisps |
| hummed | rattled |

**b** (2 27)) Listen and repeat the sentences.

1 She screamed when her friend splashed her in the swimming pool.
2 The brakes screeched and then there was a tremendous crash.
3 I hate the crunching of someone eating crisps.

**c** Write three sentences of your own, using two words from **a** in each sentence. Give them to your partner to say.

## 3 READING

**a** Read the headline and the introduction to the article on page 35. With a partner, say how you think the following aspects of Vicky's life have been affected by her phobia.

• university studies
• relationships
• work
• where she lives

**b** Read the article and check.

**c** What is each paragraph about? With a partner, match paragraphs 1–7 to summaries A–H. There is one summary that you don't need.

A ☐ how her phobia caused her to underachieve
B ☐ the physical effects of her phobia
C ☐ what she considers to be the most damaging effect of her phobia
D ☐ the effect of her phobia on where she works and lives
E ☐ her eventual diagnosis
F ☐ how therapy has helped her
G ☐ her ambivalent attitude to sounds
H ☐ how her problems originated

### LEXIS IN CONTEXT

**d** Look at the highlighted adverbs and adverbial phrases and work out the meaning of any that you don't know. Check with your dictionary.

**e** How sympathetic are you to Vicky's phobia? Do you know anyone with a phobia that seriously affects their life?

Life & style    Experience

🏠 Previous | Next | Index

# I have a phobia of sound

For the last 30 years, I have had violent physical reactions to certain noises. Everyday sounds, like someone chewing or a pen being clicked, make me want to hide, scream, and put my fingers in my ears.

I feel unreasonable complaining to people about these seemingly harmless sounds, but for me they are threatening. My body reacts in the same way as it would under attack: I am flooded with adrenaline. It is as if I were in the same room as a huge, fierce dog. I am unable to focus on anything but my terror. I often have to hang up on phone calls abruptly, leave my seat and walk around the room, trying to block out the noise.

My phobia began when I was 19 and started work in a busy office. The noise of a colleague next to me who chewed gum incessantly became unbearable. My ears tuned in to every sound until they filled my head, and I couldn't focus on my work. This cacophony was added to by another colleague who continually whistled, until I was forced to leave.

The path of my life has been dictated by the sounds around me. I have changed jobs numerous times, searching for the perfect quiet office. I have moved house, too, away from loud music or arguing neighbours. Strangely, I'd love to live near a motorway: the constant hum of traffic would be soothing to me.

My phobia has affected my ability to get on in life. During my final examinations at university, I was doing really well, translating Greek with ease, until the scratching of a pen against paper filtered into my consciousness, bringing me to a halt. During another exam, a nearby pub had a delivery and the sound of barrels being rolled along by whistling delivery men destroyed any chance of concentration. I discovered afterwards that I was two marks off a first.

My biggest regret is that it has prevented me from having a long-term relationship and children. The longest I have been with someone is two years, until the sound of their eating, breathing, just existing in proximity to me became intolerable. I would sneak off to the spare room in the night to try to get some sleep, but it would be interpreted as a rejection of them. It's hard to stay with someone who doesn't want to eat or sleep with you. I haven't ruled out love yet, though. I'm sure there is someone who could accept my limitations.

It took me 30 years to realize that what I have has a name: misophonia, or hatred of sound. When I recently discovered a support forum dedicated to it, I cried for two hours. I felt so relieved to know that other people – 900 of them on this one site – felt like I did. I wasn't the only one.

It also gave me perspective. Some sufferers wish they were deaf, but I don't. I love many, many sounds: the sea, wind in the trees, music, the human voice. Time and experience have taught me that being able to hear is a beautiful thing, too important to sacrifice. I would never wish that away.

*By Vicky Rhodes in* The Guardian

**Glossary**
**a first** the top qualification in UK university degrees

## 4 LISTENING & SPEAKING

a  (2 28))) Listen to five people talking about noises they don't like.

1  What noise does each person describe?
2  How much do you think it affects their daily life?

b  Listen again. Who…?

1 ☐ feels that a sound represents a negative emotion
2 ☐ wishes he'd / she'd complained about a noise sooner
3 ☐ is annoyed because he's / she's powerless to stop a sound
4 ☐ has to make a sound stop before he / she can relax
5 ☐ describes sounds that other people clearly like

c  Talk to a partner.

• **Are there any noises that really annoy you?**

  Are you affected by them in your daily life?

  Is there anything you can do to avoid or stop them?

• **Are there any sounds that you really love or that make you feel good?**

• **Do you prefer music or silence in these situations?**
  – in bars and restaurants
  – in a supermarket
  – in a gym
  – when a plane is taking off or landing
  – when you're put on hold on the phone
  Why?
  If you prefer music, what kind?

## 5 GRAMMAR speculation and deduction

**a** Look at this picture and answer the questions.

Boris Johnson, Mayor of London, on a zip wire.

1 When and where **could** the photo **have been taken**?
2 Why do you think Boris **might have been** on a zip wire?
3 What do you think **might have** just **happened**?
4 How do you think he **must have been feeling** while he was hanging there?

**b** ➤ **Communication** *Boris left hanging p.106*. Find out what really happened.

**c** ➤ **p.146 Grammar Bank 4A**. Learn more about speculation and deduction, and practise them.

**d** Look at these photos taken in London and make speculations and deductions about them.

## 6 LISTENING

**a** Have you had an interesting conversation with a stranger recently? Where? What about?

**b** Read about an organization called 'Talk to me London'. What do they aim to achieve? Does 'Talk to me London' sound like a good idea to you?

# TALK TO ME LONDON

 What's the idea? | Why talk? | Stories | Get started!

**Talk to me London** is all about finding ways for people to talk to each other. We know that talking brings about many benefits, from a greater sense of well-being to friendlier communities, and increased opportunities. Think about it – just one conversation can inspire us, reassure us, or brighten up our day. Our vision is to build a friendlier city through encouraging small conversations between strangers.

> 🔍 **Note-taking**
> A good way of taking notes when you are listening to a talk, a lecture, or an interview is to try to write down the key words that you hear. These are the 'content' words (usually nouns or verbs) that will help you remember the important information.

**c** **2 29 ))** Listen to an interview with Polly Akhurst, one of the founders of 'Talk to me London'. Make notes under these headings.

**The 'Talk to me London' badge**

**How Polly has benefited from talking to strangers**

**Mediterranean countries and Madrid**

**Her reaction to negative media coverage**

**What she would say to people who don't want to talk**

**d** Compare your notes with a partner and agree the main points under each heading. Then listen again. Can you add anything to consolidate your notes?

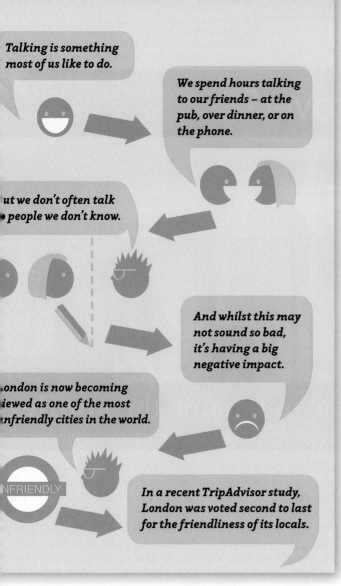

Talking is something most of us like to do.

We spend hours talking to our friends – at the pub, over dinner, or on the phone.

...ut we don't often talk ...o people we don't know.

And whilst this may not sound so bad, it's having a big negative impact.

...ondon is now becoming ...iewed as one of the most ...nfriendly cities in the world.

...NFRIENDLY

In a recent TripAdvisor study, London was voted second to last for the friendliness of its locals.

**e** **2 30**)) Listen to four true stories from the 'Talk to me London' website. Who started a conversation, and who was approached by someone else?

James   Anneka   Philippa   Alise

**f** Now listen again and match the four people to the information about the conversations. Write **Al**, **An**, **Ja**, or **Ph**.

1 ☐ met someone she knew who she hadn't seen for a long time.
2 ☐ talked to someone who had recently come to London.
3 ☐ was surprised that the other person was happy to talk.
4 ☐ was unexpectedly given something.
5 ☐ talked to four different people one after another.
6 ☐ didn't expect anyone to talk to her.
7 ☐ was given a suggestion about how to make the most of travelling time.
8 ☐ ended up chatting to a whole group of people.

**g** If you were visiting London, would you wear a 'Talk to me London' badge? Why (not)?

## 7 SPEAKING

**a** Read some online comments about 'Talk to me London'. How do you think each person feels about the project?

**say** hello@talktomelondon

**Posts** Top / All

**Alex**   I only lived in London for three months, but I experienced my fair share of conversations with people on random benches or at Tube stations late at night, etc. If you want unfriendly, try Vienna. Honestly. I've lived here for nearly a decade, but it still drives me insane. You could spend all day, every day, in the same café and you'd die, decades later, before any of the other regulars even acknowledged your presence! #talktomelondon

**Mark**   London is no different from most cities in this respect. It's an unwritten rule, you don't talk to strangers and they don't talk to you. I can imagine few things worse than someone trying to engage me in small talk on my morning commute. You keep to your private bubble and I'll keep to mine. That's how we like it. #talktomelondon

**Bella**   I just don't get this – London unfriendly, nobody talks to a stranger? Rubbish. Maybe those who find London unfriendly are in fact the ones who are unfriendly, and unwilling to initiate a conversation. No problem for many of us. #talktomelondon

**b** **2 31**)) Look at some useful phrases for giving your opinion in English. Underline the words that you think have extra stress. Listen and check.

 **Emphasizing that something is your own opinion**
1 *I'd say that...*
2 *If you ask me,...*
3 *Personally, I think that...*
4 *Personally speaking, ...*
5 *In my opinion, ...*
6 *In my view,...*
7 *I feel that...*
8 *My feeling is that...*
9 *As far as I'm concerned, ...*

**c** Answer these questions in small groups. Try to use the language from the box to express your opinions.

1 Do people in your town or city tend to chat to complete strangers, or would it be considered odd?
2 Which cities or regions in your country have a reputation for being friendly or unfriendly? Do you agree?
3 Have you ever been to a city or country that struck you as particularly friendly or unfriendly?
4 'You keep to your private bubble and I'll keep to mine.' Do you think this is a good approach to city life?

**G** adding emphasis (1): inversion
**V** describing books and films
**P** sounds and spelling: /ɔː/

> " Literature is the art of discovering something extraordinary about ordinary people, and saying with ordinary words something extraordinary "
>
> *Boris Pasternak,*
> *Russian author and poet*

# 4B From cover to cover?

## 1 READING & SPEAKING

**a** Read the extract from the Barnes & Noble book blog and answer the questions.

- What is a 'spoiler'?
- Has anyone ever spoiled a film, a book, a sports match, or anything else for you by telling you how it ended?

### B&N BOOK BLOG

**Warning:** if you like to be surprised, stop reading right now. But if you're curious about these books and their endings, then read on. (Because I'm not completely cruel, I've whited out the spoilers — just highlight the empty space to see the hidden words.)

*Don't say we didn't warn you...*

**And Then There Were None by Agatha Christie**

Most Agatha Christie novels leave you gobsmacked, but *And Then There Were None* is an absolute masterpiece of the 'whodunnit?' formula. People invited to a party in a mansion keep on being murdered, but by whom? Well, if you're sure you want to know – it was

**b** Read the title of the article and answer the question. Then read the article and check.

**c** Now read the article again and answer these questions with a partner.

1 How did the reading experiment work? What was the outcome?
2 What possible reasons does the writer give for this outcome?
3 What's the writer's overall conclusion?

**d** Talk to a partner.

- Would you ever read the last page of a book first, or ask a friend how a film or sports match ends? Why (not)?
- Do you ever re-read books or watch films or sports matches again? Which ones? Why (not)?
- Does knowing the ending change the experience for you?

# Time to rename the **spoiler**
## DOES KNOWING THE **ENDING** AFFECT YOUR ENJOYMENT?

One of my favourite movies is *When Harry Met Sally*. I can watch it again and again and love it every single time – maybe even more than I did before. There's a scene that will be familiar to any of the movie's fans: Harry and Sally have just set off on their drive to New York City and Harry starts telling Sally about his dark side. He mentions one thing in particular: whenever he starts a new book, he reads the last page first. That way, in case he dies while reading it, he'll know how it ends.

Harry will know how it ends, true, but doesn't that also ruin the book? If you know the ending, how can you enjoy the story? As it turns out, easily. A study in this month's issue of *Psychological Science* comes to a surprising conclusion: spoilers don't actually spoil anything. In fact, they may even serve to enhance the experience of reading.

Over 800 students from the University of California in San Diego took part in a series of experiments where they read one of three types of short story: a story with an ironic twist (such as Roald Dahl), a mystery (such as Agatha Christie), and a literary story (such as Raymond Carver). For each story, there was a spoiler paragraph that revealed the outcome.

The students read the stories either with or without the spoiler. Time to reconsider, it seems, what we call a spoiler. The so-called 'spoiled' stories were actually rated as more enjoyable than those that were 'unspoiled', no matter what type of story was being read. Knowing the ending, even when suspense was part of the story's goal, made the process of reading more, not less, pleasurable.

Why would this be the case? Perhaps, freed from following the plot, we can pay more attention to the quality of the writing and to the subtleties of the story as a whole. Perhaps we're more likely to spot signs and clues about what might happen, and take pleasure in our ability to identify them.

Whatever the reason, it may not be as urgent as we think it is to avoid spoilers. Harry might have the right idea after all, reading the last page first. In fact, he might be getting at the very thing that lets me watch him meet Sally over and over and over again, and enjoy the process every single time.

## 2 VOCABULARY & PRONUNCIATION
describing books and films; /ɔː/

**a** Complete some readers' comments about books and films with an adjective from the list.

| | | | | |
|---|---|---|---|---|
| depressing | entertaining | fast-moving | gripping | haunting |
| heavy-going | implausible | intriguing | moving | thought-provoking |

1 A wonderful film. So _____ it brought tears to my eyes! ★★★★★
2 A _____ novel that raised many interesting questions. ★★★
3 Rather _____ . I really had to make an effort to finish it. ★★
4 A _____ story. I was hooked from the very beginning. ★★★★★
5 A light and _____ novel, perfect for beach reading! ★★★
6 The plot was _____ . It was impossible to predict how it would end. ★★★★
7 The characters were totally _____ . I couldn't take any of them seriously. ★
8 A _____ story which jumps from past to present and back again at breakneck speed. ★★★★
9 A well-written novel, but so _____ it made me feel almost suicidal! ★★★
10 A _____ tale which stayed with me long after I'd finished reading it. ★★★★

**b** (2 32)) Listen and check.

**c** Take turns with a partner to choose an adjective from the list in **a** and name a book or a film that you could use the adjective to describe. Say why.

**d** (2 33)) Listen and write six sentences. Then circle the /ɔː/ sounds in them. What different spellings can be pronounced /ɔː/?

**e** Practise saying the sentences.

## 3 SPEAKING

Talk to a partner about as many of the topics as you can. Tell your partner about a book that…

you couldn't put down
YOU STARTED BUT COULDN'T FINISH
YOU DECIDED TO READ AFTER SEEING THE FILM
you think would make a good film
you bought, but never opened
YOU'VE READ, BUT CAN'T REMEMBER MUCH ABOUT
you were forced to read at school and hated
PEOPLE ARE TALKING ABOUT AT THE MOMENT
YOU FEEL YOU OUGHT TO HAVE READ, BUT HAVEN'T

## 4 GRAMMAR adding emphasis (1): inversion

**a** Complete extracts 1–5 with endings A–E.

1 **No sooner** had we sat down at the kitchen table… ☐
(Margaret Drabble, *A Day in the Life of a Smiling Woman*)

2 **Hardly** had she put the comb in her hair… ☐
(Grimm's Fairy Tales, *Snow White*)

3 **Only later** did I understand… ☐
(Mikhail Gorbachev, *On My Country and the World*)

4 **Never** have I seen so many people in an art gallery… ☐
(review of Matisse exhibition, *The Independent*)

5 **Not only** had Silas killed the only four people who knew where the keystone was hidden, (but)… ☐
(Dan Brown, *The Da Vinci Code*)

A looking happy.
B than the twins burst in.
C than the poison in it took effect, and the girl fell down senseless.
D he had killed a nun inside Saint-Sulpice.
E that this was not the way to proceed, that we could not live by a double standard.

**b** Look at the verbs after the **bold** adverbial expressions. What is unusual about the word order? What is the effect of putting the adverbial expression at the beginning of the sentence?

**c** ► p.147 Grammar Bank 4B. Learn more about adding emphasis using inversion, and practise it.

**d** Complete the sentences in your own words, using inversion to make them as dramatic as possible.

1 Only after the wedding…
2 No sooner…than I realized…
3 Never in the history of sport…
4 Not until the last moment…
5 Not only…, but…

## 5 WRITING

► p.116 Writing *A review*. Write a review of a book or film you have read or watched recently.

## 6 READING

**a** Would you prefer…
- to read a book written in English in the original version or translated into your language? Why?
- to watch an English-language film subtitled or dubbed? Why?

**b** Read the introduction to a blog by Daniel Hahn, a translator. Why do you think he calls translation 'both simple and impossible'?

**c** Read **Part 1** and make sure you understand every word of the 'rough translation'. How do you picture the scene? Where are the two people, and how are they feeling?

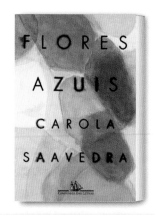

# Translation Diary

**Daniel Hahn** I'm translating a novel. It's written in Portuguese, and it needs to be written in English. There is a Brazilian novelist at one end, and an American publisher at the other, and there's me in the middle, tasked with giving the publisher exactly the same book the novelist has written, keeping it identical in absolutely every conceivable respect, except that I've got to change all the words. The novel is *Blue Flowers* by Carola Saavedra. Or, to be more accurate, the novel is still *Flores Azuis*, for now. *Blue Flowers* is what it's got to be when I'm done with it. So I have to immerse myself in Carola's book, in Portuguese, and write it again for the publishers in English. The process is both simple and impossible, and I'm going to be describing it on this blog.

**1** In this scene, A, the main woman character, describes the moment her lover leaves her:

*Eu não disse nada, não chorei, não pedi explicações, não te implorei para ficar. Eu apenas permaneci ali, imóvel, muda, deitada na cama, enquanto você se vestia, pegava a mochila e ia embora.*

A rough translation might be:

*I didn't say anything, I didn't cry, I didn't ask for explanations, I didn't implore you to stay. I merely stayed there, immobile, mute, lying on the bed, while you dressed, took your rucksack and went away.*

**2** 'Implore' isn't quite right, is it? 'Beg' would be better. And 'immobile', similarly – I prefer 'still' or 'unmoving'. In both cases my first quick version just used words that stayed close to the Portuguese ('implore' for 'implorei', 'immobile' for 'imóvel'), but we need to move away a little further in order to arrive somewhere more like normal English. I think 'merely' is a bit too formal for A's voice here, too.

*I didn't say anything, I didn't cry, I didn't ask for explanations, I didn't beg you to stay. I just stayed there, unmoving, mute, lying on the bed, while you dressed, took your rucksack and went away.*

**3** There are an awful lot of 'I's in that first sentence, aren't there? In Portuguese there's an 'Eu' ('I') at the beginning of the first sentence and an 'Eu' at the beginning of the second, so the sentences are perfectly balanced. As you can see, I've removed a pair of 'I's. And we have a 'rucksack' which should probably be a 'backpack', to minimize how UK-ish it sounds to US readers.

*I didn't say anything, I didn't cry, didn't ask for explanations, didn't beg you to stay. I just stayed there, unmoving, mute, lying on the bed, while you dressed, took your backpack and went away.*

**4** Now, that first sentence ends on the word 'stay' – which would be fine…except that 'stay' appears again, three words later. Hmm, so now I've got to change that, too. One option is 'I didn't beg you not to go', which helps because we imagine A saying 'Please don't go!' rather than 'Please stay!', which isn't quite the same.

*I didn't say anything, I didn't cry, didn't ask for explanations, didn't beg you not to go.*

**5** I've also got to decide if the man is dressing, or getting dressed, or getting himself dressed, and my decision will be as much about the rhythm of the sentence as anything else. And I don't like the ending – 'went away' is very weak. I'd rather end solidly on one word – just 'left'.

*I just stayed there, unmoving, mute, lying on the bed, while you got dressed, took your backpack and left.*

**6** Right. So – we're done now, surely? Um, not quite… I'd prefer 'picked up your backpack' to just 'took your backpack' – I think the latter might sound as though he's taking it from her? And I'm not sure about 'mute', either. I think 'silent' would do. So how about this, then?

*I didn't say anything, I didn't cry, didn't ask for explanations, didn't beg you not to go. I just stayed there, unmoving, silent, lying on the bed, while you got dressed, picked up your backpack and left.*

Better?

**d** Now read **Parts 2–6**, which show the evolution of the translation. (Circle) the changes in each version and compare with a partner.

**e** Read **Parts 2–6** again and match them to the reasons A–E Daniel gives for making the changes.

A ☐ He wants to stay close to the effects achieved in the original, and the translation needs to be accessible to American readers.

B ☐ He wants to choose the right expression to clarify exactly what is happening.

C ☐ It's better not to use the same word twice in quick succession.

D ☐ Some of the words are too close to the original and don't sound very natural in English.

E ☐ He has to decide which version of a phrase will suit the music of the sentence best.

## LEXIS IN CONTEXT

🔍 **Understanding synonyms**

It is very useful to know a variety of synonyms for common words. This will help you to use a wider lexical range in your writing and not to repeat yourself. However, it is important to make sure that your synonym has exactly the meaning or register that you want.

**f** Which synonyms does the translator consider for…?

1 implore _____
2 immobile _____ _____
3 merely _____
4 rucksack _____
5 went away _____
6 mute _____

**g** Now find synonyms in the introduction for:

1 employed to _____
2 the same _____
3 imaginable _____
4 precise _____
5 finished with sth _____

**h** What do you think you could learn from Daniel's blog about improving your own writing in English?

## 7 LISTENING

**a** You are going to listen to an interview with Beverly Johnson, a professional translator working in Spain. Before you listen, think of three questions you might ask her about her job.

**b** (2 34») Listen to the whole interview. Did she answer any of your questions?

**c** Now listen to each part of the interview again. Choose a, b, or c.

(2 35») **Part 1**

1 One of the reasons Beverly decided to become a translator was that…
   a she thought teaching English was boring.
   b she really enjoyed the postgraduate course that she took.
   c she wanted to be self-employed.

2 Which of these does she mention as one of the drawbacks of being a freelance translator?
   a A low salary.
   b No paid holidays.
   c Time pressure.

3 Beverly's advice to would-be translators is to…
   a specialize.
   b study abroad.
   c take a translation course.

(2 36») **Part 2**

4 Most people who translate novels into English…
   a don't do any other kind of translation work.
   b prefer translating authors who are no longer alive.
   c often concentrate mainly on one particular writer.

5 She mentions the advertising slogan for Coca-Cola™ as an example of…
   a how difficult it is to convey humour in another language.
   b how you cannot always translate something word for word.
   c how different cultures may not have the same attitude to advertising.

(2 37») **Part 3**

6 *The Sound of Music* was translated into German as…
   a 'All dreaming together'.
   b 'Tears and dreams'.
   c 'My songs, my dreams'.

7 Which of these is <u>not</u> mentioned as a problem when translating film scripts?
   a Having enough room on the screen.
   b Conveying the personality of the speaker.
   c Misunderstanding the actors' words.

8 The problem with translating swear words in a film script is that…
   a they may be more shocking in other languages.
   b they may not be translatable.
   c you can't use taboo words in some countries.

**d** Are there any words in your language which you think are 'untranslatable' into English? How would you try to express the ideas? Can you think of any English words which are 'untranslatable' into your language?

## 8 (2 MP3») SONG *Story of Your Life* ♫

## GRAMMAR

**a** Complete the sentences with the right word or phrase.

1 It's 2.30 now – what time do you think we'll get _____ London?
2 Unfortunately, Allie got _____ cheating in her final exam.
3 The windows are filthy. Shall we get someone _____ them?
4 I don't think Keith will ever get _____ doing his own laundry – his mother always did it.
5 My passport expires in two months, so I need to get it _____.

**b** Right (✓) or wrong (✗)? Correct any mistakes in the highlighted phrases.

1 Basic, I think she still hasn't got over the break-up of her marriage.
2 We've finished the interviews and all of all we think Joe Young is the most suitable candidate.
3 Dave's really late, isn't he? I think he might get lost.
4 The waiter didn't probably notice that they had left without paying.
5 I think it's unlikely that I'll be given a work permit.
6 What a wonderful smell! Somebody must bake some bread.
7 You definitely won't pass your driving test if you drive that fast!
8 I called you yesterday. You should have got a message on your voicemail.
9 Not only we saw the sights, we managed to do some shopping as well.
10 Only when the main character dies does her husband realize how much he loved her.

**c** Complete the sentences with the right form of the verb in brackets.

1 The traffic is quite bad – she's unlikely _____ before 7.00. (arrive)
2 Maria is bound _____ the news – everybody was talking about it yesterday. (hear)
3 My neighbour can't _____ very long hours. He's always home by early afternoon. (work)
4 No sooner _____ married than James lost his job. (they / get)
5 Never _____ such a wonderful view. It completely took my breath away. (I / see)

## VOCABULARY

**a** Complete the missing words.

1 She's quite shy, but you'll soon get to _____ her.
2 Shall we get _____ for a coffee at the weekend?
3 I've been trying to get _____ of Danny, but he's not answering his phone.
4 She's always phoning me at work – it really gets on my _____.
5 I hope I get _____ this cold by the weekend; I'm supposed to be going to a wedding.
6 His parents let him do whatever he wants, so he's used to getting his own _____.
7 When I was a student, I had to get _____ on less than £50 a week.
8 I hope I get the _____ to talk to him before he goes home.

**b** Circle the right word.

1 The English archers used their bows to fire thousands of *arrows / spears* into the air.
2 After days of fighting, both sides agreed to a *retreat / ceasefire*.
3 The city finally fell after a three-month *siege / coup*.
4 During the civil war, thousands of *refugees / allies* crossed the border to safety.
5 It was a fierce battle and *civilians / casualties* were heavy on both sides.
6 The rebels *broke out / blew up* the railway lines.
7 Even though they were surrounded, the troops refused to *surrender / defeat*.
8 The army shelled the capital with long-range *bullets / missiles*.

**c** Complete the sentences with verbs in the past simple.

buzz creak rattle screech sigh
slam whisper whistle

1 Mabel _____ the door and walked off angrily.
2 'Thanks, darling,' she _____ softly in his ear.
3 He _____ a happy tune as he walked down the street.
4 'I wish he was here – I really miss him,' she _____.
5 The wind was so strong that the windows _____.
6 The car's brakes _____ as it came to a stop.
7 A bee flew in through the window and _____ round the room.
8 The door of the old library _____ open slowly, but there was nobody there!

**d** Write the adjectives for the definitions.

1 th_____-pr_____ = making you think seriously about a particular subject or issue

2 de_____ = making you feel very sad and without enthusiasm

3 in_____ = very interesting because of being unusual or not having an obvious answer or ending

4 gr_____ = exciting or interesting in a way that keeps your attention

5 mo_____ = causing you to have deep feelings of sadness or sympathy

6 im_____ = not seeming reasonable or likely to be true

## CAN YOU UNDERSTAND THIS TEXT?

**a** Read the article once. How do you think you would feel in 'the quietest place on Earth'?

**b** Read the article again and complete it with phrases A–G. There is one phrase you do not need.

A Then, after a minute or two
B The kids were whining
C I booked a 45-minute session
D My experience in the anechoic chamber changed my life
E In an attempt to recapture some peace
F Despite my dislike of loud sounds
G Ironically, far from finding it peaceful

**c** Look at the highlighted words and phrases and work out their meaning. Check with your teacher or with a dictionary.

## ◄ CAN YOU UNDERSTAND THIS FILM?

IDEO

(2) MP3 ))) Watch or listen to a short film on the York Literature Festival. Answer the questions with a number, a date, or a few words.

1 How many literary festivals are there each year in the UK?
2 How old is the York Literature Festival?
3 What kind of people does it attract?
4 When did the city become famous for the Mystery Plays?
5 When was the classic novel *Tristram Shandy* first published?
6 How many copies were printed in York?
7 What is York Minster?
8 When did Paul Farley publish his first collection of poetry?
9 When was Tara Bergin named one of the Next Generation Poets?
10 What can writers learn at Rob O'Connor's workshop?

YORK LITERATURE FESTIVAL

Celebrating the written and spoken word in one of the UK's most beautiful cities.

Steve Orfield in the anechoic chamber

# The quietest place on Earth

**My quest started** when I was in the New York subway with my kids. ¹_____, four trains came screaming into the station at once and I put my hands over my ears and cowered – the noise was deafening. In cities, the ever-present, dull background roar of planes, cars, machinery, and voices is a fact of life. There is no escape from it and I was beginning to be driven mad by it.

²_____, I decided to go on a mission to find the quietest place on Earth; to discover whether absolute silence exists. The place I was most excited about visiting was the anechoic chamber at Orfield Laboratories in Minnesota. This is a small room, massively insulated with layers of concrete and steel to block out exterior sources of noise. It is the quietest place on Earth – 99.9% sound-absorbent.

³_____, most people find its perfect quiet upsetting. The presence of sound around you means things are working; it's business as usual. When sound is absent, that signals malfunction. I had heard that being in an anechoic chamber for longer than 15 minutes can cause extreme symptoms, from claustrophobia and nausea to panic attacks. A violinist tried it and hammered on the door after a few seconds, demanding to be let out because he was so disturbed by the silence.

⁴_____ – no one had managed to stay in for that long before. When the heavy door shut behind me, I was plunged into darkness (lights can make a noise). For the first few seconds, being in such a quiet place felt like nirvana, a balm for my jangled nerves. I strained to hear something and heard...nothing.

⁵_____, I became aware of the sound of my breathing, so I held my breath. The dull thump of my heartbeat became apparent – nothing I could do about that. As the minutes ticked by, I started to hear the blood rushing in my veins. The feeling of peace was spoiled by a tinge of disappointment – this place wasn't quiet at all. You'd have to be dead for absolute silence. Then I stopped obsessing about what bodily functions I could hear and began to enjoy it. I didn't feel afraid any more and came out only because my time was up. Everyone was impressed that I'd beaten the record, but having spent so long searching for quiet, I was comfortable with the feeling of absolute stillness. Afterwards, I felt wonderfully rested and calm.

⁶_____. I found that making space for moments of quiet in my day is the key to happiness – they give you a chance to think about what you want in life. If you can occasionally become master of your own sound environment – from turning off the TV to moving to the country, as I did – you become a lot more accepting of the noises of everyday life.

*By George Michelson Foy in* The Guardian

iTutor    43

**G** distancing
**V** expressions with *time*
**P** linking in short phrases

> Do three things well,
> not ten things badly.
>
> *David Segrove,*
> *British author*

# 5A One thing at a time

## 1 SPEAKING

**a** When you are working or studying, do you tend to do one task at a time and concentrate on it, or do you multitask, i.e. try to do several things at once? Give examples.

**b** Look at some examples of multitasking. Rate them 1–3 (1 = easy to do at the same time, 2 = possible to do at the same time, but can be distracting, 3 = very difficult or even dangerous to do at the same time).

☐ talking to a friend on the phone while you are cooking

☐ checking your email or chatting online while you are working or studying

☐ having a conversation with a friend when you are out jogging together

☐ checking an alternative route on your satnav when you are driving

☐ talking on a hands-free phone while you are driving

☐ listening to music while you are studying or working

☐ listening to music while you are exercising

☐ sending a message while talking to a friend

**c** Talk to a partner.

1 Compare your scores for **b**, and explain your ratings.
2 Which of the pairs of activities above do you do? To what extent do you think doing one thing affects how well you do the other?
3 Do you think multitasking helps you to use your time better?

## 2 READING

**a** You are going to read two extracts about time management: one from a newspaper article and one from a science website. Read the extracts once. With a partner, look at the four headings and choose the best one for each extract.

Get started, get finished
Increased efficiency, increased satisfaction
You think you can do it, but can you really?
The sport of saving time

**b** Read the extracts again. Mark the sentences **T** (true) or **F** (false). Correct the **F** ones.

1 It is often dangerous to chat to a friend while walking in the street.
2 It is more difficult to make a decision when you are doing two things at the same time.
3 It is difficult to maintain a conversation when you are driving if you also have to read a road sign.
4 Researchers have discovered that people trained in mindfulness are unable to multitask.
5 Mindfulness training develops people's ability to concentrate.
6 The quality of your work is not affected by how much you enjoy it.

### LEXIS IN CONTEXT

🔍 **Learning verbs with dependent prepositions**
Some verbs are always followed by a particular preposition before an indirect or direct object, e.g. depend **on**, worry **about**, etc. It is important to make a note of these prepositions when you learn new verbs.

**c** Look at some common verbs and verb phrases from the texts. Complete the gaps with the preposition that normally follows them.

1 deal _____ sth
2 concentrate _____ sth
3 be capable _____ sth
4 focus _____ sth
5 become aware _____ sth
6 be faced _____ sth

**d** Talk to a partner.

1 Have you ever made a mistake or had an accident because you were multitasking? Does the first text explain in any way why it might have happened?
2 What advice do you get from the two texts about how to multitask successfully?

## A

**M**ULTITASKING is a natural everyday occurrence. We can cook dinner while watching TV and we can talk to a friend while walking down the street without bumping into anybody or getting run over. However, research suggests that there is an enormous difference between how the brain can deal with what are referred to as 'highly practised tasks', such as cooking or walking, and how it responds when, for example, you think about adding another ingredient or you decide to change the direction you are walking in. In this case, our brains require us to concentrate on the activity at hand.

Problems also arise when we try to carry out two or more tasks that are in some way related. Most people feel they are perfectly capable of driving and having a conversation at the same time. This is fine until they need to process language while driving, for example, read a road sign. Then the language channel of the brain gets clogged and the brain can no longer cope. A similar thing occurs if the conversation is about something visual, for example your friend describing what his new flat looks like. In this case, as you try to imagine what he is describing, the visual channel of the brain is overloaded and you can no longer concentrate on the road.

| SPACE | TECHNOLOGY | ENVIRONMENT | HEALTH | SCIENCE IN SOCIETY |
| --- | --- | --- | --- | --- |

## B

**MINDFULNESS** refers to moment-by-moment awareness of thoughts, feelings, bodily sensations, and the surrounding environment. It focuses the brain on the present moment, instead of on the past or the future, and is gaining popularity as a practice in daily life.

A recent experiment conducted by psychologists in the USA looked at the effects of mindfulness training on the multitasking behaviour of workers in high-stress environments. They found that when asked to do multiple tasks in a short period of time, those who had been trained in mindfulness had a better memory for details and were able to maintain more focus on each task. They did not get distracted by worrying about the other tasks that still needed doing. This may well be because mindfulness training helps us to become more aware of where we are focusing our attention, so it makes sense that we are then better equipped to deal with a demanding work environment.

According to another study, mindfulness training can help improve people's attitudes towards work. Let's say you are faced with a large pile of invoices to process. If your mind starts to look for more interesting things to do, it is going to take you longer and you will probably make mistakes. If you can look at this task with a calm, clear, and engaged mind, you will be more efficient and you might even find some enjoyment in the process.

💬 Comment  🖶 Print

## 3 LISTENING

**a** You are going to listen to *The Chocolate Meditation*, a well-known exercise used to introduce people to the idea of mindfulness. Before you listen, with a partner, say what you think these verbs mean.

unwrap  inhale  pop (sth) into  melt  chew  swallow

**b** **3 2 ))** Close your eyes and listen. Imagine doing all the stages.

**c** Listen again. What does the speaker say about …?
1 the type of chocolate to choose
2 what to do before you unwrap it
3 what to notice as you unwrap it
4 what to do before you eat it
5 what to notice and do as you eat it
6 when to swallow it

**d** What is the main message of the meditation? Do you agree that mindfulness could 'change your whole day'? Can you think of any other everyday activities you could try this approach with?

## 4 GRAMMAR distancing

**a** Read some sentences about the origins of mindfulness. Then focus on the highlighted phrases. What do they have in common? What effect would it have on the meaning if they were left out?
1 Jon Kabat-Zinn, Professor of Medicine at the University of Massachusetts, is considered to be the 'father' of mindfulness.
2 He claims to help patients cope with stress, pain, and illness.
3 It appears that mindfulness is beneficial in lowering blood pressure and decreasing anxiety.

**b** ➤ **p.148 Grammar Bank 5A.** Learn more about distancing, and practise it.

## 5 WRITING

You are a journalist. Your editor has asked you to write three breaking news stories for the website. However, you have to be careful what you say, as the facts haven't been confirmed yet. Write two or three sentences for each headline, using the prompts and appropriate distancing expressions.

### Politician's wife seeks divorce

Which politician? After how many years of marriage? What do people say is the reason?

### Footballer linked to cheating scandal

Which footballer? What did he do? What are his club planning to do about it?

### Sugar: the new health benefits

What are the benefits? How much sugar do you need to eat? When / In what form should you eat it?

## 6 SPEAKING & LISTENING

a Read an article about a survey by the watch manufacturer Timex. With a partner, complete the information with a time from the list.

### Things we hate waiting for – and how long before we freak out!

According to a US survey, there's a limit to how long people will wait for something before getting annoyed and trying to do something about it. The average wait in different situations before people lose patience is:

## Survey Results

| Survey Results | Length of time |
|---|---|
| for a blind date to arrive | |
| for a bus / train | |
| for a car in front of you to start moving when the light turns green | |
| for a table in a restaurant | |
| for people to stop talking during a film at the cinema | |
| for the doctor | |
| for your partner to get ready to go out | |
| in a queue at a coffee shop | |

| | | | |
|---|---|---|---|
| 5 seconds | 2 minutes | 7 minutes | 15 minutes |
| 20 minutes | 21 minutes | 26 minutes | 32 minutes |

b ➤ **Communication** *The Timex survey p.106.* Check your answers to **a**. Then with your partner, say:
- how long <u>you</u> would wait.
- what you would do or say when you had got frustrated with waiting.

c (3 3)) Now listen to six people talking about waiting for things. What situations do they complain about?

d Listen again. Who…?

1 ☐ wishes other people would just be as quick and efficient as they are
2 ☐ says that the person they're waiting for always comes at the last possible minute
3 ☐ uses a strategy to try to avoid having to wait
4 ☐ doesn't mind waiting if other people follow the rules
5 ☐ says how long they're prepared to wait before getting very annoyed
6 ☐ gets frustrated by sitting watching something happen very slowly

e Do you identify with any of the speakers? In what other circumstances do you hate having to wait?

## 7 VOCABULARY expressions with *time*

a Can you remember the missing words in these sentences from the listening?

1 …but more often they'll say, 'Could be _____ **time** 7 a.m. to 7 p.m.'
2 …you actually sort of see one line loading _____ **a time**.
3 …I always turn up _____ **time**, in fact usually at least five minutes early.

b (3 4)) Listen to the extracts and check.

c ➤ **p.165 Vocabulary Bank** *Expressions with* time.

d Complete these sentences so that they're true for you, or reflect what you think. Then compare with a partner.

1 By the time I'm _____, I'll be _____.
2 Everyone should _____ from time to time.
3 It's only a matter of time before _____.
4 _____ is taking up a lot of my time at the moment.
5 I think _____ is a waste of time.
6 It's going to take me a long time to _____.
7 It's about time I _____.
8 I find _____ very time-consuming.
9 If I had more time off, I'd _____.

## 8 PRONUNCIATION

linking in short phrases

**a** (3 8)) Listen to sentences 1–10. Why are the words linked? Read the information box and check.

1  We need‿to make‿up for lost‿time.
2  He gave me a really hard‿time.
3  We're going to run‿out‿of time.
4  Could‿I have some time‿off next week?
5  At‿times‿I feel like giving‿up completely.
6  Time's‿up. Please‿stop writing.
7  Let's not waste‿time‿on that.
8  It's‿only a matter‿of time before they break‿up.
9  Did you have‿a good‿time last night?
10  It's‿about‿time you learnt‿to cook!

> #### Understanding linking
> When people speak quickly, many phrases are linked together so they sound like one word. This is often because:
> 1  a consonant sound at the end of a word is linked to a vowel sound at the beginning of the next, e.g. *I met him‿a long time‿ago.*
> 2  a word ending with a consonant sound is followed by a word beginning with the same consonant sound, e.g. *I need some‿more time.* This also applies to two very similar sounds, e.g. /d/ and /t/, e.g. *Have a good‿time!*, and /z/ and /s/, e.g. *Please‿sit down.*
> 3  a word ending with a silent *r* or *re*, e.g. *quarter, spare* is followed by a word beginning with a vowel sound. In this case the words are linked and a /r/ sound is added, e.g. *a quarter‿of an‿hour.*

**b** (3 9)) Listen to some three-word phrases which are often heard as one word. First you will hear the phrase on its own, and then you'll hear it in context. What are the phrases?

1  _____ _____ _____
2  _____ _____ _____
3  _____ _____ _____
4  _____ _____ _____
5  _____ _____ _____

**c**  Practise saying the sentences and phrases in **a** and **b**, trying to link the words.

## 9 SPEAKING

With a partner, answer the questions in *Time and you*. Give examples to illustrate your answers using language from the box.

> #### Giving examples
> 1  *For example, ...*      3  *...such as...*      5  *...like...*
> 2  *For instance, ...*     4  *...like...*         6  *An example of this is...*

# Time and you

When you do an exam or test, do you tend to **have time left** at the end or do you usually **run out of time**?

When you were younger, did your parents **give you a hard time** if you came home late? Is there anything else that they used to give you a hard time about?

On a typical weekday morning, are you usually **short of time**? Is there anything you could do to **give yourself more time**?

Do you have any apps that you think really **save you time**? How often do you use them?

What do you usually do to **kill time** while you're waiting at an airport or a station? In what other situations do you sometimes have to kill time?

When you go shopping, do you like to buy things as quickly as possible or do you prefer to **take your time**?

Is there anything or anybody who is **taking up a lot of your time** at the moment? How do you feel about it?

Are you usually **on time** when you meet friends? Does it bother you when other people aren't on time?

Do you usually get to the airport or station **with time to spare** or at the last minute? What do you think this says about your personality?

What do you most enjoy doing when you have some **me time**?

**G** unreal uses of past tenses
**V** money
**P** US and UK accents

> Too many people spend money that they haven't earned to buy things that they don't want to impress people they don't like.
>
> *Will Rogers,*
> *US actor*

# 5B A material world

## 1 READING & SPEAKING

**a** How important do you think the following are for people who are looking for a long-term partner? Number them in order of importance for both men and women. Are there any other important criteria?

| | men look for… | women look for… |
|---|---|---|
| a good education | ☐ | ☐ |
| a healthy bank balance | ☐ | ☐ |
| good looks | ☐ | ☐ |
| an attractive personality | ☐ | ☐ |

**b** Read the first part of the article. What points in **a** does it back up? Did you find the studies mentioned surprising?

**c** Now read the two opposing viewpoints in the article. Answer with **JL** (Jemima Lewis) or **JM** (JoJo Moyes).

**Who…?**
1. ☐ thinks that women are influenced by previous generations' lifestyles
2. ☐ admits that she understands the other viewpoint when she is under a lot of pressure
3. ☐ admits to occasional feelings of jealousy
4. ☐ says that rich husbands are hard to find
5. ☐ thinks that working mothers with children have particularly difficult challenges to deal with
6. ☐ thinks that if you marry for money you have to accept the consequences

**d** Now read the whole article again. With a partner, say what the writer means by:
1. By logical extension, it would appear men are keen to 'marry down'… (lines 9–10)
2. We call them 'trophy wives', as if to distinguish them from the real thing… (lines 28–29)
3. …calibrate your work-life balance to suit yourself, rather than your mortgage provider. (lines 41–42)
4. But marry rich and you may marry a man who views you as a commodity. (lines 51–52)
5. …the shattered dreams of traded-in middle-aged wives… (lines 56–57)
6. Earning my own money means I don't have to justify my shoe habit… (lines 61–62)
7. I wouldn't be delighted if my daughter ended up with a dropout. (line 65)

# Do women really want to marry for money?

1　According to a report from the London School of Economics, women are now more determined than ever to find a partner who will improve their financial prospects. 'Women's aspirations to "marry up", if they can,
5　to a man who is better-educated and higher earning persists in most European countries,' says the report's author, Catherine Hakim. 'Women continue to use marriage as an alternative or supplement to their employment careers,' she concludes. By logical extension, it would appear men
10　are keen to 'marry down', although nobody seems to query, much less gather statistics on, their matrimonial motives. Arguably, there's nothing surprising in these findings, especially when you consider women with young children. A recent study by the National Centre for Social Research
15　revealed that a third of all mothers would prefer to give up their jobs if they could afford to and three-fifths said they would want to work fewer hours.

We asked journalist **Jemima Lewis** and novelist **JoJo Moyes** what they thought.

## Yes, **says Jemima Lewis**

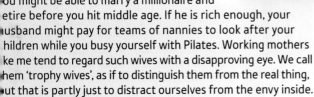

Women want rich husbands. Perhaps we don't often say it – perhaps we don't even like to admit it to ourselves – but women are practical creatures. A rich husband gives you options.

One of the perks of being female is that you grow up knowing there's a slim chance that you might be able to marry a millionaire and retire before you hit middle age. If he is rich enough, your husband might pay for teams of nannies to look after your children while you busy yourself with Pilates. Working mothers like me tend to regard such wives with a disapproving eye. We call them 'trophy wives', as if to distinguish them from the real thing, but that is partly just to distract ourselves from the envy inside.

Whether you fill your days with Pilates or child-rearing, not having to work is…well, less like hard work. Unfortunately, rich husbands, like handsome princes, are not easy to come by. Most of us, not moving in millionaire circles, are likely to fall in love with and marry a more normal bloke. In the meantime, you might have built up a career that you are proud of, and reluctant to give up. If you then have a baby, you are doomed to an inner life of conflict and guilt as you try to find a way to bring up your child without going bankrupt or insane.

Like a winning lottery ticket, a rich husband would solve your problems at a stroke, allowing you to calibrate your work-life balance to suit yourself, rather than your mortgage provider.

## No, **says JoJo Moyes**

Today's young women, having observed their mothers juggling a full-time job and all the domestic responsibility, having the odd nervous breakdown and still having to look glamorous, have now decided they'd prefer to be kept by a wealthy husband. Who can blame them? There are times – usually when sick children and deadlines collide – that I think the same thing.

But marry rich and you may marry a man who views you as a commodity. You may spend much of your time alone; a high-flying career often means an absent husband and father. You can marry for money, but it's not a marriage. It's a deal. And I suspect only the toughest of women can see that with the clarity it requires. The divorce courts are littered with high earners, as well as the shattered dreams of traded-in middle-aged wives who have been replaced by a younger, more glamorous model. My children have long played a game called 'Who's got the sourest face?' in Waitrose. It's always the wives in the really expensive cars.

My husband and I have taken turns as the highest earner. Earning my own money means I don't have to justify my shoe habit, and he doesn't shoulder the mortgage alone. And having a career brings me more contentment than having a designer handbag.

So, I wouldn't be delighted if my daughter ended up with a dropout. But I'd feel worse if she thought the most important thing about a man was his bank balance.

*By Judith Woods in* The Telegraph

**Glossary**
**Pilates** a physical fitness system which focuses on posture
**Waitrose** an upmarket UK supermarket chain

---

## LEXIS IN CONTEXT

🔍 **Understanding metaphors**
These are words or phrases not used literally, but used to describe somebody or something in a more dramatic way to make a description more powerful, e.g. *doomed to an inner life of conflict and guilt* (line 37) where *doomed* doesn't literally mean *certain to fail, die, or be destroyed.*

**e** Look at the highlighted metaphors in the 'No' text. What is their literal meaning? What do they mean here?

**f** Who do you agree with more, Jemima Lewis or JoJo Moyes? Do you think it's acceptable for men and women to consider finance as well as romance when they choose a partner?

## 2 **GRAMMAR** unreal uses of past tenses

**a** Look at the highlighted verbs in these sentences and answer the questions with a partner.
- Which ones refer to things that really happened in the past?
- What do the others have in common? Which ones refer to the present or future? Which ones refer to the past?

1 When we got married, my husband and I were penniless students.
2 If he got promoted, we'd be able to afford a new car.
3 I wish we were better off.
4 It's time we thought about buying a bigger house.
5 I wasn't at all surprised when I heard that they had divorced.
6 I'd rather my husband stayed at home with the children.
7 I wish I'd accepted when he asked me to marry him!
8 If I'd married him, I would have a much better standard of living.

**b** ▶ p.149 Grammar Bank 5B. Learn more about unreal uses of past tenses, and practise them.

**c** Ask and answer the questions in small groups.

Do you ever wish…?
- you could meet a wealthy partner
- you had been born in another decade or century
- you could have a year off to travel
- you could learn a new skill
- you had chosen to study different subjects at school or university
- you had more free time for your hobbies
- you lived in another town or city

## 3 ③ MP3 )) **SONG** *Material Girl* 🎵

## 4 VOCABULARY money

**a** Look at some idioms related to money. With a partner, say what you think they mean.

1 Money doesn't grow on trees.
2 He's really tight-fisted.
3 It must have cost an arm and a leg.
4 They can't make ends meet at the moment.
5 We're in the red. (opp *in the black*)
6 It's daylight robbery!
7 We're going to have to tighten our belts.
8 Those two are definitely living beyond their means!

**b** ➤ **p.166 Vocabulary Bank** *Money*.

**c** Choose the right word from each pair according to meaning, collocation, or register.

1 Mum, can you lend me some money? I'm *broke* | *penniless*.
2 I'm trying to get *a loan* | *a mortgage* from the bank to buy a car.
3 We're going to have to be a little careful this month if we don't want to end up *in the red* | *in the black*.
4 He took part of his pension as *a lump sum* | *a deposit* when he retired.
5 One of my cousins is absolutely *affluent* | *loaded* – she inherited a fortune from her parents.
6 When you're abroad, you get a better *currency* | *exchange rate* if you take money out at a cash machine.
7 We like living here because we have a much better *cost* | *standard* of living.
8 **A** Is breakfast included in the price of the room?
  **B** No, sir. It's 12 *quid* | *pounds* extra.

**d** Choose two or three of the options and tell a partner about them.

### Do you know anybody who...?

## is a bit tight-fisted
## lives beyond their means
### was given a grant to study abroad
buys and sells shares on the stock market
## charges very high fees
## for what they do
### has difficulty making ends meet
often gives donations to charity

## 5 LISTENING

**a** Read the biographical information about Sarita Gupta and Muhammad Yunus. What is the link between them?

| Article | Talk | | Read | Edit | View history |

### Sarita Gupta
*From Wikipedia, the free encyclopedia*

**Sarita Gupta** is an executive with more than 25 years' experience of promoting awareness and raising funds for international non-profit organizations. She's worked for different initiatives that fight poverty around the world. From 2007 to 2010, she was the Vice-President of Development and Communications at Women's World Banking. The mission of Women's World Banking is to strengthen and expand its global network of microfinance institutions and banks, to help low-income women to have access to financial services and information.

### Muhammad Yunus

**Muhammad Yunus** is a social entrepreneur, banker, economist, and civil society leader who was awarded the Nobel Peace Prize for founding the Grameen Bank and pioneering the concepts of microcredit and microfinance. These loans are given to entrepreneurs who are too poor to qualify for traditional bank loans. In 2008, Yunus was rated #2 in *Foreign Policy* magazine's list of the 'Top 100 Global Thinkers'.

**b** **3 15))** Now listen to Sarita Gupta talking about microfinance. Complete the information with two-word phrases.

1 The idea of microfinance started in the _____ _____.
2 The Western world had been _____ _____ to developing countries for many years.
3 Yunus realized that poor people need access _____ _____.
4 Poor people can't _____ _____ relatives because their relatives are poor as well.
5 Yunus's first innovation was to make a group of people responsible for _____ _____ a loan.
6 Poor people can't repay a loan all at once with a _____ _____.
7 However, they can make small _____ _____ and repay a loan little by little.
8 Yunus's system doesn't encourage poor people to borrow a _____ _____.
9 If they pay back a small amount successfully, they can apply for a _____ _____.

**Glossary**
**aid** /eɪd/ money, food, etc. that is sent to help countries in difficult situations
**collateral** /kəˈlætərəl/ *noun* property or sth valuable that you promise to give to sb if you cannot pay back money that you borrow
**peer** /pɪə/ *noun* a person who has the same social status as you

**c** (3 16)) (3 17)) (3 18)) You're going to listen to Sarita Gupta talk about three success stories. Make notes for each case study in the chart.

| | The Dominican Republic | Jordan | India |
|---|---|---|---|
| The situation she was in | | | |
| The business she set up | | | |

**d** Do you think there are people in your country who would benefit from microfinance?

> **Glossary**
> **the DR** the Dominican Republic
> **cantina** /kæn'tiːnə/ *noun* Spanish for a cafeteria or kitchen
> **recourse** /rɪ'kɔːs/ *noun* being able to use sth that can provide help in a difficult situation
> **embroider** /ɪm'brɔɪdə/ *verb* to decorate cloth with a pattern of stitches usually using coloured thread
> **sari** /'sɑːri/ *noun* a long piece of cloth that is worn as the main piece of clothing by women in south Asia
> **amass** /ə'mæs/ *verb* to collect sth, especially in large quantities
> **middleman** /'mɪdlmæn/ *noun* a person or company that buys goods from the company that makes them and sells them to sb else

## 6 PRONUNCIATION  US and UK accents

🔍 **Distinguishing between US and UK accents**
Although people speaking US English will almost always be understood in the UK, and vice versa, there are several differences in pronunciation between Standard English and General American, apart from all the regional accents. Understanding these differences will help you to follow American English more easily.

**a** (3 19)) Sarita Gupta was born in India. She speaks English with a US accent, since she studied at Columbia University in the USA and lives and works in New York. Listen to an extract from her interview. Focus on how she says the highlighted words.

'And the answer is obvious, they need money and all of us, in order to get started, have had access to credit. So, the poor can't get access to credit, they can't go to relatives to borrow because generally the relatives are as poor as they themselves are.'

**b** (3 20)) Now listen to the same passage read by a British speaker. How does the pronunciation of the highlighted words change?

**c** (3 21)) Listen to some more examples of words spoken by UK and US speakers. Can you hear the difference?

| | | UK | US |
|---|---|---|---|
| 1 | twenty | a | b |
| 2 | internet | a | b |
| 3 | party | a | b |
| 4 | clever | a | b |
| 5 | turn | a | b |
| 6 | honest | a | b |
| 7 | coffee | a | b |
| 8 | awesome | a | b |
| 9 | new | a | b |
| 10 | route | a | b |
| 11 | vase | a | b |
| 12 | leisure | a | b |
| 13 | enquiry | a | b |
| 14 | moustache | a | b |
| 15 | address | a | b |

**d** (3 22)) Now listen and circle a if you hear UK pronunciation and b if you hear US pronunciation.

**e** When you listen to English, e.g. in songs or on TV, which accent do you hear more often? Which do you find easier to understand?

## 1 █◄ THE INTERVIEW Part 1
VIDEO

**a** Read the biographical information about Jordan Friedman. Would you be interested in participating in one of his stress reduction programmes?

**Jordan Friedman**, also known as 'The Stress Coach', lives in New York City and is a specialist in the field of stress and stress reduction. He has been developing stress management programmes and resources for individuals, companies, and universities worldwide for over 20 years, and his client list includes Harvard University, the Massachusetts Institute of Technology, and the New York City Department of Education. He is the author of *The Stress Manager's Manual*, and his work has been featured by *The New York Times*, *The Wall Street Journal*, and *The Today Show*. Jordan is an expert on student stress, and has developed a programme called Stressbusters, which helps nearly 250,000 university students and staff.

**b** **③23** ⟩⟩ Watch or listen to **Part 1** of the interview. Why does he think it's important to reduce stress?

**c** Now listen again. Complete sentences 1–5.

1 The biggest causes of stress are…
2 Compared with 20 years ago, life today is more stressful because…
3 Nowadays we don't have time to…
4 If our immune systems are weakened by stress…
5 If we don't sleep well…

**Glossary**
**stressor** *(technical)* something that causes stress
**the immune system** the system in your body that fights infection and disease
**punching bag** *AmE* a heavy leather bag on a rope, used by boxers when they train (*BrE* **punchbag**)
**stroke** a sudden serious illness when a blood vessel in the brain bursts or is blocked, which can cause death or the loss of the ability to move or to speak clearly

## █◄ Part 2
VIDEO

**a** **③24** ⟩⟩ Now watch or listen to **Part 2**. Mark the sentences **T** (true) or **F** (false).

1 Different people should choose different ways of dealing with stress.
2 The stress management techniques Jordan Friedman mentions all take a minute or less.
3 The most important thing about stress management techniques is to make them a habit.
4 Friedman worked with a student who felt very stressed when he had to drive.
5 The student's classmates suggested that he should travel at a different time of day.
6 The solution to the student's problem was difficult for him to see for himself.

**b** Listen again. Say why the **F** sentences are false.

**Glossary**
**salad bar** a counter in a restaurant where customers can serve themselves from a variety of salad ingredients
**walk around the block** go for a quick walk near where you live or work in a town or city
**subway car** a carriage on an underground train

## █◄ Part 3
VIDEO

**a** **③25** ⟩⟩ Now watch or listen to **Part 3**. Do students in your country suffer from similar stress?

# stress and relaxation

**b** Listen again and answer the questions.

1 At what age do people tend to be most stressed?
2 What main reasons does Jordan Friedman give for student stress?
3 How does stress affect memory? How might this affect students?
4 What two things does the Stressbusters programme give students?
5 What feedback have students given about Stressbusters?

> **Glossary**
> **back rub** a short back massage
> **campus** the buildings of a university and the land around them
> **wellness resources** facilities for helping people to stay healthy

## 2 LOOKING AT LANGUAGE

> 🔍 **Compound nouns**
> Jordan Friedman frequently uses compound nouns, e.g. *stress response*, *stress management*, etc. Remember that when you hear new compound nouns, the first noun usually describes the second one – this will help you to work out the meaning.

**a** Try to complete the compound nouns in these extracts from the interview.

1 '…when you have emails coming in and t_____ messages left and right…'
2 'Stress is really important, and, in fact, it can be a l_____saver…'
3 'Er, stress contributes to high **bl**_____ pressure, which contributes to **h**_____ problems and stroke.'
4 'So these are all reasons to really pay attention to our **st**_____ levels and to take action to reduce the stress.'
5 'The great thing about stress **m**_____ is that it's like a salad bar.'
6 'We can do one-minute **br**_____ exercises, we can, er, exercise, we can take a ten-minute walk around the block…'
7 'Stress is a very democratic occurrence, so older people are stressed, **c**_____ students are stressed, babies get stressed…'
8 '…there's a greater need to get help for, er, them while in school, but if you're not with your usual **s**_____ network it's even more challenging sometimes to do so.'

**b** ③26 ))) Watch or listen again and check.

## 3 ◼◀ IN THE STREET
VIDEO

**a** ③27 ))) Watch or listen to five people talking about stress. Who do you think is the most / least stressed? Why?

| Simon, *English* | Stephanie, *English* | Jim, *American* | Myfannwy, *English* | Sean, *English* |

**b** Watch or listen again. Match the people (**Si, St, J, M,** or **Se**) to something they do to de-stress.

☐ focuses on a certain part of their body
☐ blocks out a particular sound
☐ has a favourite meal
☐ goes on holiday
☐ tries not to think about anything

**c** ③28 ))) Watch or listen again and complete the Colloquial English phrases. What do you think they mean?

1 '…to just _____ _____ the sound of the babies.'
2 '…for the past three years I've been kind of _____-_____, really.'
3 'I experience very little stress, except those rare periods when I'm _____ _____ a deadline.'
4 'Um, but I am giving a lecture on Tuesday, and so that's _____ _____ _____ a bit.'
5 '…and every half an hour _____ _____, just if I concentrate on relaxing…'

## 4 SPEAKING

Answer the questions with a partner or in small groups.

- Are you currently more stressed at work or school, or at home? Why?
- How stressful do you find the following? Why?

  buying clothes   driving   exams   travelling

- If you feel stressed when you get home in the evening, what's the first thing you do to unwind?
- Do you ever have back rubs or massages when you feel stressed? Do they help you?
- Where would you go for the weekend if you wanted to get away from it all? Why?
- A recent survey found that Nigeria was the most stressful country in the world to live in, and Norway the least. Where do you think your country would come? Why?

# Communication

## 1A WHAT'S YOUR PERSONALITY?
### Students A + B

**a** Use your four types to find out which personality you have and read the description.

**b** Now find out what your partner's personality is and read the description.

**PLANNER + FACTS + HEAD + INTROVERT = REALIST**
**How you see yourself** mature, stable, conscientious
**What you are like** loyal, straightforward, good at meeting deadlines, respect facts and rules, can be obsessed with schedules, critical of others, may not have faith in other people's abilities

**PLANNER + FACTS + HEAD + EXTROVERT = SUPERVISOR**
**How you see yourself** stable, practical, sociable
**What you are like** natural organizer and administrator, irritated when people don't follow procedures, other people find you bossy

**PLANNER + FACTS + HEART + INTROVERT = NURTURER**
**How you see yourself** gentle, conscientious, mature
**What you are like** caring, may have trouble making decisions that could hurt others, tend to avoid conflict, others may take advantage of you

**PLANNER + FACTS + HEART + EXTROVERT = PROVIDER**
**How you see yourself** sympathetic, easy-going, steady
**What you are like** warm, caring, traditional, tend to avoid conflict, not afraid to express your beliefs

**PLANNER + IDEAS + HEAD + INTROVERT = MASTERMIND**
**How you see yourself** logical, thorough, bright
**What you are like** efficient, independent, rarely change your mind, critical of those who don't understand you

**PLANNER + IDEAS + HEAD + EXTROVERT = LEADER**
**How you see yourself** bright, independent, logical
**What you are like** organized, good at solving large-scale problems, can be critical and aggressive

**PLANNER + IDEAS + HEART + INTROVERT = COUNSELLOR**
**How you see yourself** gentle, peaceful, cautious
**What you are like** relaxed and creative, deeply private, can be difficult to get to know

**PLANNER + IDEAS + HEART + EXTROVERT = MENTOR**
**How you see yourself** intelligent, outgoing, sensitive
**What you are like** articulate, warm, lively, extremely sensitive to people's needs, may become overbearing

**SPONTANEOUS + FACTS + HEAD + INTROVERT = RESOLVER**
**How you see yourself** understanding, stable, easy-going
**What you are like** independent, rational, good at finding solutions, natural risk taker, enjoy an adrenaline rush, often focus on short-term results, sometimes lose sight of the bigger picture

**SPONTANEOUS + FACTS + HEAD + EXTROVERT = GO-GETTER**
**How you see yourself** inventive, enthusiastic, determined, alert
**What you are like** resourceful, tough-minded, may become frustrated by routines and constraints

**SPONTANEOUS + FACTS + HEART + INTROVERT = PEACEMAKER**
**How you see yourself** steady, gentle, sympathetic
**What you are like** sensitive to the feelings of others and the world around you, can be self-critical, often difficult to get to know

**SPONTANEOUS + FACTS + HEART + EXTROVERT = PERFORMER**
**How you see yourself** enthusiastic, sociable, sensitive
**What you are like** fun-loving, outgoing, often a good motivator, can be unreliable

**SPONTANEOUS + IDEAS + HEAD + INTROVERT = STRATEGIST**
**How you see yourself** bright, logical, individualistic
**What you are like** quiet, easy-going, intellectually curious, logical, may be critical or sarcastic, can be insensitive to the emotional needs of others

**SPONTANEOUS + IDEAS + HEAD + EXTROVERT = BIG THINKER**
**How you see yourself** talkative, curious, logical, self-sufficient
**What you are like** ingenious, bored by routine, can be rude, rebellious, critical of others

**SPONTANEOUS + IDEAS + HEART + INTROVERT = IDEALIST**
**How you see yourself** bright, forgiving, curious
**What you are like** generally easy-going, flexible, can be stubborn, may refuse to compromise

**SPONTANEOUS + IDEAS + HEART + EXTROVERT = INNOVATOR**
**How you see yourself** imaginative, sociable, sympathetic
**What you are like** energetic, sensitive, creative, sometimes illogical, rebellious, unfocused

◀ p.7

## 3A BLIND DATE  Student A

**a** Read what Stef says about her blind date with Graham.

Previous | Next | Index

### Life & style  Blind date

#### Stef on Graham

**First impressions?** Friendly, funny, attractive, and forgiving: I was late.

**What did you talk about?** Music, comedy, food, bad dancing.

**Any awkward moments?** Only when we were playing pool – neither of us are fabulous players.

**Good table manners?** Impeccable, even though it was burgers. He faced the ultimate date challenge well.

**Best thing about him?** Really genuine and friendly.

**Did you go on somewhere?** No, but then we didn't leave till 2 a.m.

**Marks out of 10?** 9 (being a teacher, I can never give full marks).

**Would you meet again?** I'd really like to, yeah.

**b** Using your own words, tell **B** about Stef's opinion of the date.

> When Stef met Graham at the restaurant her first impressions were positive. She thought he was...

**c** Now listen to **B** describing Graham's opinion of the date. How do you think their relationship might develop?

**d** Turn to p.106 and see if you were right!

◀ p.26

## 3B GUESS THE SENTENCE  Student A

**a** Look at sentences 1–5 and guess what the missing phrase could be. Remember: + = positive verb and − = negative verb.

1 A lot of people say the book is better than the film, but actually I _____ . +
2 It wasn't a particularly nice day for the barbecue, but at least it _____ . −
3 The sea was blue, the sun was shining, and the picnic was marvellous. All in all, it was _____ . +
4 On the one hand, dogs are much better company than any other pets, but on the other hand, you have to _____ at least twice a day. +
5 Make sure your suitcase weighs less than 20 kilos, otherwise you may _____ . +

**b** **B** has the complete sentences 1–5. Read your sentences to **B**. Keep trying different possibilities until you get each sentence exactly right.

**c** Listen to your partner's sentences. Tell them to keep guessing until they get it exactly the same as yours.

6 I'm not sure you would enjoy the play, and in any case it will be very difficult **to get tickets**.
7 Some of the teachers aren't very inspiring, but on the whole I think it's **a good school**.
8 Laura's husband only thinks of himself and he always gets his own way. In other words, **he's totally selfish**.
9 I don't feel like going to Miranda's birthday party and besides, I **don't have anything to wear**.
10 It's no big surprise that Leo didn't do very well in his exam. After all, he **didn't study at all**.

◀ p.31

# Communication

## 4A BORIS LEFT HANGING
Students A + B

# Boris left hanging

**By Hannah Furness**
1:58PM BST  01 Aug 2012

Boris Johnson was featuring as a special guest in Victoria Park, east London, during the 2012 Olympics, to ride the 1,050ft (320m) zip wire, wearing a hard hat and waving two Union Jack flags as he attempted to sail down. Instead, he came to a halt about 65ft (20m) before the end of the wire, and was left dangling inelegantly in front of a watching crowd. The Mayor spent around five minutes hanging comically from the line, as spectators took video footage and photographs of his misfortune. When one asked how he was feeling, he replied 'Very, very well, thank you', before shouting: 'Get me a rope, get me a ladder'.

◀ p.36

## 5A THE TIMEX SURVEY  Students A + B

### Survey Results

| | Length of time |
| --- | --- |
| for a blind date to arrive | 26 minutes |
| for a bus / train | 20 minutes |
| for a car in front of you to start moving when the light turns green | 5 seconds |
| for a table in a restaurant | 15 minutes |
| for people to stop talking during a film at the cinema | 2 minutes |
| for the doctor | 32 minutes |
| for your partner to get ready to go out | 21 minutes |
| in a queue at a coffee shop | 7 minutes |

◀ p.46

## 3A BLIND DATE  Students A + B

Life & style  Blind date

🏠  Previous | Next | Index

**Stef and Graham on their wedding day**

◀ p.26

## 3A BLIND DATE Student B

**a** Read what Graham says about his blind date with Stef. Then listen to **A** describing Stef's opinion of the date.

**b** Now, using your own words, tell **A** about Graham's opinion of the date.

> *When Graham met Stef he thought she was beautiful. Unfortunately...*

How do you think their relationship might develop?

---

### Life & style  Blind date

.....................................................................

🏠 Previous | Next | Index

.....................................................................

**Graham on Stef**

.....................................................................

**First impressions?** Effortlessly beautiful and unforgivably late. But she had phoned.

**What did you talk about?** Music, cooking, and why Abba are the greatest pop band ever.

**Any awkward moments?** Not really.

**Good table manners?** I've never seen a burger crammed into a face with such grace and finesse.

**Best thing about her?** Anyone who knows the full routine to *Saturday Night Fever* and is prepared to strut their stuff scores highly with me.

**Did you go on somewhere?** Cash machine, bus stop.

**Marks out of 10?** 9. Would have been higher, but I lost a game of pool.

**Would you meet again?** Yes, it'd be great to do it again.

---

**c** Turn to p.106 and see if you were right!

◀ *p.26*

## 3B GUESS THE SENTENCE
### Student B

**a** Look at sentences 6–10 and guess what the missing phrase could be. Remember: ➕ = positive verb and ➖ = negative verb.

6  I'm not sure you would enjoy the play, and in any case it will be very difficult _____ . ➕

7  Some of the teachers aren't very inspiring, but on the whole I think it's _____ . ➕

8  Laura's husband only thinks of himself and he always gets his own way. In other words, _____ . ➕

9  I don't feel like going to Miranda's birthday party and besides, I _____ . ➖

10  It's no big surprise that Leo didn't do very well in his exam. After all, he _____ . ➖

**b** Listen to your partner's sentences. Tell them to keep guessing until they get it exactly the same as yours.

1  A lot of people say the book is better than the film, but actually I **preferred the film**.

2  It wasn't a particularly nice day for the barbecue, but at least it **didn't rain**.

3  The sea was blue, the sun was shining, and the picnic was marvellous. All in all, it was **a great day**.

4  On the one hand, dogs are much better company than any other pets, but on the other hand, you have to **take them for a walk** at least twice a day.

5  Make sure your suitcase weighs less than 20 kilos, otherwise you may **have to pay extra**.

**c** **A** has the complete sentences 6–10. Now read your sentences to **A**. Keep trying different possibilities until you get each sentence exactly right.

◀ *p.31*

# Writing  A job application

## ANALYSING A MODEL TEXT

**a**  You see the following advertisement on the Skyscanner website. Would you be interested in applying for the job? Why (not)?

### Receptionist

**Location: Edinburgh**

The receptionist is the first point of contact for staff and visitors. The role involves a variety of tasks including answering and directing calls, welcoming visitors, scheduling meetings, and general admin support.

Core hours are 8 a.m.–6 p.m. and you will need to be available to work earlier shifts some days and later shifts other days.

**About you:**

The ideal candidate will have a customer-focused personality with a strong can-do attitude. We're looking for someone with proven communication skills for liaising with individuals at all levels in a very fast-moving environment.

**Interested? The closing date for applications is Wednesday 18 June – click 'Apply' before this opportunity flies away!**

**b**  Read the first draft of an email written in response to the advertisement. What information does Agata give in the three main paragraphs?

| To: | irena.foster@skyscanner.net |
|---|---|
| From: | Agata Beck |
| Subject: | Application |

Dear ~~Miss~~ *Ms* Foster,

~~My name is Agata Beck.~~ I am writing to apply for the post of receptionist advertised in your website.

1  I have recently graduated from the University of Berlin, where I completed a degree in business studies. I have a high level of spoken english (C1 on the CEFR), as I lived in the United States during six months as part of an exchange programm between my school and a high school in Utah. I made many American friends during this period, but we lost touch when I came home.

2  As you will see from my CV, I have some relevant experience because I am currently an intern at a leading German travel company. I have worked in various roles, including marketing asistant and administrator and my tasks have included organizing and running meetings and dealing with clients by phone and email. The director of company would be happy to provide a reference. He is, in fact, my uncle.

3  I am very enthusiastic on travel and would welcome the chance to be part of such a high-profile and successful company. I believe I would be suitable for the job advertised as, apart of my work experience, I am an outgoing person and get along well with people. Friends describe me as calm and consciensious and I would enjoy the variety and excitement the job would offer. I would definitely not panic when things got busy!

I attach a full CV and if you require a further information, I would be very happy to provide it.

I look forward to hearing from you.
Yours sincerely,
Agata Beck

> 🔍 **Improving your first draft**
> Check your writing for correct paragraphing, mistakes, irrelevant information, and language which is in an inappropriate register.

**c**  Read the draft email again and try to improve it.

  1  Cross out three sentences (not including the example) which are irrelevant or inappropriate.
  2  Correct ten more mistakes in the highlighted phrases, including spelling, capital letters, grammar, and vocabulary.

**d**  Do you think Skyscanner would have given her an interview if she had sent her first draft?

112

## SEFUL LANGUAGE

Look at 1–9 below. How did Agata express these ideas in a more formal way? Use the **bold** word(s) to help you remember. Then look at the text again to check your answers.

1 This letter is to ask you to give me the job of receptionist. **apply**
*I am writing to apply for the post of receptionist.*

2 I've just finished uni, where I did business studies. **graduate / degree**

3 I can speak English very well. **high**

4 I've done this kind of job before. **relevant**

5 My tasks have included talking to people on the phone. **dealing / clients**

6 I'd love to work for such a famous company. **welcome / high-profile**

7 I'm sending a full CV with this email. **attach**

8 If you need to know anything else, I'll tell you. **require / provide**

9 Hope to hear from you soon! **forward**

## PLANNING WHAT TO WRITE

a Read the job advertisement below and underline the information you will need to respond to. Then make notes about:

- any qualifications you have.
- any relevant experience you could include.
- what aspects of your personality you think would make you suitable for the job and how you could illustrate them.
- any other information you think you need to include.

---

**Festival staff required to work at Global Stage UK**,
a world music event in the west of England, from 12th to 14th July

### Responsibilities
- To ensure the safety and comfort of the public and to assist in the running of a successful festival.
- To help to manage any crowd-related problems, including maintaining a state of calm to minimize any injury.
- To prevent unauthorized access to the site by members of the public.

### Requirements
- You must be aged 18 or over on the date of the festival and be eligible to work in the UK.
- You must be physically fit and healthy and able to work under pressure in a demanding atmosphere.
- You should speak English well and have some experience of dealing with the public.

### How to apply
Send an email and full CV to Emma Richards:
e.richards@globalstage.org

---

b Compare notes with a partner and discuss how relevant you think each other's information is, what you think you should leave out, and what else you might want to include.

**TIPS** for writing a covering email / letter to apply for a job, grant, etc.

- Use appropriate sentences to open the email / letter.
- Organize the main body of the email / letter into clear paragraphs.
- Use a suitable style:
  Don't use contractions or very informal expressions.
  Use formal vocabulary where appropriate, e.g. *require* instead of *need*, *as* instead of *because*.
  The use of a conditional can often sound more polite, e.g. *I would welcome the chance to...*
- When you say why you think you are suitable for the job, be factual and positive, but not over-confident. Be careful not to sound arrogant.
- Use appropriate phrases to close the email / letter.

## WRITING

You have decided to apply for the festival job advertised opposite. Write a covering email of between 200 and 250 words.

**DRAFT** your email.

- Write an introductory sentence to explain why you are writing.
- Paragraph 1: Give personal information including skills and qualifications.
- Paragraph 2: Talk about any relevant experience you have.
- Paragraph 3: Explain why you think you would be suitable for the job.
- Write a closing sentence.

**EDIT** the email, checking paragraphing, cutting any irrelevant information, and making sure it is the right length.

**CHECK** the email for mistakes in grammar, spelling, punctuation, and register.

◀ *p.11*

# Writing An article

## ANALYSING A MODEL TEXT

a You are going to read an article about childhood covering the areas below. What information would you include if you were writing about your country?

- What are the main differences between children's lives 50 years ago and children's lives now?
- Why have these changes occurred?
- Do you think the changes are positive or negative?

b Now read the article. Did the writer include any of your ideas? With a partner, choose what you think is the best title from the options below and say why you prefer it to the others.

> **How childhood has changed**
> **Children of the past**
> **My childhood**

c Answer the questions with a partner.

1 What is the effect of the direct question in the introduction? Where is it answered?

2 What does paragraph 1 focus on? What examples are given?

3 What are the changes that the writer focuses on in paragraph 2 and what reasons are given for the changes? Do you agree?

4 Underline the discourse markers that are used to link the points in paragraphs 2 and 3, e.g. *First…*

**Children's lives have changed enormously over the last 50 years. But do they have happier childhoods?**

1 It's difficult to look back on one's own childhood without some element of nostalgia. I have four brothers and sisters and my memories are all about being with them, playing board games on the living room floor, or spending days outside with the other neighbourhood children, racing around on our bikes, or exploring the nearby woods. My parents hardly ever appear in these memories, except as providers either of meals or of severe reprimands after some particularly hazardous adventure.

2 These days, in the UK at least, the nature of childhood has changed dramatically since the 1960s. First, families are smaller and there are far more only children. It is common for both parents to work outside the home and far fewer people have the time to bring up a large family. As a result, today's boys and girls spend much of their time alone. Another major change is that youngsters today tend to spend a huge proportion of their free time at home, inside. This is due more than anything to the fact that parents worry much more than they used to about real or imagined dangers, so they wouldn't dream of letting their children play outside by themselves.

3 Finally, the kinds of toys children have and the way they play is totally different. Computer and video games have replaced the board games and more active pastimes of my childhood. The fact that they can play electronic games on their own further increases the sense of isolation felt by many young people today. The irony is that so many of these devices are called 'interactive'.

4 Do these changes mean that children today have a less idyllic childhood than I had? I personally believe that they do, but perhaps every generation feels exactly the same.

## USEFUL LANGUAGE

**○ Using synonyms**

Try not to repeat the same words and phrases too often in your writing. Instead, where possible, use a synonym or similar expression if you can think of one. This will both make the text more varied for the reader and help to link the article together. A good monolingual dictionary or thesaurus can help you.

**1** Find synonyms in the article for…

1  at the present time _____ , _____
2  children _____ , _____ , _____
3  alone, without adults _____ , _____

**○ Using richer vocabulary**

You can make your writing more colourful and interesting to read by trying to use a richer range of vocabulary instead of the most obvious words.

**2** Can you remember how the words in *italics* were expressed in the article, to make the style more interesting?

1  Children's lives have changed *in a big way*… _____
2  …spending days outside with the other *children who lived near us*… _____
3  …*going* around *fast* on our bikes… _____
4  My parents *don't* appear *very often* in these memories… _____
5  …after some particularly *dangerous* adventure. _____
6  …*usually both parents* work outside the home _____
7  …that children today have a less *happy* childhood than I had? _____

## PLANNING WHAT TO WRITE

**a** Look at the exam question below.

Many aspects of life have changed over the last 30 years. These include:
**marriage   dating   the role of women and / or men**

Write an article for an online magazine about how <u>one</u> of these areas has changed in your country and say whether you think these changes are positive or negative.

With a partner, brainstorm for each topic…

1  what the situation used to be like.
2  whether the situation has changed a lot in your country.
3  whether you think the changes are positive or negative and why.

Now decide which topic you are going to write about and which ideas you want to include.

**b** Think of a possible title for your article.

**TIPS** for writing an article:

* Remember that this is not an essay. In an essay, you would focus on the most important points, but for an article, you should choose the points that you could say something interesting about, or where you can think of any interesting personal examples.
* There is no fixed structure for an article, but it is important to have clear paragraphs. Use discourse markers to link your points or arguments.
* Use a suitable style, neither very formal nor very informal.
* Make the introduction reasonably short. You could use a question or questions which you then answer in the article.
* Try to engage the reader, e.g. by referring to your personal experience.
* Vary your vocabulary using synonyms where possible.

## WRITING

Write an article of between 200 and 250 words.

**DRAFT** your article.

* Write a brief introduction which refers to the changes and asks a question.
* Write two or three main paragraphs saying what the situation used to be like and how it has changed.
* Write a conclusion which refers back to the question in the introduction and which says whether you think the changes are positive or negative.

**EDIT** the article, checking paragraphing, cutting any irrelevant information, and making sure it is the right length.

**CHECK** the article for mistakes in grammar, spelling, punctuation, and register.

◀ *p.19*

# Writing A review

## ANALYSING A MODEL TEXT

a   Which of the following would normally influence you to read a book?

- a friend of yours recommended it
- it's a bestseller – everybody is reading it
- you saw and enjoyed a film based on it
- you were told to read it at school
- you read a good review of it

b   Read the book review. In which paragraph 1–4 do you find the following information? Write **DS** if the review doesn't say. Does the review make you want to read the book?

- [ ] the strong points of the book
- [ ] the basic outline of the plot
- [ ] what happens in the end
- [ ] where and when the story is set
- [ ] the weakness(es) of the book
- [ ] whether the reviewer recommends the book or not
- [ ] who the author is
- [ ] who the main characters are
- [ ] how much the book costs
- [ ] who the book will appeal to

c   Look at these extracts from a first draft. Which words did the reviewer leave out or change to make it more concise? Then read the information box about **Participle clauses** to check.

**1**

A thriller, **which is set in the present day** in a small town in Missouri in the USA, it immediately became an international bestseller.

**2**

…a couple, Nick and Amy Dunne, **who are now living in Nick's home town** of Carthage,…

**3**

Nick now owns a bar, **which was opened with his wife's money**, which he runs with his sister Margo.

---

**1** *Gone Girl* is the third novel by American writer Gillian Flynn. A thriller, set in the present day in a small town in Missouri in the USA, it immediately became an international bestseller.

**2** The main characters in the novel are a couple, Nick and Amy Dunne, now living in Nick's home town of Carthage, after Nick lost his job as a journalist in New York City. Nick now owns a bar, opened with his wife's money, which he runs with his sister Margo. On the day of his fifth wedding anniversary, Nick discovers that his wife, Amy, is missing. For various reasons, he becomes a prime suspect in her disappearance. The first half of the book is told in the first person, alternately by Nick, and then by Amy through extracts from her journal. The two stories are totally different: Nick describes Amy as stubborn and antisocial whereas she makes him out to be aggressive and difficult. As a result, the reader is left guessing whether Nick is guilty or not. In the second half, however, the reader realizes that neither Nick nor Amy have been telling the truth in their account of the marriage. The resulting situation has unexpected consequences for Nick, Amy, and the reader.

**3** The great strength of this book is how the characters of Nick and Amy unfold. Despite having the typical devices common to thrillers, for example, several possible suspects and plenty of red herrings, the novel is also a psychological analysis of the effect on personalities of failure and disappointed dreams. My only criticism would be that the first half goes on too long and perhaps could have been slightly cut down.

**4** Not only is this a complex and absolutely gripping novel, but it also tackles real problems in society, such as the unhappiness that is caused by problems with the economy and the effect of the media on a crime investigation. For all lovers of psychological thrillers, *Gone Girl* is a must.

> **Glossary**
> **red herring** an unimportant fact, event, idea, etc. that takes people's attention from the important one

### 🔍 Participle clauses
The writer uses participles (*set, living, opened*) instead of a subject + verb. Past participles replace verbs in the passive, and present participles (*-ing* forms) replace verbs in the active. The subject of the clause is usually the same as the subject of the main clause.

Participle clauses can be used:
- instead of a conjunction (*after, as, when, because, although*, etc.) + subject + verb, e.g. *Having run out of money…* instead of *Because she has run out of money…*
- instead of a relative clause, e.g. *set in the present day / opened with his wife's money* instead of *which is set… / which was opened…*

When you use a participle clause, you do not need to link the next clause with *and*, e.g. *It is set in 1903 and it tells the story of a young girl…* → *Set in 1903, it tells the story…*

**d** Rewrite the sentences, making the highlighted phrases more concise by using participle clauses.

1 As she believes him to be the murderer, Anya is absolutely terrified.

2 Armelle, who was forced to marry a man she did not love, decided to throw herself into her work.

3 Simon, who realizes that the police are after him, tries to escape.

4 It was first published in 1903 and it has been reprinted many times.

5 When he hears the shot, Mark rushes into the house.

6 It is based on his wartime diaries and it tells the story of a young soldier.

## USEFUL LANGUAGE

**e** Underline the adverbs of degree in these phrases from the review. What effect do they have on the adjectives?

> The two stories are totally different...

> ...and perhaps could have been slightly cut down.

**f** Cross out any adverbs that don't fit in these sentences. Tick (✓) if all are possible.

1 My only criticism is that the plot is *somewhat* | *slightly* | *a little* implausible.

2 The last chapter is *really* | *very* | *absolutely* fascinating.

3 The end of the novel is *rather* | *pretty* | *quite* disappointing.

4 The denouement is *absolutely* | *incredibly* | *extremely* thrilling.

## PLANNING WHAT TO WRITE

**a** Think of a book or film that you have read or seen recently. Make a list of the main things about the characters and plot that you should cover in a review. Don't include a spoiler. Use the present tense and try to include at least one participle clause.

**b** Exchange your list with other students to see if they can identify the book or film.

**TIPS** for writing a book / film review:

- Choose a book or film that you know well.
- Organize the review into clear paragraphs.
- Use a suitable style, neither very formal nor very informal.
- Give your reader a brief idea of the plot, but do not give away the whole story. This is only part of your review, so choose only the main events and be as concise as possible.
- Use the present tense when you describe the plot. Using participle clauses will help to keep it concise.
- Use a range of adjectives that describe as precisely as possible how the book or film made you feel, e.g. *gripping, moving*, etc. (see p.39). Use adverbs of degree to modify them, e.g. *absolutely gripping*.
- Remember that an effective review will include both praise and criticism.

## WRITING

A student magazine has asked for reviews of recent books and films. Write a review of between 200 and 250 words.

**DRAFT** your review.

- Paragraph 1: Include the title of the book or film, the genre, the author or director, and where / when it is set.
- Paragraph 2: Describe the plot, including information about the main characters.
- Paragraph 3: Talk about what you liked and any criticisms you may have.
- Paragraph 4: Give a summary of your opinion and a recommendation.

**EDIT** the review, making sure you've covered all the main points, checking paragraphing, cutting any irrelevant information, and making sure it is the right length.

**CHECK** the review for mistakes in grammar, spelling, punctuation, and register.

◀ p.39

# Listening

🔊 **1** 2»)

Frida Kahlo is Latin America's best-known twentieth century painter, and a key figure in Mexican art. She has also become a kind of cultural legend. She was born in Mexico in 1907, the third of four daughters, and when she was six she caught polio – a disease which left her with one leg shorter than the other. Her second tragedy came when she was 18: she was riding in a bus when it collided with a tram. She suffered serious injuries, which affected her ability to have children. Although she recovered, she was in pain for much of her life and had three miscarriages. But it was this accident and the long periods of recuperation that changed Frida's career plans: she had wanted to study medicine, but instead she started to paint. This work is an unfinished one – you can see patches of bare canvas behind the row of women at the bottom of the picture and some of the faces have been painted over, suggesting she may have wanted to repaint them. Frida started it in 1949, five years before the end of her short life – she died in 1954 at the age of 47. She actually carried on trying to finish it on her deathbed, which suggests that it had a strong meaning for her.

As with many of her other works, the image contains at least one self-portrait: she is the third woman from the left in the bottom row, but the unborn child next to her may also be a representation of her – it is placed below her father, to whom she was very close. The painting is a kind of visual family tree: at the top are both sets of grandparents. On the left are her father's parents, whose ancestors were German–Hungarian. On the right are her maternal grandparents: her grandfather Antonio had American Indian origins, while her grandmother Isabel was the great-granddaughter of a Spanish general. Her parents Matilde and Guillermo, who were dead by the time this picture was painted, are in the middle of the picture. Their portraits are based on photographs and it is interesting that they are shown turning away from each other – their marriage was an unhappy one. They appear with their dead parents in a kind of cloud above their four daughters. From left to right the daughters are Matilde, the eldest, then Adriana, followed by Frida herself (with her niece Isolda) and then, with a blanked-out face, her sister, Cristina. Frida was very close to Cristina, but also jealous of her, especially because she had an affair with Frida's husband, the painter Diego Rivera. The next figure is Cristina's son Antonio, but it is not clear who the last unfinished face in the very bottom right-hand corner might be.

🔊 **1** 13»)

**Interviewer** Well, today I'm very pleased to be visiting the Edinburgh offices of Skyscanner, a company which did extremely well in this year's *Sunday Times* Best Companies to Work For awards, coming sixth overall and winning outright in the categories for most exciting future and best personal growth. So, welcome to Lisa Imlach. Lisa, could you start by telling us a bit about what you do?

**Lisa** So I am the PR, PR Manager for the Danish, Swedish, and Turkish markets. I look after the, our PR agencies there, and what that really means is that I work with them to get Skyscanner messages and stories into the media, so that could be anything from a big report on trends, on the future of travel, to smaller stories about where the Turkish people are going on summer holidays.

**I** And how long have you worked at Skyscanner?

**L** I have just celebrated my year anniversary.

**I** Oh, well, congratulations!

**L** Lots has changed in a year, but all good changes.

**I** And what was it that attracted you to apply for a job here?

**L** I had always want, wanted to work somewhere that was kind of travel-focused, my previous job was in a very dry environment, so much so that I decided I would go travelling and then the day before I flew to South

America for a few months, I had an interview here and found out when I was in the Bolivian Salt Flats that I got the job, so really nice, yeah.

**I** Skyscanner did very well in this year's *Sunday Times* survey of Best Companies to Work For. Do you agree that it's a good place to work?

**L** Yeah, absolutely it's, it's a very funny thing, actually, because it very quickly becomes the norm for someone who works here, all these amazing benefits we have, so when you talk to someone else, you know, in another company, you suddenly think 'Wow, we're so lucky,' so, you know, anything from flexible working to the small things like free fruit, to people being able to work from their home country, they are all massive benefits that you quite quickly get used to, but I think everyone really does appreciate it.

**I** So I guess it would be difficult to go anywhere else after this?

**L** Yes, very much – maybe that's the plan, maybe that's the ploy that they've gone with!

**I** Is, is there one thing that you'd identify for you as a particularly significant benefit?

**L** I have to admit what I really love is, the flexible working policy, it's a quite casual thing, there is no formal procedure, but it, it very much places the trust with the, the employees, so, you know, if I want to leave early on a Friday, there is kind of this, relaxed understanding, 'Do you know what? You'll make up the time when you can, you're in charge, you're the, you're the one who knows your workload and your own role,' which is really nice, it's quite refreshing because it's quite unusual, especially within quite a large corporate–, you know, organization and so I particularly like that.

**I** Is there anything that you might change about, about the company or about its, the way it treats its employees?

**L** I think, so we're growing at quite a, kind of rapid pace and I think because we have six different offices – you know, Beijing, Miami – I think as we grow it will probably be something that we need to tackle in terms of how we all work together across different time zones, so I think at some point that will be something that becomes more of an issue – it's not at the moment, but I'm pretty confident that Skyscanner will be able to tackle that, and tackle that in good time.

**I** Wonderful. OK, well, thank you very much indeed, Lisa, thanks for your time.

**L** Thank you.

🔊 **1** 19»)  **Part 1**

**Interviewer** Eliza Carthy, could you tell us a bit about your family background, your parents and grandparents?

**Eliza** Um, I come from a musical family; my parents are folk singers, my father is a guitarist who is known for playing for playing the guitar, um, and inventing a particular style of English folk guitar. Um, he started playing when he was 17, back in the fifties, and, um, really was, was quite instrumental in his youth in sort of building the, the sixties folk club scene in London. He was a friend of Bob Dylan and Paul Simon many, many years ago, and, um, is known for reconstructing old traditional ballads, traditional English ballads. My mother comes from a folk-singing family called The Watersons, and they were from the north of England, they're from Hull, which is in the north of England, and they were also instrumental in the beginning of the sixties folk revival, the formation of the folk clubs, and the, the beginning of, basically, the professional music scene that I work on now.

**I** And were your parents both from musical families?

**E** Um, really, both sides of my family are musical: my, my mother's side of the family were all travellers and gypsies, my– er, her grandmother, she was brought up by her grandmother, both of her parents died when she was very young. She had an uncle that played the

trumpet, you know, her father played the banjo, he used to listen to American radio in– during the Second World War and he used to learn the songs off the radio like that. Her grandmother was very into the sort of old romantic ballads like *The Spinning Wheel* and things like that, and she used to– she used to sing when they were little; the whole family sang, the whole family danced. And I was brought up in that kind of a family: my mother and her, her brother and her sister were in a singing group, my dad joined that singing group, and then, when I was old enough, I joined the family as well.

**I** So you had a very musical upbringing?

**E** My upbringing was– I suppose some people might think it was quite a hippy upbringing. I was brought up on a farm, um, that had three houses in a row, with me and my mum and dad in the end house, my uncle – my mum's brother – and his wife and their four children in the middle house, and then my mum's sister and her husband and their two children on the other end house. And we grew up basically self-sufficient, we had animals and we had chickens and goats and pigs and horses and things like that, and we, we grew up singing together and living together in that environment in North Yorkshire in the 1970s. Um, we had– Because my parents were professional musicians and touring musicians, we had a lot of touring musician friends who would come and stay at the farm and they would sing and play all the time and there was music all around when I was a child, and that really, that really formed the basis of, of, of how I live now.

🔊 **1** 20»)  **Part 2**

**Interviewer** Do you think it was inevitable that you'd become a professional musician?

**Eliza** Well, if you if you were ever to ask any of us, were it– we would definitely have all said no. I wanted to be, I wanted to be a writer; my mum certainly didn't want me to go on the road. My mum retired in 1966 – 65 / 66 from professional touring to raise me. I mean, the road is a difficult place, whether you're travelling with your family or with a band or on your own, and she certainly didn't want that for me. My dad also probably never thought that I would do it, but I ended up following– exactly following his footsteps and quitting school when I was 17 and going on the road, and I've been on the road ever since.

**I** Can you tell us about your first public performance?

**E** My dad says that my first public performance was at the Fylde Folk Music Festival in Fleetwood in Lancashire when I was six, and we were at the Marine Hall and they were singing, The Watersons, the family– the family group were, were singing, and I asked if I could– I asked if I could go up on stage with them, and I was six. And Dad said, 'Well, you know, you probably don't know everything so just stand next to me on stage and we'll start singing and if you, if you know the song just pull on my leg and I'll lift you up to the microphone and you can, you can join in.' God, I must have been awful! But yes, apparently I just– the first song they started up singing, tugged on his leg, and he picked me up and held me to the microphone and I sang that, and he was like, 'Did you enjoy that?' 'Yes, I did!' Put me down again and they started singing the next one, tugged on his leg, same thing! And he just ended up doing the whole concert with me sitting on his hip! Which er– now I have a six-year-old and I know how heavy she is – it must have been quite difficult, God bless him!

**I** Has having children yourself changed your approach to your career?

**E** Er, yes, in a way. Yes, in a way it has. I've just reordered my working year because my eldest daughter has just started school, so I, you know– I'm, I'm not free to, to take the children with me on the road anymore and, and I'm now bound by the school terms. So I try to work only on the weekends and in school holidays now and I try to, to be Mummy from Monday to Friday, taking them to school, bringing them back again. I'm not getting a great deal of sleep, but then I don't know many mothers of– many mothers of six- and four-year-olds that are getting a great deal of sleep!

**21 ))) Part 3**

**nterviewer** You do a lot of collaborations with other musicians. What is it that appeals to you about working like that?

**liza** I like working with other– I don't like working alone. I don't know if that's because I don't trust myself or I just don't like being alone; I like being surrounded by a big crowd of people. I suppose that's, that's partly to do with my upbringing, there were always so many people around, that, um, I, I'm at my best, I'm at my best in a, in a large event where loads of people are running around doing things and we're all sort of collaborating with each other and there's lots of ideas and everyone's having, you know, a creative time, and that's how I feel– yeah, that's how I feel I, I work best, and that's why at the moment I have a 13-piece band and it's just heaven for me being with so many people and just feeling like a part of a big machine, I love that.

Is there a difference between playing with your family and playing with other people?

Um, yes, very much so. I'm not sure if I could tell you how different or why it's different. My dad is very eloquent on how and why it's different and he, he knows that uniquely because he joined The Watersons, and The Watersons was, was a brother and two sisters, and he joined that, and of course he was married to my mum, but he wasn't related to her. And there is this thing within family groups, this blood harmony thing, this intuition, you have similar sounding voices, you know where a relative is going to go, and that may be because you know each other so well, but it also may be whatever it is that binds a family together anyway.

Would you like your children to follow in your footsteps?

I get very, very excited when the children, um, when the children love music, I get very excited. My daughter Florence is very, very sharp, she listens and she can already– she plays *Twinkle, Twinkle* on the violin, plucking like that, and on the guitar as well, and she's– yeah, she has a very, very good sense of rhythm. And she loves foreign languages as well, there's a real, um, there's a real sort of correlation there between, between language and singing, she has great pitch, she is able to learn songs and things very, very quickly, and I love that. And Isabella, my youngest as well, she's really, she's really showing interest in it and I love it when they do that. As to whether or not I'd want them to be touring musicians, I think I'm probably of the same opinion as my mother, which is, 'No, not really!' But, you know, I, I think the– I think the world is changing anyway, I don't know how many touring musicians there are going to be in the world in 20 years when they're ready, I don't know.

**23 )))**

**nterviewer** How much do you know about your family tree?

**om** Erm, actually a surprisingly large amount. Er, my dad's quite into genealogy and the family tree, erm, so he's actually traced my surname back to, I think it's twelfth century, er, Durham, um, and we've gone to there and seen our crest on the family, er, on the font at the church and everything. So yeah, quite far back – it's a Saxon name and, you know, no Normans or anything in it. So yeah, quite a lot.

Is there anyone in your family that you'd like to know more about?

Erm, I think, yeah, there, um, one called Elizabeth Elstob. Um, she was a poet in London actually, erm and it would be quite interesting to know a bit more about her, because she was quite famous, by all means, but I don't know enough about her to be able to talk about it really, so yeah.

**nterviewer** How much do you know about your family tree?

**ent** I know a fair about– amount about my family tree. Um, I know we come back from ancestors in Sweden and, er, England, and I know we've traced it back I think to, to the 1500s for some of the lines.

Have you ever researched it?

**K** Erm, you know, I haven't personally done a lot of research about my ancestors. I know we have the books and we have the stories and the journals and it's all there, so I guess I, I, I'd be interested to know a little bit about, er, what my my ancestors did, er, before they came to America. Um, 'cause I think they were farmers, I'm not entirely sure.

**Interviewer** How much do you know about your family tree?

**Alison** Um, I know a little bit because, um, my dad's done some research into his side of the family. Um, we know that my father's side stretches back to the 1700s in Cornwall. Um, my great-great-grandfather went down on the *Titanic*. Interesting piece of family history. Um, and we've got some family artefacts for that.

**I** Is there anyone in your family that you'd like to know more about?

**A** Um, probably the wife of the man who went down with the *Titanic*. I think she had quite an interesting and quite difficult life. Um, she had a baby, er, brought it up by herself, so sounds like a, an amazing woman.

**Interviewer** How much do you know about your family tree?

**Marylin** Um, I know quite a lot because a relative of my father's, um, did some research on our family tree, oh about 20 years ago. So, well, I know that my father's family, um, is from Luxembourg and in fact when I worked there I tried to get in touch with some distant relatives, but they weren't interested.

**I** Is there anyone in your family that you'd like to know more about?

**M** Um, well, guess what, it's precisely those relatives who are still living in Luxembourg. But what can I do, if they didn't want to meet me, oh well, I guess it's just destiny.

**Interviewer** How much do you know about your family tree?

**Hannah** You know, I, I know a little bit about my family tree because I was lucky enough to grow up with having great-grandparents in my life until about, like, ninth grade, so I know a lot from them and they told me a lot of stories about their parents and grandparents, but it doesn't go much further than that and that's only on my dad's side. I know about, um, immigration from Russia but that's all I know and then my mum's side I really don't know a lot about, but it's something that I'm interested in looking into.

**I** Have you ever researched it?

**H** I've tried to research it a little bit, er, like doing the ancestry dot com thing, but um I haven't really gotten much further than that.

**I** Is there anyone in your family that you'd like to know more about?

**H** I'd love to know more about my great-grandmother's grandmother. So I guess that would be my great-great-great grandmother. Um, she was involved with Prohibition and I heard stories of her, um, like, bringing, like making alcohol in their house and then, like, smuggling it to other areas of– they actually lived in New York, so other areas of the city. Yeah.

**1 30 )))**

1 I'm from a small village on the south-east coast of Scotland, it's a very small place, not very many people live there. I liked growing up there, but I think it's a better place to visit than it is to actually live because there isn't very much for young people to do there. The people are quite nice and friendly, but most people have spent their whole lives there and their families have been there for several generations, so sometimes it can seem a bit insular.

2 I'm from Tipperary which is in the middle of Ireland. It's quite a rural place. The town I'm from has a population of around 2,000, so it's quite small, but that means that most people know each other. So I'd say the people there are friendly and quite welcoming.

3 I'm from Oxford in the south-east of England, I, I was born here and I've, I've lived here my whole life. Difficult to say what the people are like because it's, in a way it's a city of two halves, famous for its university, but also, which obviously has people from all over the world, but also, it's a city in its own right, it has a very large BMW factory where they make Minis, so, but it's a nice place, I like it, I've lived here my whole life pretty much, so, so there we are.

4 So I'm from Melbourne which is on the south-east coast of Australia, just in, in the state of Victoria, this is a really cultural city, very European, you've got everything from beaches to art galleries, lots of shopping, and bars and restaurants, so it's a fantastic city to be in. The people are really laid back and and quite friendly there. We've got a very big mixture of cultures there, so a very multicultural city. So it's quite diverse and a really interesting place to be.

5 I'm from New Jersey and it's a nice mix between rural and city life because it, it has a lot of nature and nice kind of mountain landscapes where you can go hiking or walking, but it also has nice access to the city and lots of nice little shops and restaurants as well.

6 OK, I was born in Johannesburg in the late, in the late 50s. I moved to Cape Town when I went to university and of course it's a very beautiful old colonial centre, with lovely buildings, and the aspect of Table Bay with the beautiful backdrop of Table Mountain, wonderful vegetation and a wonderful friendly community of people. It's very vibrant and exciting, people like bright colours in the strong sunlight, it's a very creative environment.

**1 31 )))**

**Interviewer** Are there any native speaker accents that you find especially difficult to understand?

**Joanna** Anyone with a broad regional accent is, is going to be a challenge for non-native speakers, and from my personal experience, the accents that I would put into this category are, in no particular order: Ireland, Liverpool, the north-east, Glasgow, and the, the far north of Scotland. And I've, again personally, never been to, to the States, but just watching films, I sometimes struggle with accents from the Deep South. One of my favourite films is *No Country for Old Men*, but until this day I've got no idea what Tommy Lee Jones says in the closing scenes of the film.

**I** How comfortable do you feel with your own accent?

**J** I think I've reached a good place with my accent, it's, it's mine, and, and I'm happy with it, but it's, it's been a journey to get to this place, and when I was a student at Warsaw University, I did a comparative Polish-English phonetics class, which was very, very useful, along that journey, and I learnt lots about the mistakes that I was making in English because of my mother tongue. And so I consciously worked to improve my pronunciation, and in the end, I sort of sounded like a bit like the Oxford English Dictionary. And when I first came to England, the people I met would say, just after a few exchanges, would say 'Cor, you sound posh!' Funnily enough, it didn't sound like a compliment...but of course, living here, I, I lost the posh edge quite quickly.

**I** Do you find it easier to understand native or non-native speakers of English?

**J** I think the closer any speaker is to the standard pronunciation, whether they are native or non-native, it, it's going to be relatively easy to understand, and, at the same time, a strong regional accent or a really strong foreign accent is going to be an issue, and it can make communication really difficult. But at the same time, again, if, if you, are exposed to a certain type of accent for quite a long time, that sort of familiarity really helps, because you get used to the, the 'melody' of, of how somebody speaks. And I suppose the–, just to give you an example, the people who come from the Nordic countries are actually really easy to understand, they've got a very clear, very beautifully articulated, way in which they speak English, so they're a pleasure to listen to.

**1 32 )))**

**Interviewer** How do you feel about having your English corrected?

**Joanna** I actually really appreciate it, because otherwise I would just not know that I've made a mistake. In fact sometimes I remember either a specific context or a place in which I was corrected and that just helps me recall the correct version much easier. And of course, a lot depends on who the person is who corrects me and how they do it. So if they're going to be nice and friendly, I will listen to them willingly, but if they're not, then I will naturally assume that they just wanted to be mean and point out that my English is not that good after all.

**I** Is there anything you still find difficult about English?

**J** There are so many words in English. I find I come across a new one pretty much every single day. And I think it'll always be a challenge, but also an adventure because there will be something new and something to learn for me, always. And just yesterday I learnt a new word, the word is 'intrepid' and I found it in a description of a film that I wanted to watch, which was *The Raiders of the Lost Ark*.

**I** Do you feel in any way a different person when you're speaking English compared to when you're speaking in your own language?

**J** This is, actually a really interesting question. If you Googled 'two languages two personalities', it's amazing how many different blogs and newspaper articles actually talk about it. I wouldn't say that I'm a, a different person, I don't think it's a split personality disorder we have to deal with, but I think that what does change is that, my behaviour, and the way that I communicate with people is affected by the language in which I speak at the time. Without trying to sound stereotypical, but, I'm more polite and tentative in English, and I'm much more direct when I speak Polish. And I think you can you can see it most obviously in writing, so if I have to write an email in Polish, and it, it's sort of squeezed somewhere in between messages that I write in English, then after a few sentences I, I've realized that I've just used so many *could haves* and *would haves*, and I still haven't got to the point. So basically, it's just a question of delete and start again.

**I** Do you have any stories about not understanding someone?

**J** For me personally, the most traumatic experience linguistically was when I visited my partner's family, who live in Buckie, which is, a really charming small fishing village in the north of Scotland, it's in the Moray Firth, and I have to say that as I, I thought I spoke pretty good English, but, my confidence was crushed because I realized that I was understanding about 30% of what everyone around me was saying. And it wasn't just the accent, it was the actual words, they, they were completely different! So, turns out that, for example, I've got one 'bairn', and to go to the shops I have to go 'doon the brae', which, if you translate it, means that I actu– 'I've got one child' and to get to the shops I have to go 'down the hill'.

**1 39**

1 My, my earliest memory, I must have been about three, I guess, possibly two, was, when we'd been to, to a funfair and I would have gone with my brother, who's a bit older than me, and my parents, and I'd been bought, a, a helium balloon, and for some reason the balloon had a snowman inside it, it was only September; I don't know why there was a snowman, but, but there was, and I took it out into the back garden and because it was full of helium, obviously, it was pulling on the string, it wanted to, to fly away, and I let go, I didn't let go by accident, I remember letting go on purpose, to see what would happen, and of course what happened was the balloon flew up into the sky over the neighbours' trees and disappeared, and I was absolutely devastated, heartbroken by the loss of the balloon, and stood there crying and crying, and my dad had to go back to the funfair and get me another identical balloon, which did nothing to console me, I kept crying and crying and crying and that's my, my earliest memory, not a very happy one!

2 My earliest memory is probably from when I was about three or four years old and it was Christmas and I was at my nana's house with, all my family and my uncle was reading to me, he was reading *The Little Mermaid*, except that he was making it up, he wasn't actually reading the words in the book, he was just saying things like 'Ariel went to buy some fish and chips' and things like that, and that made me quite annoyed because I was at an age where I couldn't really read myself, but I knew that he was reading it wrong. So I got quite annoyed with him and told him to read it properly, but yeah, that's my earliest memory.

3 My earliest memory is from when, I must have been nearly three, and we were moving house, we moved to a block of flats and I remember arriving and it was, it was dark and we'd had quite a long journey and we arrived and we went in the door and we turned the lights on and nothing happened, and the whole flat was completely black and dark, no power, no electricity, no lights, and I thought this was fantastic, and we had a torch and I was just running around, running around the, the hall and the rooms, finding all these new rooms all with a torch, and I imagined that it was always going to be like that, that we'd, we'd arrived in a house that wasn't going to have lights, so I was always going to have to use a torch. And I thought that was going to be brilliant. My mother was in tears, obviously she, she was very stressed from the journey and arriving somewhere and having no power. But I, I was really, really excited by it, and the next day when the power came on I was really disappointed.

**1 40**

**Presenter** Are our first memories reliable, or are they always based on something people have told us? What age do most people's first memories come from? John Fisher has been reading a fascinating new book about memory by Professor Draaisma called *How Memory Shapes Our Past*, and he's going to answer these questions for us and more. Hello, John.

**John Fisher** Hello.

**P** Let's start at the beginning, then. At what age do first memories generally occur?

**J** Well, according to both past and present research, 80% of our first memories are of things which happened to us between the ages of two and four. It's very unusual to remember anything that happened before that age.

**P** Why is that?

**J** There seem to be two main reasons, according to Professor Draaisma. The first reason is that before the age of two, children don't have a clear sense of themselves as individuals – they can't usually identify themselves in a photo. And you know how a very small child enjoys seeing himself in a mirror, but he doesn't actually realize that the person he can see is him. Children of this age also have problems with the pronouns *I* and *you*. And a memory without *I* is impossible. That's to say, we can't begin to have memories until we have an awareness of self.

**P** And the second reason?

**J** The second reason is related to language. According to the research, first memories coincide with the development of linguistic skills, with a child learning to talk. And as far as autobiographical memory is concerned, it's essential for a child to be able to use the past tense, so that he or she can talk about something that happened in the past, and then remember it.

**P** I see. What are first memories normally about? I mean, is it possible to generalize at all?

**J** Early memories seem to be related to strong emotions, such as happiness, unhappiness, pain, and surprise. Recent research suggests that three quarters of first memories are related to fear, to frightening experiences like being left alone, or a large dog, or having an accident – things like falling off a swing in a park. And of course this makes sense, and bears out the evolutionary theory that the human memory is linked to self-preservation. You remember these things in order to be prepared if they happen again, so that you can protect yourself.

**P** Are first memories only related to emotions or are there any specific events that tend to become first memories?

**J** The events that are most often remembered, and these are always related to one of the emotions I mentioned before, are the birth of a baby brother or sister, a death, or a family visit. Festive celebrations with bright lights were also mentioned quite frequently, much more frequently than events we might have expected to be significant, like a child's first day at school. Another interesting aspect is that first memories tend to be very visual. They're almost invariably described as pictures, not smells or sounds.

**P** First memories are often considered unreliable, in that perhaps sometimes they're not real memories, just things other people have told us about ourselves or that we have seen in photos. Is that true, according to Professor Draaisma?

**J** Absolutely! He cites the famous case of the Swiss psychologist Jean Piaget...

**1 41**

**Presenter** First memories are often considered unreliable, in that perhaps sometimes they're not real memories, just things other people have told us about ourselves or that we have seen in photos. Is that true, according to Professor Draaisma?

**John Fisher** Absolutely! He cites the famous case of the Swiss psychologist Jean Piaget. Piaget had always thought that his first memory was of sitting in his pram as a one-year-old baby when a man tried to kidnap him. He remembered his nanny fighting the kidnapper to save him. The nanny was then given a watch as a reward by Jean's parents. But many years later, I think when Jean was 15, the parents received a letter from the nanny in which she returned the watch to them. The nanny, who was by now an old woman, confessed in the letter that she'd made up the whole story, and that was why she was returning the watch. Of course, Jean had heard the story told so many times that he was convinced that he'd remembered the whole incident.

**2 8**

**Presenter** A first date is loaded with expectation. Will I like them, and will they like me? Is this person going to be 'the one' or will I want to run for the door before the starter? Will we have anything to talk about and, if not, how will we get through the evening? Here's relationships expert Jenny with some suggestions on how to make sure that your first date is the best it can be – even if it turns out to be your only date.

**Jenny** Hello there. My first tip is 'Choose the venue carefully', that is, the place where you're going to meet. Try to avoid very noisy places where you can't hear each other, or places where you can't talk, like cinemas. So a good place to meet might be a quiet bar for an after-work drink, for example, or lunch in a little local place you know. The advantage of keeping the first date short and sweet, meeting for a drink or for lunch rather than dinner, is that if you don't like each other, you don't have to make it through a seven-course meal together. And of course if you do like each other, you can either extend the date, or plan a longer one for next time.

Tip number two is 'Make an effort with your appearance'. Obviously you don't want to make so much of an effort that your date wouldn't recognize you if they saw you in the street the next day. But getting your hair done, say, or wearing something you know you look good in, those kinds of things show that you care – and that you want to make a good impression. I mean, if you turn up with unwashed hair, wearing yesterday's clothes, you aren't likely to win anyone over.

The third tip, and it's an important one, is 'Be kind', even if you think the date is going nowhere. It doesn't cost anything, and it'll make a big difference to how much the other person enjoys themselves. Of course being kind also means not lying or giving your date false hope. Don't tell someone that you'll phone and that you can't wait to see them again if you have absolutely no intention of following through!

Tip number four, which is sort of related to number three, is 'Don't forget your manners'. Make sure you turn up on time, and if you're going to be late for whatever reason, let your date know. Try not to yawn even if you're getting a bit tired. Turn off your phone, and if the other person is footing the bill, do remember to say 'thank you'. And one last thing while we're on the subject of manners – you can tell a lot about a person by how they treat waiters and waitresses. So don't just be polite to your date, be polite to the other people, too.

Number five is 'Don't pretend to be anything you're not'. It can be very tempting to exaggerate, or to dress up the truth, or just to plain lie to try to get your date interested. Of course, you may get away with it if you don't see the person again after the first date, but if the relationship does last any longer, you may find yourself in a tricky situation further down the line. So, for example, if you're separated, don't say that you're divorced. If you hate football, don't say that you can't think of a better way to spend a Saturday afternoon than cheering on Manchester City. And if you work part-time in a call centre, don't say you're something big in communications.

Finally, and this is my last tip, 'Don't make an instant judgement'. Many of us make up our minds whether we like someone in the first few seconds or minutes of meeting them. But you know, first impressions can be misleading, so try not to rule someone out straightaway. It's much better to spend a bit of time getting to know them, and if you're not sure about someone, it may take two or three dates before you can really decide. If you make a snap decision, you may risk missing out on the love of your life.

Jenny, thank you very much for the advice. And now we turn to the next…

### 2 14 Part 1

**nterviewer** How important is historical accuracy in a historical film?

**Adrian** The notion of accuracy in history is a really difficult one in drama because you know, it's like saying, well, 'Was *Macbeth* accurate? Was– is Shakespearean drama accurate?', the iro– the thing is, it's not about historical accuracy, it's about whether you can make a drama work from history that means something to an audience now. So I tend to take the view that, in a way, accuracy isn't the issue when it comes to the drama, if you're writing a drama you, you have the right as a writer to create the drama that works for you, so you can certainly change details. The truth is nobody really knows how people spoke in Rome or how people spoke in the courts of Charles II or William the Conqueror or Victoria, or whoever, you have an idea from writing, from books, plays, and so on. We know when certain things happened, what sort of dates happened. I think it's really a question of judgement, if you make history ridiculous, if you change detail to the point where history is an absurdity then obviously things become more difficult. The truth is, the, the more recent history is, the more difficult it is not to be authentic to it. In a way it's much easier to play fast and loose with the details of what happened in Rome than it is to play fast and loose with the details of what happened in the Iraq War, say, you know. So it, it, it's all a matter of perspective in some ways. It, it, it's something that you have to be aware of and which you try to be faithful to, but you can't ultimately say a drama has to be bound by the rules of history, because that's not what drama is.

Do you think that the writer has a responsibility to represent any kind of historical truth?

**A** Not unless that's his intention. If it's your intention to be truthful to history and you, and you put a piece out saying 'This is the true story of, say, the murder of Julius Caesar exactly as the historical record has it,' then of course, you do have an obligation, because if you then deliberately tell lies about it, you are, you know, you're deceiving your audience. If, however, you say you're writing a drama about the assassination of Julius Caesar purely from your own perspective and entirely in a fictional context then you have the right to tell the story however you like. I don't think you have any obligation except to the, to the story that you are telling. What you can't be is deliberately dishonest, you can't say 'This is true,' when you know full well it isn't.

### 2 15 Part 2

**nterviewer** Can you think of any examples where you feel the facts have been twisted too far?

**Adrian** Well, I think the notion of whether a film, a historical film has gone too far in presenting a dramatized fictional version of the truth is really a matter of personal taste. The danger is with any historical film that if that becomes the only thing that the audience sees on that subject, if it becomes the received version of the truth, as it were, because people don't always make the distinction between movies and reality and history, then obviously if that film is grossly irresponsible or grossly fantastic in its in its presentation of the truth, that could, I suppose, become controversial. I mean, if you– you know, the only thing anybody is ever likely to know about *Spartacus*, for example, the movie, is Kirk Douglas and all his friends standing up and saying 'I am Spartacus, I am Spartacus', which is a wonderful moment and it stands for the notion of freedom of individual choice and so on. So *Spartacus*, the film made in 1962, I think, if memory serves, bec– has become, I think, for nearly everybody who knows anything about Spartacus, the only version of the truth. Now in fact we don't know if any of that is true, really. There are some accounts of the historical Spartacus, but very, very few, and what, virtually the only thing that's known about is that there was a man called Spartacus and there was a rebellion and many people were, you know, were crucified at the end of it, as in, as in the film. Whether that's irresponsible I don't know, I, I can't say that I think it is, I think in a way it's, it's, it's *Spartacus* is a film that had a resonance in the modern era.

There are other examples, you know, a lot of people felt that the version of William Wallace that was presented in *Braveheart* was really pushing the limits of what history could stand – the whole, in effect, his whole career was invented in the film, or at least, yeah, built on to such a degree that some people felt that perhaps it was more about the notion of Scotland as an independent country than it was about history as an authentic spectacle. But you know, again, these things are a matter of purely personal taste, I mean, I enjoyed *Braveheart* immensely.

### 2 16 Part 1

**Interviewer** Professor Beard, what's the secret to getting people interested in the Romans, in ancient history?

**Mary** Well, you have to go about it in the right way, really. Um, you know, I think perhaps starting from rather arcane and difficult bits of literature isn't the right way. But, you know, one thing that you see in Britain, you know, one thing that we know is that an awful lot of our culture and our geography and our place names and so on are actually formed by the Romans, you know. You ask somebody, um, 'Why do you think so many English place names end in *-chester* or *-caster*, you know, Manchester, Doncaster?' And they'll often say, 'I don't know'. And then you say, 'That's because that bit – *-caster* – is from the Latin for 'military camp', and every place that ends *-caster* or *-chester* once had a Roman fort on it'. And I've got a pretty 99% success record with getting people interested after that, because suddenly it is a question, not of these, um, uh, remote people who wrote some literature that you probably suspect would be boring; it's the people who formed the geography of our country and much of Europe. Why is London the capital of, of Britain? It's because the Romans made it so.

**I** What do you think we can learn from Roman history?

**M** In political terms many of the issues and questions and dilemmas that we face now, uh, were faced by the Romans. And in many ways we're still thinking about and using their answers. I mean, one classic example of that is a famous incident in Roman history in 63 BC where there's a terrorist plot in, in the City of Rome to, to assassinate the political leaders, to torch the city, um, and to take over – revolution. Um, and that plot is discovered by, uh, one of the most famous Romans of all, Marcus Tullius Cicero, the great orator and wit of Roman culture. And he discovers the plot. He lays it before the Senate. He then decides to execute the leading conspirators without trial, summary execution. Um, and a couple of years later he's exiled. Now, in many ways that's the kind of problem we're still facing, uh, with modern responses to terrorism. I mean, what…how far does, how far should homeland security be more important than civil rights, you know? Uh, you know, what about those people in Guantanamo Bay without trial? Um, you know, where, where does the boundary come between the safety of the state and the liberty of the citizen? Now, the Romans were debating that in the 60s BC. And in many ways we're debating it, uh, along the same terms. And in part we've learned from how they debated those rights and wrongs.

### 2 17 Part 2

**Interviewer** If you could go back in time, is there one particular historical period that you'd like to go back to?

**Mary** I think it would be a terrible kind of, er, punishment to be made to go back in history, you know, particularly if you're a woman, you know. There's, you know, there is not a single historical period in world history where women had halfway as decent a time as they do now. So, deciding to go back there, uh, you know, that would, that would be a self-inflicted punishment. I think I'd rather go in the future. Um, and there's also, I mean, even for men there's considerable disadvantages about the past, you know, like, you know, no antibiotics and no aspirin.

**I** Today we live in a celebrity culture, but in *Meet the Romans*, you focus on the lives of the ordinary people in Rome. Was that a conscious decision, to try to get people away from celebrity culture?

**M** I was rather pleased that people did actually find, you know, the non-celebrity, um, version of the Romans interesting. Um, and in some ways if it, if it was a small antidote to modern celebrity culture, I'm extremely pleased. Um, I think that, that wasn't quite what was driving me, though, because, uh, I think the celebrities of the ancient world are so remote from us in some ways. Um, and one of the things that puts people off ancient history is that, you know, you know, the big narrative books, the kind of the history of 'the big men', you know, never seem to answer all those questions that we know we all want to know about the ancient world, you know, or any period in the past, you know: where did they go to the loo, you know. Um, and actually I think people are often short-changed, uh, about, um, the…in, in terms of providing an answer to questions which are really good ones, you know. Um, you know, in the end most of us, most women – don't know about men – most women, you know, do really want to know what having a baby was like, um, uh, before the advent of modern obstetrics, you know. That's a big question. It's not a– it's not, simply because it's, uh, intimate and female doesn't mean it's a less important question than why Julius Caesar was assassinated. And actually world history contains a lot more people like me and my family and women and slaves and people who, you know, want to do many of the things that we want to do, you know. But they can't clean their teeth 'cause there's no such thing as an ancient toothbrush, you know. Now, how does that feel? And I'm not saying in that I guess that those big blokeish issues aren't important, you know. The assassination of Julius Caesar, you know, is an event in world history that has formed how we look at every other assassination since, you know. When Kennedy's assassinated we see that partially in relation to that, that formative defining bit of political assassination in Rome. But it's not the only way that Rome is important.

### 2 18 Part 3

**Interviewer** As a historian, how important do you think it is that historical films should be accurate?

**Mary** I'm not sure quite how keen I am on accuracy above everything else. The most important thing, if I was going to make a historical movie, I'd really want to get people interested. And I think that, that, um, film and television, um, programme makers can be a bit, can be a bit sort of nerdish about accuracy. I remember a friend of mine once told me that, uh, he'd acted as advisor for some Roman film and the, the crew were always ringing up when they were on location, um, saying things like, 'Now, what kind of dog should we have?' You know, 'Should it, you know, if we're going to have a dog in the film, should it be an Alsatian or, you know, a Dachshund or whatever?' And to start with, he said he'd go to the library and he'd kind of look up and he'd find a breed. And eventually after question after question he'd think, look, these guys are getting the whole of Roman history in, in the big picture utterly wrong, and yet there they are worrying about the damned dogs, you know.

**I** Can you think of any historical films that you've really enjoyed?

**M** I absolutely loved *Gladiator*. Um, you know, never mind its horribly schmaltzy plot, you know; I thought in all kinds of ways it was just a wonderful, uh, brilliant, and I don't know if it was accurate, but a justifiable recreation of ancient Rome. Um, the, the beginning scenes of *Gladiator* which show, you know, Roman combat, um, just in a sense punctured the kind of slightly sanitized version of, you know, legionaries standing, you know, with all their shields, you know, face to–, you know, facing the enemy, um, you know, all looking ever so kind of neat and tidy. I mean, it was messy and it was bloody and it was horrible. And it was such a different kind of image of, uh, Roman combat that I remember we set it in Cambridge as an exam question, you know, um, you know: how, how would, how would students judge that kind of representation of Roman warfare.

I It's very interesting that there seem to be more and more historical films recently, and many have won Oscars. Is that because history has all the best stories?

M Yes, there's no such good story as a true story – and that's what history's got going for it, you know, actually. Um, you know, non-fiction in a, in a kind of way is always a better yarn than fiction is. Um, and I think it's, you know…I feel very pleased because, uh, I think, you know, for one thing it gets, it gets some of the best stories from history into the popular, into popular attention, popular consciousness. But I think also, I mean, it shows that you don't always have to be deadly serious about history. I mean, you know, history, like classics, you know, is often treated as something which is good for you; but isn't actually going to be much fun, you know. You'll be improved by knowing about it, but it probably will be a bit tedious in the process. And I think that, you know, showing that history can be larky, it can be funny, it can be surprising, um, it can be something that you can sit down and have a good two and a half hours at the cinema enjoying, is really all to the good.

**2 20 )))**

**Interviewer** Is there a period of history that you would like to go back to?

**Daisy** I'd really like to go back to Tudor England, sixteenth-century England.

I Why that period?

D Well I'm doing a PhD in the music of that period and I just think it's such a fascinating time because there was so much change happening and the way people lived their lives, their religion, the way the politics of the country was working. It must have been a really exciting time to live.

I Is there a person from history that you admire or find especially fascinating?

D There was a lady called Bess of Hardwick, um, who owned a lot of property in Derbyshire. She was a real social climber, and she lived through Henry VIII, Edward VI, Mary I, and Elizabeth I and into a bit of James I as well. Um, so she had a really long life, a really exciting life and she started from absolutely nothing and worked her way right to the top. I think she must have been a really amazing lady to know.

**Interviewer** Is there a period of history that you would like to go back to?

**Heather** I think I would have loved to be around in California in the sixties. I think it, it sounds like it was a really exciting time. I think, er, there was a lot of frightening things happening, in Vietnam, and, but it– but people were excited and, um, excited about the potential, I think of, of something new and really exploring their freedom, I guess.

I Is there a person from history that you admire or find especially fascinating?

H I think I most admire Nelson Mandela. I'm South African. So, er, he's the first person that comes to mind. I think he was, um, an incredible person and an amazing leader. So, um, yeah, I would have loved to have met him.

**Interviewer** Is there a period of history that you would like to go back to?

**Harry** Um, ooh, that's a really, that's a weird one. I don't know. Um, history was pretty brutal, life was really quite hard. Um, I mean, there are some parts, some aspects of it that I'd like, where time was slower, life was defined by the seasons and daylight, um, and you didn't have the same sort of pressures as you do now. So, I'd like aspects of it, but I'm not sure I'd really like to go back to the actual way of life.

I Is there a person from history that you admire or find especially fascinating?

H Um, probably, er, probably Queen Elizabeth I, because she, she managed to be the queen in a society where women weren't expected to have or hold or command any power and respect and that they were meant to do the bidding of men and their families and she actually stood up and was a person to be counted.

**Interviewer** Is there a period of history that you would like to go back to?

**Adam** Yes, there's a period I'd like to go back to, absolutely! I love ancient Greece. I love, er, ancient Athens. I think it would be so amazing to spend time there and see what it was like being in the Agora with, you know, er, Plato and Aristotle and talking. And, er, that entire world be very, very interesting to me.

I Is there a person from history that you admire or find especially fascinating?

A Hmm. A person from history that I find, eh, that I admire. There are a lot of people, I study a lot of ancient history, so I would love to meet Julius Caesar or someone like that who really transformed the entire world with his actions and you know he has a very unique personality, he was a very cocky person and it'd be fun to, er, just see what he was like in person and see how he was able to kind of take over the entire Roman Empire by himself.

**Interviewer** Is there a period of history that you would like to go back to?

**Richard** Oh, there's so many. Um, I kind of have this romantic idea of the 1920s maybe, when there was, a motor car had been invented, but not many people were driving so I like the idea of wandering and walking the quieter roads of, of England.

I Is there a person from history that you admire or find especially fascinating?

R Erm, it would probably be one of the ordinary men. So not a, a big person, a big name, but one of the hundreds of men who were like, on, say, Nelson's ship, the *Victory*, who were maybe firing cannons or pulling up the sails. So one of those characters, so just an ordinary seaman, sailor.

**2 28 )))**

1 Sounds or noises that particularly annoy me, I would say dogs barking, very irritating, they just don't stop, especially the small yappy dogs, they just go on and on and on and just keep yapping at you and I just find that extremely irritating because there isn't any real way to shut them up like a child, or something – you can tell them to shut up, but a dog, no, they'll just keep going.

2 Any noises that annoy me? I suppose I'm annoyed by excessively creative cell phone ringers, that can be of overly popular songs or themes from television series that people obviously think are really cute, but I probably don't think they are as cute.

3 The one sound I really hate is car horns, which you hear an awful lot of in cities. And the reason I hate them is because in my mind, at least, a car horn is meant as a warning, but of course nobody uses them for warnings any more, they use them because they're angry and impatient, and it, it seems to me that it's like shouting at somebody, and I don't like hearing that expression of anger all around me from dozens of cars.

4 For me, the most annoying sound is the buzzing noise of a mosquito. When you're just falling asleep in your bedroom at night and you hear that sound, and it's just terrible. I actually can't sleep until I've stopped the sound by killing the mosquito. So what I tend to do is, I tend to leave the light off actually, and just follow the sound, and just search the room for the sound for as long as I can until I can track it down and kill it, 'cause otherwise I, I can't sleep knowing that I will wake up in the morning covered in bite marks.

5 I work in an office, and the person who sits next to me, Julie, she crunches on rice cakes every lunchtime, and it's really annoying, and I don't know what to say to her, or how to put it, and if I do tell her now, she'll know I've been annoyed for the last four years, but I think she's leaving soon, so maybe I'll just have to bear with it for the next few weeks, or months.

**2 29 )))**

**Interviewer** London has often been accused of being an unfriendly place, but is it really, and if it is, does it matter and what could or should we do about it? Today I'm talking to Polly Akhurst, one of the co-founders of 'Talk to me London', an organization that aims to get Londoners chatting to each other. Hello, Polly.

**Polly** Hello.

I Could you start by telling us a bit about 'Talk to me London'?

P Sure. 'Talk to me London' is all about finding ways for people to talk to other people they don't know. And we

do this through fun activities including a badge, which says *Talk to me London* on it and shows you are open to conversation, as well as through regular events that, that get people talking, and we are also organizing, a 'Talk to me London' day at the end of August.

I And how did you get the idea for it, I mean, do you personally find London unfriendly?

P Well I personally talk to a lot of people I don't know, and I think that is where the idea came from, I found that the conversations that I have with people just kind of randomly, have been hugely, kind of, beneficial, really, so I've made, I might have made new friends, new business connections, sometimes they just kind of just cheer up my day. So 'Talk to me London' comes from this idea of, you know, what happens if we do start talking to each other more and you kind of, you know, are able to see more opportunities and possibilities there.

I Have you ever been anywhere either in the UK or abroad, a, a large city, which you thought really was a friendly place, which made you think you wish London was like that?

P There are definitely places that I've found friendlier than London, but I think that we all kind of change a bit when we travel and when we're out of our normal circumstances, we feel like, you know, more free to, to do things and perhaps talking to people is one of them. There is a tendency for, people say that Mediterranean countries are friendlier, however, or Latino countries even, but there was a similar initiative to this which was set up in Madrid a couple of years ago which I think indicates that, that they're facing the same problem as us, and perhaps, you know, points to the fact that this is a phenomenon in all large cities.

I So you wouldn't say it was a uniquely London problem?

P No, I wouldn't, no.

I You've had some quite high profile support of 'Talk to me London', on your website I think there's a quote from Boris Johnson saying what a wonderful idea it sounds. But on the other hand there's, there's been some quite negative media coverage which must have been a bit discouraging for you?

P I mean, I don't think so, I think that this idea is quite controversial in some ways because we're trying to encourage people to think about the way that they act and to reflect on that and to possibly change that, so, it hasn't really been surprising for us that we've had the negative coverage.

I And what would you say to people, and there are plenty of them I think, people who would say, 'I'm sitting on the bus, I'm sitting on the Tube, I really don't want to talk to anybody, I really don't want anyone to talk to me, I just want to read my book or listen to my music, whatever it is'. What would you say to those people?

P I would say that it's not about everyone talking to everyone else, it's about enabling those people who want to talk to do so, basically, so that's why all the things that we do are opt in, so the badge, for example, you wear it if you want to talk, if you don't want to talk you don't have to wear it, so you know, this, this isn't something for everyone, but we want to give people the choice between talking or not talking and currently there doesn't really seem to be that choice.

I Well, I wish you all the best with the project, I hope it's extremely successful and thank you very much for talking to us.

P Thanks a lot.

**2 30 )))**

**James's story**

I was heading home at rush hour a few weeks ago. I was tired and bored, and there was this guy standing beside me reading a book. So I started reading it over his shoulder – it was all about the history of popular social movements. I couldn't see the title, so I asked him what it was called. Surprisingly, he reacted quite positively and told me the name. He told me that he commuted for two hours each day and that he always tried to read something enlightening cause it made him feel a bit better about his life and being productive by the time he got home! It was such a nice unexpected conversation – and it got me thinking about my own reading habits!

**Anneka's story**

I was getting the last Tube back home one evening, and I had to wait for ages on the platform, so I started talking to the girl sitting next to me. She was Czech and had just come over to the UK with her boyfriend for work. She was a science graduate in the Czech Republic, but was working at a sandwich chain. I suppose in many ways it was a pretty typical story, but she was so upbeat and positive about London and living in the UK. At the end of the journey she emphasized how good it was to talk, and pulled out a sandwich from her bag and gave it to me. I was both shocked and grateful! Perhaps my stomach had been rumbling too loudly...

**Philippa's story**
I was on the Tube home today and this young man asked me how my day had been. We chatted about the area and iPads and TV and that kind of thing. Then I mentioned the concept of 'Talk to me London' and encouraged him not to stop talking to people. An older lady in the meantime had sat down by us and thought the fact that we were chatting was lovely! And then I bumped into an old neighbour from about ten years ago, and we caught up. When he got off the Tube, the guy opposite me mentioned how nice it was to see us catching up, and then we got talking too. It was enthusing. It was quite contagious. I had a smile across my face for the rest of the day.

**Alise's story**
I was standing on a bus, and I would have thought I'd looked unapproachable, but instead a man sitting close by saw I was carrying a guitar. He gave me a big smile and asked if I'd play him a song! Before long we were chatting about travelling and living in different countries and cities around the world, and about music. He was leaving the next day for a few months travel around South America. Because the man was a small distance away from where I was standing, quite a few people nearby were able to hear us talk, and many of them also joined in. It felt a little surreal, stepping off the bus later, smiling and saying goodbye to a bunch of strangers as though they were long-time friends.

**2 34**

**Interviewer** What made you want to be a translator?
**Beverly** It was something that I'd done when I was at university and when I moved to Spain it was difficult to get a job that wasn't teaching English, so I went back to England and I did a postgraduate course in translation. After doing the course I swore that I would never be a translator, I thought it would be too boring, but I kept doing the odd translation, and eventually I, I came round to the idea because I liked the idea of working for myself, and it didn't require too much investment to get started. And, and actually, I enjoy working with words, and it's, it's very satisfying when you feel that you've produced a reasonable translation of the original text.
**I** What are the pros and cons of being a translator?
**B** Well, um, it's a lonely job, I suppose, you know, you're on your own most of the time, it's hard work, you're sitting there and, you know, you're working long hours, and you can't programme things because you don't know when more work is going to come in, and people have always got tight deadlines. You know, it's really rare that somebody'll, 'll ring you up and say 'I want this translation in three months' time'. You know, that, that just doesn't really happen.
**I** And the pros?
**B** Well the pros are that it, it gives you freedom, because you can do it anywhere if you've got an internet connection and electricity, and I suppose you can organize your time, cause you're freelance, you know, you're your own boss, which is good. I, I like that.
**I** What advice would you give someone who's thinking of going into translation?
**B** I'd say that– I'd say, in addition to the language, get a speciality. Do another course in anything that interests you, like, economics, law, history, art, because you really need to know about the subjects that you're translating into.
**I** What do you think is the most difficult kind of text to translate?
**B** Literary texts, like novels, poetry, or drama because you've got to give a lot of consideration to the author, and to the way it's been written in the original language.
**I** In order to translate a novel well, do you think you need to be a novelist yourself?
**B** I think that's true ideally, yes.
**I** And is that the case? I mean are most of the well-known translators of novels, generally speaking, novelists in their own right?
**B** Yes, I think in English anyway, people who translate into English tend to be published authors, and they tend to specialize in a particular author in the other language. And of course if it's a living author, then it's so much easier because you can actually communicate with the author and say, you know, like, what did you really mean here?
**I** Another thing I've heard that is very hard to translate is advertising, for example, slogans.
**B** Yeah, well, with advertising, the problem is that it's got to be something punchy, and, and it's very difficult to translate that. For example, one of the Coca-Cola adverts, the slogan in English was 'the real thing', but you just couldn't translate that literally into Spanish – it, it just wouldn't have had the same power. In fact it became *Sensación de vivir*, which is 'sensation of living', which sounds, sounds really good in Spanish, but it, it would sound weird in English.
**I** What about film titles?
**B** Ah, they're horrific, too. People always complain that they've not been translated accurately, but of course it's impossible because sometimes a literal translation just doesn't work.
**I** For example?
**B** OK, well, think of, you know, the Julie Andrews film, *The Sound of Music*. Well, that works in English because it's a phrase that you know, you know like 'I can hear the sound of music'. But it doesn't work at all in other languages, and in Spanish it was called *Sonrisas y Lágrimas* which means 'Smiles and tears'. Now let me– in German it was called *Meine Lieder, meine Träume* which means 'My songs, my dreams', and in Italian it was *Tutti insieme appassionatamente* which means I think, 'All together passionately' or, I don't know, something like that. In fact, I think it was translated differently all over the world.
**I** Do you think there are special problems translating film scripts, for the subtitles?
**B** Yes, a lot. There are special constraints, for example the translation has to fit on the screen as the actor is speaking, and so sometimes the translation is a paraphrase rather than a direct translation, and of course, well, going back to untranslatable things, really the big problems are cultural, and humour, because they're, they're just not the same. You can get across the idea, but you might need pages to explain it, and, you know, by that time the film's moved on. I also sometimes think that the translators are given the film on DVD, I mean, you know, rather than a written script, and that sometimes they've simply misheard or they didn't understand what the people said. And that's the only explanation I can come up with for some of the mistranslations that I've seen. Although sometimes it might be that some things like, like humour and jokes, especially ones which depend on wordplay are just, you know, they're, they're simply untranslatable. And often it's very difficult to get the right register, for example with, with slang and swear words, because if you literally translate taboo words or swear words, even if they exist in the other language they may well be far more offensive.

**3 2**

Again and again people tell us that mindfulness greatly enhances the joys of daily life. In practice, even the smallest of things can suddenly become captivating again. For this reason one of our favourite practices is the chocolate meditation. In this, you ask yourself to bring all your attention to some chocolate as you're eating it. So if you want to do this right now, choosing some chocolate, not unwrapping it yet, choosing a type that you've never tried before, or one that you've not eaten recently. It might be dark and flavoursome, organic, or fair-trade, or whatever you choose. Perhaps choosing a type you wouldn't normally eat, or that you consume only rarely.

Before you unwrap the chocolate, look at the whole bar or packet – its colour, its shape, what it feels like in your hand – as if you were seeing it for the very first time. Now very slowly unwrapping the chocolate, noticing how the wrapping feels as you unfold it, seeing the chocolate itself. What colours do you notice? What shapes? Inhaling the aroma of the chocolate, letting it sweep over you. And now taking or breaking off a piece and looking at it as it rests on your hand, really letting your eyes drink in what it looks like, examining every nook and cranny. At a certain point, bringing it up to your mouth, noticing how the hand knows where to position it, and popping it in the mouth, noticing what the tongue does to receive it. See if it's possible to hold it on your tongue and let it melt, noticing any tendency to chew it, seeing if you can sense some of the different flavours, really noticing these.

If you notice your mind wandering while you do this, simply noticing where it went, then gently escorting it back to the present moment.

And then when the chocolate has completely melted, swallowing it very slowly and deliberately, letting it trickle down your throat.

What did you notice? If the chocolate tasted better than if you'd just eaten it at a normal pace, what do you make of that? Often we taste the first piece and perhaps the last, but the rest goes down unnoticed. We're so often on autopilot, we can miss much of our day-to-day lives. Mindfulness is about bringing awareness to the usual routine things in life, things that we normally take for granted. Perhaps you could try this with any routine activity, seeing what you notice? It could change your whole day.

**3 3**

1 One thing I really hate waiting for is waiting at home for a delivery to arrive, 'cause sometimes you get, like, a two-hour delivery window, and that's fine, but more often they'll say 'Could be any time 7 a.m. to 7 p.m.', and you're stuck in the house – you don't even dare go and buy a pint of milk – and of course it always ends up arriving at five to seven in the evening, and you've spent the whole day waiting.
2 It annoys me if I have to wait for web pages to load, if there's a really bad internet connection and the pages are very slow to load and you actually sort of see one line loading at a time, pixel by pixel it seems, but, you know, invariably, if you need the information you sit and wait as long as it takes.
3 Is there anything I really hate having to wait for? Not particularly, I'm, I'm fairly patient. If I'm in a queue I'm fairly patient, but I will get annoyed if people start to disregard the laws of queues, and try and jump them or, or try and get to the front in some other way. As long as there's a system to follow, it, that usually keeps me calm.
4 I really hate waiting for anything where I've been given an appointment time for a specific hour, you know, a specific time, and then having to wait for ages before I have it, so, well, you know, for example a hairdresser or, or a dentist or a doctor. I think particularly things like hairdressers and dentists, because I think they must know how long the previous person's going to take, you know, they don't have to deal with emergencies or anything like that, so why can't they give me a correct time? I mean, I'm very punctual so I always turn up on time, in fact usually at least five minutes early, and it really, really annoys me if I have to wait for a long time. Anything more than fifteen minutes over the appointment time drives me completely insane.
5 Waiting for Jerry, my husband, is a complete nightmare, because he's never ready on time and I always tell him to be ready fifteen minutes before we need to be ready, and even so he's so late, it drives me completely bananas. I don't know why it drives me completely bananas because, in fact, often we don't need to be there on time, or it doesn't need to be that kind of precise, but it does. I hate it. He's preening himself, you know, getting his jacket on and looking at himself in the mirror, I mean, he takes much more time than I do.
6 I can't abide waiting in check-in queues at airports, because I'm standing in the queue watching people take ages and ages and ages to check in, and I know when I get to the front of the queue I'll do my check-in in twenty seconds. I don't know why these other people can't do the same.

**3 15**

**Interviewer** Where did the idea of microfinance come from?

**Sarita** The idea behind microfinance again goes back to the mid-70s. There had been, by that time, several decades of what we call the Western World giving massive amounts of aid to the developing world and a realization that a lot of it was not working, there were still many people who were left poor. So, you know, Muhammad Yunus is credited as being the father of microfinance, he's an economist living in Bangladesh, a very poor country, and he looked around and he said – what, what is it that the poor lack, what is that they need? And the answer is obvious, they need money and all of us, in order to get started have had access to credit. So, the poor can't get access to credit, they can't go to relatives to borrow because generally the relatives are as poor as they themselves are and they certainly cannot go into a bank and borrow because they have no collateral.

**I** How did Dr Yunus solve these problems?

**S** There are really three innovations that he came up with that are brilliant in, in hindsight. One was, OK, the poor have no collateral, but let's figure out a way to create collateral which means, collateral is basically if you're not going to pay back the loan, that somebody's held responsible. So he came up with a lending methodology where there was a group of peers that were given the loan and they would be lending to each other and the group held each member accountable for paying back. The second innovation that he came up with is that it is very difficult for the poor to gather a lump sum to pay back a loan, but if you can break up that payment into very small regular payments that are coming out of your daily income, then it's feasible to pay back the loan. So what micro-credit did was, to break up the, the loan payment into these very sort of regular small payments. And the third was really an incentive system, that the poor were not encouraged to borrow a large amount, they only borrowed what they could use in their business and then pay back, and if they paid back successfully then they were eligible for a larger loan.

**3 16**

**Interviewer** Do you have any examples of individual success stories?

**Sarita** Oh, I love talking about, individual success stories, because this is what, sort of gets us up in the morning and, you know, gets us to come to work and stay late, and, and do this, this work, since I've been at Women's World Banking I have been to the Dominican Republic, Jordan, and India, so I am happy to give you a story from each, each, each of the three countries.

The DR is a more established economy, if you will, and so the, the woman I met had already had successive loans that she had taken from our partner in the DR and what she did was to start out, she was basically selling food from her, kitchen, making excess food and selling it to the factory workers, took out a loan, sort of increased that business and then set up a little cantina out of her living room. So that along with food she was selling cigarettes, beer, candy, etc. That business did well, took out another loan and built a room on top of her house and started to rent it out and so over seven years what she's been able to do is to completely build a new home for herself and rent out the old one, and this is going to ensure income in her old age, because at some point she's going to be too old to, to work in the kitchen, and to be, you know, standing on her feet behind the cantina counter and she's looking at the, the, these rental rooms that she has been able to put on as her, her old age security.

**3 17**

In Jordan, I'll, I'll tell you about a young women that, that we met, you know, sort of the, the cultural, norm in Jordan is that, a fairly old husband can marry again and marry a, a fairly young woman, so the one that we met, her husband was now too old and sick so while, while, he took care of the…having a roof over her head, she had absolutely no means of earning more money for herself or her kids, and at her socio-economic level it's not considered proper for a woman to go out and work. So the only thing that she was able to do, was she had taken a loan to buy cosmetics, and was selling them from her living room to her neighbours and this was considered to be an OK business for her because primarily she was dealing with other women, but it gave her that sort of extra money, to use for herself.

**3 18**

And then in India where I was recently in the city of Hyderabad, and Hyderabad is this up-and-coming city, you know, it's gleaming, it's, Indians themselves are thinking of it as the next cyber city. But across town they have slums, where even now, both men and women have not gone to school, they're not educated and their only recourse is to work in the informal economy, so the family that we met, the husband, was a vegetable cart– a vegetable seller, so he took his cart and went out into the more affluent neighbourhoods, the son had dropped out of school to join his father, to push a similar car…cart, and the mother had taken a loan to embroider saris, and, she did this at home, sort of in her spare time and what she really wanted to do was to, amass enough income so that she would cut out the middleman, because she basically got half of what the sari was worth, because she was handing it over to a, a middle man, so that if she could buy the materials herself, embroider it herself, and sell it herself to the store she could in effect double her income without doubling her labour.

**3 23 Part 1**

**Interviewer** In your experience, what are the main causes of stress?

**Jordan** My clients and audiences tell me that their big stressors are, er, too much to do, too little time, er, money stressors, commuting is a big stressor. I think that the opportunities to be stressed are everywhere.

**I** Do you think life is more stressful now than it was, say, 20 years ago?

**J** I think that today there are many more opportunities to be stressed, there are many more distractions, especially ones that are technology-driven. And I'm a big fan of technology, we can use technology to help us reduce stress, but when you have emails coming in and text messages left and right, and Twitter feeds and Facebook messages, and, er TV, and the kids and a job, and maybe school, it really divides our attention and it produces a stress response that is often ongoing, continuous within us. And all of that stuff can take away the time to just relax, er, take a walk, not think about who's trying to communicate with us, and not needing to be on all of the time. So, er, so I think there are just more chances to be stressed today, er, and therefore we need to really pay more attention to reducing stress.

**I** Can you tell us something about the effects of stress on the body and mind?

**J** Stress impacts the body because it produces wear and tear, and when we are constantly stressed, our organs, our immune system, become the punching bags of our stress response. Stress is really important, and, in fact, it can be a lifesaver, but when it kicks into action all the time, it, er, has a corrosive effect on us. So, for example, our immune systems are weakened when we are under a lot of stress, and especially for a long period of time. When our immune systems are weaker, it opens us up to be more susceptible to illnesses in the environment. Er, stress contributes to high blood pressure, which contributes to heart problems and stroke. Stress impacts our sleep, so when we get stressed during the day it often makes it more difficult for us to fall asleep at night or to stay asleep or to have a quality night's sleep, and if we don't get a good night's sleep, then we are tired the next day, which makes us more stressed in many cases, so it becomes a stress–poor-sleep cycle that is stressful and tiring. So these are all reasons to really pay attention to our stress levels and to take action to reduce the stress.

**3 24 Part 2**

**Interviewer** How can you help people deal with stress and how long does it take to find a solution?

**Jordan** The great thing about stress management is that it's like a salad bar. There are 30 different choices on a salad bar and some of us like most of the things that are offered, but some of us don't like everything, but we get to choose what works for us and what we enjoy. Same thing with stress management – there are more than 30 different ways you can manage stress, there are probably, er, 30 million and counting, and we should pick the techniques, many of them easy and simple and fun, that we like, and therefore we'll be more likely to use them on an ongoing basis. So stress management can take as little as ten seconds. You can look at a beautiful picture that you took on your last vacation, you can put it on your computer screen, you can put it next to your bed, you can put it on your desk, and just focusing on that photo of the ocean or a mountain or a beach can alleviate stressed feelings immediately. We can do one-minute breathing exercises, we can exercise, we can take a ten-minute walk around the block, we can meditate each day. So there are many different ways to prevent and reduce the stress that we're experiencing and the, the key is to do it on a regular basis.

**I** Are the solutions to stress physical, mental, or both?

**J** Stress management involves both the mind and the body, they make great partners when we're trying to feel better and to cut down on the stress that we're experiencing. I once worked in a school where a student identified his stressor as riding on the subway. He felt very stressed going to school every day and very stressed when it was time to go home, because the subway made him feel very closed in and like he wanted to escape, he couldn't stand the, the crowds. And then we opened up to the rest of the group and we asked them for different ways that this student might think about this stressor and different ways that he might act to try and reduce it. And the group came up with all sorts of great possibilities, including that he ride in a different car, in the first car or the last car, because it's often less crowded compared to the centre car, which is where he always used to ride. And he liked that idea, and I heard from the principal of the school a few weeks later that he in fact had started riding in the first car, and for the first time in his subway-taking life, he didn't feel stressed, he didn't feel anxious, because the car was less crowded and he felt so much better. And you might think, 'Well, that's such an easy answer, why didn't he think of that himself?' The truth is, and I think we all identify with this, we get into very fixed ways, habits almost, of thinking and acting, because we, we deal with our stressors and have dealt with them in similar ways for a long, long time, so we lose the perspective, we don't take as much time to think about how we could deal with our stressors in different ways. So this is an example of how the mind and body and actions and thoughts can work together to really make a big difference in the way we feel.

**3 25 Part 3**

**Interviewer** Are some age groups more susceptible to stress than others?

**Jordan** Stress is a very democratic occurrence, so older people are stressed, college students are stressed, babies get stressed, 30-somethings get stressed, men are stressed, women are stressed, so, er, it's hard to say if one group is more stressed than another.

**I** What makes students stressed? How does stress affect their lives or their studies, and what are the most stressful times in a typical student's life?

**J** College, and being a student can be really fun and exciting and rewarding. There are also a lot of stressors associated with it: there's the studying, there's the pressure to do well on exams so that you can get a better job and perhaps make more money. You are in a different environment that doesn't have the same support that you used to have, especially if you were back home. Er, there is the social stress of needing to meet new people, and also for a lot of young people, especially those in their teens and twenties, we see a lot of mental, er, health issues arise and there's a greater need to get help for, er, them while in school, but if you're not with your usual support network it's even more challenging sometimes to do so. Stress makes it difficult to study, to focus, to concentrate. When you're sitting down to take an exam and you studied really hard for the exam, and then all of a sudden you're having trouble remembering what you studied, stress can play a big role in making it more difficult for us to recall information. If you're doing a presentation, public speaking, that can be very stressful for a lot of students as well as professionals. In fact, still, public speaking is feared more than death by most people. Then there's the financial stress of being in school, not only, er, not having a lot of money to spend on things that you want to do, fun activities, but what awaits you when you graduate, which for many, er, students is a lot of financial, er, stress and loans to repay. So being a student – great fun, and also can provide a lot of – great stress.

You set up Stressbusters as an anti-stress programme for students. Can you tell us something about it and how it works?

We train teams of students to provide five-minute free back rubs at events all over campus, all year long, and people on campus come to the events, and not only do they get an amazing stress-relieving back rub, but they also learn about other stress reduction and wellness resources on campus that we train our students to provide. And we have seen incredible reductions in feelings of stress, tension, anxiety, lowering of feelings of being overwhelmed, from before someone has the Stressbusters experience to after. We also find students telling us that they're better able to cope with their stressors and they're better able to complete the tasks that they have at hand after they have one of our Stressbusters experiences.

3 27 ))

**Interviewer** Are you currently more stressed at work or at home?

**Simon** Am I more stressed – er, I'm more stressed at home at the moment because my wife, um, has just had, or, I say my wife has had, we have just had twin little girls. Eight months old or eight and half months old now, so it is far more stressful being at home than being at work. I found work easy compared to being at home at the moment.

When things are stressful, what do you do to try to de-stress?

I put my earphones on and listen to music, to drown out the sound of the babies.

**Interviewer** Are you currently more stressed at work or at home?

**Stephanie** OK definitely at work. Er, why? Because, er, I work for myself, I'm self-employed and, er, I'm, I'm working for, er, I'm a consultant for restaurant groups, um, and at the moment London is, is booming with new restaurants, so, er, yeah, for the past three years I've been kind of non-stop, really.

When things are stressful, what do you do to try to de-stress?

OK, um, I have a couple of holidays a year. I disappear off to Wales. Er, so the weekend after next, I'm going to disappear for a couple of weeks. I'm currently looking for a place to buy out there. Er, ultimately I will disappear for good. But, er, yeah, I like my holidays and I also like to go out eating and spend some time with friends.

**Interviewer** Are you currently more stressed at work or at home?

**Kim** Er, well, I work at home, er, I'm a self-employed writer and, er, I experience very little stress, except those rare periods when I'm up against a deadline. So, er, I have no commute, I – my commute is walking from one room to the other, and I have a cosy little office and I'm very happy, er, and unstressed with work, which I think is very unlike most New Yorkers and I'm very fortunate.

When things are stressful, what do you do to try to de-stress?

Ah, I de-stress by, er, sitting er down and breathing calmly and thinking about nothing, or sometimes thinking about the cosmos and thinking about, er, the illusory nature of time. And, um, that usually works, er, but as I say, I experience very low levels of stress, er, because I actually spend a lot of time thinking about cosmological matters and that has a very calming effect, I think, and, er, I commend it to my fellow New Yorkers.

**Interviewer** Are you currently more stressed at work or at home?

**Myfannwy** I don't think I'm very stressed in either place. Um, but I am giving a lecture on Tuesday, and so that's stressing me out a bit.

When things are stressful, what do you do to try to de-stress?

**M** To de-stress, I like to eat really good food and to watch TV.

**Interviewer** Are you currently more stressed at work or at home?

**Sean** I would say definitely more stressed at work. Um, I think stress is quite contagious. I think I spend a lot of my time around stressed people, um, either in a room with them, or on the phone to them, or, or just having emails from them, so I think that that builds a lot of stress, um, just from the environment, really.

**I** When things are stressful, what do you do to try to de-stress?

**S** I've realized quite recently that when I am stressed, I build a lot of tension in my shoulders, um, and I think it's not just a metaphor when we say we have things, we carry the weight of things on our shoulders. So I think it really helps just to be conscious of that and every half an hour or so, just if I concentrate on relaxing my shoulders, everything seems to be a little bit more bearable.

# 1A  *have*: auxiliary or main verb?

## *have* as a main verb

> 1  We **have** a large extended family.
>    **Do** you **have** any money on you?
>    She **has** a really bad cold at the moment.
> 2  He **doesn't have** lunch at home.
>    I**'m having** problems with my Wi-fi.
> 3  **Do** we really **have to** spend Christmas with your parents again?
> 4  We're going to **have** the kitchen **repainted** next week.
>    I **had** my eyes **tested** when I got my new glasses.
>    Where do you **have** your hair **cut**?

When *have* is a **main verb**, we use auxiliary verbs, e.g. *be* or *do*, to make questions and negatives. We don't usually contract *have* when it is a main verb.
1  We use *have* as a main verb for possession.
   *have* with this meaning is a stative (non-action) verb and is not used in continuous tenses.
   • *have* is also a stative verb when used to talk about relationships or illnesses.
2  We use *have* + object as a main verb for actions and experiences, e.g. *have a bath, a drink, a chat, a problem,* etc.
   *have* with this meaning is a dynamic (action) verb and can be used in continuous tenses.
3  We use *have to* as a main verb to express obligation, especially obligation imposed by others, and rules and regulations.
4  We use *have* as a main verb + object + past participle to say that you ask or pay another person to do something for you.

## *have* as an auxiliary verb

> 1  How many children **have** you **got**? I**'ve got** three, two boys and a girl.
>    They **haven't got** much money.
> 2  I **haven't** the time to go to the bank.
> 3  I**'ve got to** go now – I'm meeting my girlfriend for lunch.
> 4  They**'ve been** married for 15 years.
>    How long **has** Anna **been going** out with James?
> 5  She'll **have** finished lunch in a few minutes so you can phone her then.
>    I want to **have** started a family by the time I'm 30.
>    If I **hadn't** taken a taxi, I wouldn't **have** arrived in time.

When *have* is an auxiliary verb, we make questions by inverting *have* and the subject, and negatives with *haven't | hasn't*. *have* as an auxiliary verb is often contracted to *'ve | 's*; *had* is contracted to *'d*.
1  We often use *have got* for possession. The meaning is exactly the same as *have*.
   • *have* here is an auxiliary verb.
   • *have got* has a present meaning. We normally use *had* for the past, not *had got*.
   • *have got* is very common in informal English.
2  In negative sentences, we occasionally leave out *got*, especially in fixed expressions like *I haven't time., I haven't a clue.*
3  We use *have got to* to express obligation, especially in informal English.
   • *have got to* is normally used for a specific obligation rather than a general or repeated obligation. Compare:
   *I've got to make a quick phone call.* (= specific)
   *I have to wear a suit to work.* (= general)
4  We use *have* as an auxiliary verb to form the present perfect simple and continuous.
5  We also use *have* for other perfect forms, e.g. the future perfect, the perfect infinitive, the past perfect, etc.

**a** Right (✓) or wrong (✗)? Correct the mistakes in the highlighted phrases.

> A  You look exhausted.
> B  Yes, I've been looking after my sister's kids all day. ✓

1  I don't think you should drive until you've had your brakes fixed.
2  A  Why don't you want to come?
   B  I haven't got any money.
3  Has your husband to work tomorrow or is he taking the day off?
4  The staff don't have to dress formally in this company – they can wear what they like.
5  How long have you been having your flat in London?
6  What time are we having dinner tonight?
7  My parents had got a lot of problems with my sister when she was a teenager.
8  I don't have a holiday for 18 months. I really need a break.
9  Have we got to do this exercise now, or can we do it later for homework?

**b** Rewrite the sentences using a form of *have* or *have got*.

Her brother moved to Canada in 2011 and he still lives there.
Her brother*'s been living in Canada since 2011.*

1  She's an only child.
   She _____
2  We used to pay someone to take a family photograph every year.
   We used _____
3  Buying car insurance is obligatory for all drivers.
   All _____
4  He last saw his father in 2009.
   He _____
5  He lacks the right qualifications for this job.
   He _____
6  It's not necessary for us to do it now; we can do it later.
   We _____
7  The sea was amazingly clear and warm – we swam every morning.
   The sea was amazingly clear and warm – we _____
8  When did you start to get on badly?
   How long _____ badly?
9  I need someone to fix the central heating. I think the thermostat is broken.
   I need _____. I think the thermostat is broken.

◄ p.5

# 1B discourse markers (1): linkers

## result

1 I have a job interview next week, **so** I've bought myself a suit!
2 It had snowed hard all night. **As a result**, the airport was closed until 11.00 a.m.
   We regret that you do not have the necessary qualifications and **therefore** / **consequently** we are unable to offer you the job.

*so* is the most common way of introducing a result or a logical connection.
*as a result*, *therefore*, and *consequently* (more formal than *so*) are often used at the beginning of a sentence or clause.
• *therefore* and *consequently* can also be used before a main verb, e.g. *We have therefore / consequently decided not to offer you the job.*

## reason

1 I have stopped writing to her, **because** / **as** / **since** she never answers me.
   Why did your boss resign? **Because** his wife was ill.
2 The plane was late **because of** the fog.
   Flight 341 has been delayed **due to** / **owing to** adverse weather conditions.

*because*, *as*, and *since* (more formal) are synonyms and are used to introduce clauses giving a reason. *as* and *since* are often used at the beginning of a sentence, e.g. *As / Since the rain hasn't stopped, we've decided not to go out.*
• We use *because* (not *as* or *since*) to answer a *Why…?* question.
*because of*, *due to*, and *owing to* also express the reason for something. They are usually followed by a noun, a gerund, or *the fact that* + clause.
• *due to* and *owing to* are more formal than *because of*.

## purpose

1 I did a language course **to** / **in order to** / **so as to** improve my English.
2 She closed the door quietly **so as not to** / **in order not to** wake the baby.
3 They moved to London **so (that)** they could see their grandchildren more often.
4 I'm not going to tell Ann **in case** she tells everyone else.

*to*, *in order to*, and *so as to* introduce a clause of purpose and are all followed by an infinitive. *to* is the most informal.
For negative purpose we use *so as not to* or *in order not to*.
You can also use *so (that)* + *can* / *could* + verb or *will* / *would* + verb to express purpose. You can leave out *that* in informal English.
• Use *so (that)* when there is a change of subject in the clause of purpose, e.g. *She put a blanket over the baby so (that) he wouldn't be cold.*
We use *in case* + a clause when we do something in order to be ready for future situations / problems or to avoid them.

## contrast

1 We enjoyed the concert, **but** the journey home was a nightmare.
   Agnes was attracted to the stranger, **yet** something in her head was telling her not to get close to him.
   It's a really good idea. **However**, it may be too expensive.
   The moon shone brightly. **Nevertheless**, it was hard to find our way.
2 We enjoyed the film **although** / **even though** / **though** it was long.
3 **In spite of** being 85, she still travels all over the world.
   **Despite** her age…
   **Despite** the fact that she's 85…

*but* is the most common and informal way of introducing contrast and is normally used to link two contrasting points within a sentence.
*yet* is used in the same way, but is more formal / literary.
*however* and *nevertheless* are normally used at the beginning of a sentence to connect it to the previous one and are usually followed by a comma.
• *nevertheless* (or *nonetheless*) is more formal / literary than *however*.
*even though* is more emphatic than *although*. *though* is more common in informal speech.
After *in spite of* and *despite* use a gerund, a noun, or *the fact that* + clause.

---

**a** (Circle) the right linker.
(*Even though*) / *Despite* she's working really hard, I don't think she'll be able to catch up.

1 We can't afford to have a holiday this year *as* / *so* we've got an overdraft at the bank.
2 Could we rearrange my timetable *so that* / *in case* I don't have so many classes on Fridays?
3 I got to the interview on time *due to* / *in spite of* the fact that my train was late.
4 The restaurant chain has had a very difficult year. *Nevertheless* / *As a result*, they haven't had to close any of their restaurants.
5 He gets a good salary *though* / *since* the job itself is quite monotonous.

**b** (Circle) the better option according to register.
Sales have increased over the last three months. *So* / (*Therefore*) we will be taking on five new employees.

1 I've been off work for the last three days *because of* / *owing to* this nasty cough I've got.
2 The organization has severe financial problems, and *so* / *consequently* half the staff have been laid off.
3 The company has reported declining sales this year. *Nevertheless* / *But* they have so far managed to avoid any staff cuts.
4 I stopped at a service station *to* / *in order to* fill up with petrol.
5 I thought it was an amazing film. It was quite depressing, *though* / *however*.
6 It has been announced that the last match of the season has been cancelled *due to* / *because of* the severe weather.

**c** Join the sentences using the **bold** word(s), making any necessary changes.
We only use energy-efficient light bulbs. We don't want to waste electricity. **so as**
*We only use energy-efficient light bulbs so as not to waste electricity.*

1 Our seats were a long way from the stage. We enjoyed the play. **In spite**
   We _____
2 It took us ages to get there. The traffic was heavy. **because of**
   It _____
3 I took the price off the bag. I didn't want Becky to know how much it had cost. **so**
   I _____
4 Keep the receipt for the sweater. Your dad might not like it. **in case**
   Keep _____
5 Susanna is an only child. She isn't at all spoilt. **Even though**
   Susanna _____
6 Prices have risen because production costs have increased. **due to**
   Prices _____

◄ p.11

# 2A pronouns

## generic pronouns

1 **You** can learn a language faster if you go to live in a country where it is spoken.
2 **One** tends to have problems understanding very strong accents.
3 When **we** talk about an accent, **we** must not confuse this with pronunciation.
4 **They** always say that it's never too late to learn a new language.
  **They** should make it compulsory for people to learn two foreign languages at school.
5 If someone goes to live in a foreign country, **they** will have to get used to a different way of life.
  Could the person who left **their** bag in the library please come and see me?

1 We often use *you* to mean people in general.
2 We can also use *one* + third person singular of the verb to mean people in general. *one* is much more formal than *you* and rarely used in spoken English.
  • We can also use *one's* as a possessive adjective, e.g. *When confronted with danger, one's first reaction is often to freeze.*
3 *we* can also be used to make a general statement of opinion which includes the reader / listener.
4 In informal English, we often use *they* to talk about other people in general, or people in authority, e.g. **They** *always say…* (*They* = people in general); **They** *should make it compulsory…* (*They* = the government).
5 We use *they, them,* and *their* to refer to one person who may be male or female, instead of using *he or she, his or her,* etc.

## reflexive and reciprocal pronouns

1 You need to look after **yourself** with that cold.
  He's very egocentric. He always talks about **himself**.
2 I managed to complete the crossword! I was really pleased with **myself**.
3 We decorated the house **ourselves**.
  There's no way I'm going to do it for you. Do it **yourself**!
4 I don't feel very comfortable going to the cinema **by myself**.
5 My ex-husband and I don't talk to **each other** any more.
  My mother and sister don't understand **one another** at all.

1 We often use reflexive pronouns when the subject and object of a verb are the same person.
  • We don't usually use reflexive pronouns with some verbs which may be reflexive in other languages, e.g. *wash, shave,* etc. NOT ~~He got up, shaved himself, and …~~
  • *enjoy* is always used with a reflexive pronoun when not followed by another object, e.g. *Enjoy your meal!* BUT *Did you enjoy* **yourself** *last night?*
2 We can also use reflexive pronouns after most prepositions when the complement is the same as the subject.

> 🔍 **Object pronouns after prepositions of place**
> After prepositions of place we use object pronouns, not reflexive pronouns, e.g. *She put the bag next to her on the seat.* NOT ~~next to herself~~

3 We can use reflexive pronouns to emphasize the subject, e.g. *We decorated the house ourselves.* (= we did it, not professional decorators)
4 *by* + reflexive pronoun = alone, on your / her, etc. own.
5 We use *each other* or *one another* for reciprocal actions, i.e. A does the action to B and B does the action to A.

## it and there

1 **It's** 10 o'clock. **It's** 30 degrees today. **It's** five miles to the coast.
2 **It was** great to hear that you and Martina are getting married!
  **It used to be** difficult to buy fresh pasta in the UK, but now you can get it everywhere.
3 **There have been** a lot of storms recently.
  **There used to be** a cinema in that street.

1 We use *it* + *be* to talk about time, temperature, and distance.
2 We also use, e.g. *it* + *be* as a 'preparatory' subject before adjectives. *It was great to hear from you.* NOT ~~To hear from you was great.~~
3 We use *there* + *be* + noun to say if people and things are present or exist (or not). You cannot use *It…* here. NOT ~~It used to be a cinema in that street.~~

a Circle the right pronoun. Tick (✓) if both are possible.

  They helped (one another) / themselves to prepare for the exam.

1 *One* / *You* can often tell where people are from by the way they speak.
2 Can you put my case on the rack above *yourself* / *you*?
3 Sally and her sister look incredibly like *each other* / *one another*. Are they twins?
4 Steve's a really private person and he rarely talks about *him* / *himself*.
5 Either Suzie or Mark has left *her* / *their* bag behind, because there's only one in the back of the car.
6 When a person goes to live abroad it may take *them* / *him* a while to pick up the language.
7 *They* / *One* say that eating tomatoes can help protect the body against certain diseases.

b Complete with a pronoun.

  Don't tell him how to spell it. Let him work it out by *himself*.

1 If anyone has not yet paid _____ course fees, _____ should go to registration immediately.
2 Isabel is very quick-tempered. She finds it very hard to control _____.
3 I wouldn't stay in that hotel – _____ say the rooms are tiny and the service is awful.
4 There is a total lack of communication between them. They don't understand _____ at all.
5 Did they enjoy _____ at the festival?
6 Are you going to have the flat repainted or will you and Jo do it _____?
7 It's always the same with taxis. _____ can never find one when _____ need one!

c Complete with *it* or *there*.

  *There* was a very interesting article about language learning in *The Times* yesterday.

1 _____'s illegal to use a handheld mobile while you're driving. _____ used to be a lot of accidents caused by this.
2 Look. _____'s a spelling mistake in this word. _____ should be *j*, not *g*.
3 How many miles is _____ to Manchester from here?
4 _____'s scorching today. _____ must be at least 35 degrees.
5 _____'s no need to hurry. The train doesn't leave for ages.
6 _____'s not worth buying the paper today. _____'s absolutely nothing interesting in it.

◀ p.15

# 2B the past: habitual events and specific incidents

## narrative tenses: describing specific incidents in the past

This **happened** when I **was** about five years old. My father **had gone away** on business for a few days and my brother and I **were sleeping** in my parents' bedroom. Before we **went** to bed that night, I **had been reading** a very scary story about a wicked witch. In the middle of the night, I **woke up** with a start and **saw** that a figure in a dark coat **was standing** at the end of my bed. I **screamed** at the top of my voice.

When we describe specific incidents in the past, we use **narrative tenses**, i.e. the past simple, past continuous, and past perfect simple or continuous.

- We use the past simple to talk about the main actions in a story (*We went to bed… I woke up… I screamed*).
- We use the past continuous to set the scene (*We were sleeping in my parents' bedroom*) and to describe actions in progress in the past (*Somebody was standing at the end of my bed*).
- We use the past perfect and the past perfect continuous to talk about the earlier past, i.e. things which happened before the main event (*My father had gone away… I had been reading a story*).

## used to and would: describing habitual events and repeated actions in the past

1 Every summer, my family **used to rent** an old house in the south of France. My sister and I **often walked** to the harbour in the morning, where we **used to watch** the fishermen cleaning their nets.
2 Every night before we went to bed, my mother **would tell** us stories, but she **would never read** them from a book – she **would always make them up** herself.
3 When I was a teenager, my friends **were always teasing** me because of my red hair.

We often use *used to* + infinitive as an alternative to the past simple to talk about things that we did repeatedly in the past.
- We can also use *used to* + infinitive to talk about situations or states which have changed, e.g. *I used to have much longer hair when I was younger.*

We use *would* + infinitive as an alternative to *used to* to talk about things that we did repeatedly in the past.
- We <u>don't</u> use *would* with stative verbs, i.e. to talk about situations or states which have changed. NOT *I would have much longer hair when I was younger.*
- We don't use *would* without a time reference, e.g. *I used to play the violin.* NOT *I would play the violin.*

We can also use *always* + past continuous for things that happened repeatedly, especially when they were irritating habits.

🔍 **Variety in descriptions of past events**
When we describe past habits or repeated past actions we tend, for reasons of variety, to alternate between *used to*, *would*, or the past simple (with adverbs of frequency).

---

a ⬭Circle the right verb form. Tick (✓) if both are possible.

Corinne and I ⬭used to be⬭ | *would be* very close, but recently we've grown apart.

1 When I came into the room, my aunt *sat | was sitting* with her back to me. When she turned round, I could see that she *had been crying | had cried.*
2 Our grandmother *always used to have | would always have* a surprise waiting for us when we visited.
3 My sister *used to live | would live* on her own, but then she *used to buy | bought* a flat with her boyfriend.
4 My brother *didn't use to look | wouldn't look* at all like my father, but now he does.
5 When I was small, I *was always getting | always used to get* into trouble at school and my parents *used to punish | would punish* me by not letting me play with my friends at the weekend.
6 Suddenly we heard a tremendous crash and we saw that a car *crashed | had crashed* into a tree and petrol *poured | was pouring* onto the road.

b Complete with the verb in brackets using a narrative tense or *would | used to*.

**My earliest memory**

When I was about four or five, my grandmother, who was Polish, <u>was living</u> (live) in London and we children often
1 _____ (spend) weekends at her flat. My grandfather
2 _____ (die) a couple of years earlier, so I suppose she was in need of company. We loved going there, as my grandmother 3 _____ (cook) special meals for us and
4 _____ (take) us for lovely walks in Regent's Park, which was quite nearby. One occasion that I remember really well was when I 5 _____ (invite) to stay with her on my own, without my brothers and sisters. On the first day, after lunch, my grandmother 6 _____ (go) for her rest. I 7 _____ (try) to sleep, but I couldn't, so after a while I 8 _____ (get up) and 9 _____ (decide) to explore the flat. Everything was very quiet, so I was convinced that my grandmother 10 _____ (sleep). The room I most 11 _____ (want) to explore was my grandfather's study, I imagine, precisely because I 12 _____ (tell) not to go in there. I opened the door and went in, and was immediately drawn to his large old desk. I 13 _____ (climb) onto the chair and
14 _____ (see) on the desk a green pen in a kind of stand, with a bottle of ink. I 15 _____ (ask) my parents for a real pen for a long time, but they
16 _____ (refuse), foreseeing the mess that I was almost bound to make with the ink. I picked up the pen and then tried to open the bottle of ink. At that moment I 17 _____ (hear) my grandmother's voice saying, 'Christina? Where are you? What are you doing?' To my horror, I 18 _____ (realize) that my grandmother
19 _____ (get up) out of bed and
20 _____ (come) towards the study. Two seconds later, she 21 _____ (open) the door. I will never forget the awful feeling of shame that she 22 _____ (catch) me doing something that she 23 _____ (forbid) me to do.

◀ *p.19*

# 3A  *get*

1 I **got** an email from Marc today saying that he was leaving me!
  If you're going to the post office, could you **get** me some stamps?
  Let's not bother with a taxi – we can **get** the bus.
  When do you think we'll **get to** Paris?
2 We'd better go home. It's **getting dark**.
  I seem to have **got** very **forgetful** recently.
  The traffic **gets worse** in the city centre every day.
  I don't think my mother will ever **get used to** living on her own.
3 Did you know Dan **got sacked** last week?
  My husband **got caught** on the motorway driving at 150 km/h.

4 I'm going to **get my hair cut** next week.
  I need to **get my passport renewed** – it runs out in a couple of months.
5 We need to **get someone to fix** the central heating – it's not working properly.
  Could you **get Jane to finish** the report? I'm too busy to do it this afternoon.

---

*get* is one of the most common verbs in English and can be used in many different ways.

1 *get* + noun / pronoun usually means 'receive', 'bring', 'fetch', 'obtain', 'buy', or 'catch'; with *to* + a place it means 'arrive at / in'.
2 We use *get* + adjective or comparative adjective to mean 'become'.
  • Compare *be* + adjective and *get* + adjective:
    *It's dark. It's getting dark.*
    *I'm used to the climate in England now. I'm getting used to the climate in England.*
3 We can use *get* + past participle instead of *be* to make a passive structure. This is more informal than using *be* and is often used to talk about bad or unexpected things that have happened.
4 In informal spoken English, we sometimes use *get* + object + past participle instead of *have* + object + past participle to say that you ask or pay another person to do something for you.

◀ **See 1A p.140.**

5 We can use *get* + object + infinitive with *to* to mean 'make', 'tell', 'persuade', or 'ask' somebody (to) do something.

**a**  Replace *get* with another verb in the correct form so that the sentences mean the same.

He **got** blamed for the break-up of their marriage.  *was*

1 My father **is getting** increasingly forgetful in his old age. _____
2 Do you know anywhere near here where I can **get** a newspaper? _____
3 Could you **get** your brother to lend you the money? _____
4 We had to **get** the roof repaired, as it was damaged in the storm. _____
5 I **got** an email out of the blue today from an old school friend. _____
6 If I **get** the 7.30 train, would you be able to pick me up at the station? _____
7 Do you think they'll **get** here in time for lunch? _____
8 If you're going upstairs, could you **get** me my jacket? It's on the bed. _____
9 She's going to **get** caught if she's not careful. _____
10 How can I **get** you to change your mind? _____

**b**  Complete with the right forms of *get* and the words in brackets
  I think we ought to stop playing now. It*'s getting dark*. (dark)

1 I only just _____ in time. It was about to run out. (my work permit / renew)
2 My husband has only been in the UK for two months and he just can't _____ on the left. (used / drive)
3 Monica's fiancé _____ in a car crash. He only just survived. (nearly / kill)
4 I can _____ tomorrow night so we can go out. (my sister / babysit)
5 If you can't find your keys, we'll have to _____. (all the locks / change)
6 We _____ by the police today. They were looking for a stolen car. (stop)
7 I went to the optician's yesterday to _____. (eyes / test)
8 **A** What happened to your hand?
  **B** I _____ by our neighbour's dog yesterday. (bite)

◀ *p.27*

discourse markers (2): adverbs and adverbial expressions

| Expression | Use |
|---|---|
| **A** I really like your shirt. Hasn't Harry got one just like it? **B** Yes he has. **Talking of** Harry, did he get the job he applied for? | To change the direction of a conversation, but making a link with what has just been said. |
| So let's meet at five o'clock then. **By the way / Incidentally**, could you possibly lend me some money until the weekend? | To introduce something you have just thought of, or to change the subject completely. |
| **A** Did you see the match last night? **B** No, I didn't. **Actually / In fact / As a matter of fact** I don't really like football. | To introduce additional surprising or unexpected information. |
| We didn't go away at the weekend because I had too much work. **In any case / Anyway** the weather was awful, so we didn't miss anything. | To introduce the idea that what you said before is less important than what you are going to say now, or to return to the main topic after a digression. |
| Yes, it was a bad accident. **At least** nobody was killed, though. Tom's coming to the meeting, or **at least** he said he was. | To introduce a positive point after some negative information, or to qualify what you have just said or to make it less definite. |
| **As I was saying**, if Mark gets the job we'll have to reorganize the department. | To return to a previous subject, often after you have been interrupted. |
| **On the whole**, I think that women make better journalists than men. | To generalize. |
| I like both flats, but **all in all**, I think I prefer the one next to the cathedral. | To say that you are taking everything into consideration. |
| I think we should buy them. **After all**, we'll never find them anywhere cheaper than this. | To introduce a strong argument that the other person may not have taken into consideration. |
| I don't think I'll come to Nick's party. It will finish very late. **Besides**, I won't know many people there. | To add additional information or arguments. |
| **Basically**, my job involves computer skills and people skills. | To introduce the most important or fundamental point. |
| **Obviously** you can't get a real idea of life in Japan unless you can speak the language. | To introduce a fact that is very clear to see or understand. |
| She's very selfish. **I mean**, she never thinks about other people at all. | To make things clearer or give more details. |
| A lot of people booed and some people even left early. **In other words**, it was a complete disaster. | To say something again in another way. |
| Please try not to make a mess when you make the cake. **Otherwise** I'm going to have to clean the kitchen again. | To say what the result would be if something did not happen or if the situation were different. |
| ...and that's all you need to know about the travel arrangements. **As far as** accommodation is **concerned**, … **As regards / Regarding** the accommodation, the options are living with a family or living in a hall of residence. | To introduce a new topic or to announce a change of subject. |
| The government are going to help first-time buyers. **That is to say**, they are going to make mortgages more easily available. | To introduce an explanation or clarification of a point you have just made. |
| **On the one hand**, more young people today carry knives. **On the other hand**, the total number of violent crimes has dropped. | To balance contrasting facts or points.<br>• *On the other hand* is also used alone to introduce a contrasting fact or point. |

**a** Circle the right discourse marker.

**A** What a good film! I really enjoyed it. Didn't you?

**B** *Actually / Incidentally* I didn't like it very much.

**A** Why not?

**B** [1]*Basically / After all*, I thought the plot was completely unbelievable.

**A** I wouldn't call it unbelievable. [2]*In other words / In any case* it wasn't supposed to be a true story.

**B** I know, but it was set in a specific historical period. [3]*Otherwise / Obviously* you can't expect the dialogue to be totally authentic, [4]*I mean / on the other hand*, nobody knows exactly how people spoke in Roman times, but [5]*besides / at least* the details should be right. There were cannons in the battle scene and they weren't invented till a thousand years later! [6]*All in all / That is to say*, I thought it was a pretty awful film.

**A** We'll have to agree to disagree then. [7]*By the way / As a matter of fact*, do you know what time the last bus leaves? I don't want to miss it. [8]*Otherwise / In any case* I'll have to get a taxi home.

**B** 11.40. Don't worry, we've got plenty of time. [9]*In fact / Besides* I think we've even got time to have something to eat. There's a good Italian restaurant just round the corner.

**A** Good idea. [10]*As I was saying / Talking of* Italian food, I made a wonderful mushroom risotto last night…

**b** Complete with a discourse marker. Sometimes more than one answer may be possible.

The film was a box office disaster. *That is to say*, it cost more to produce than it made in receipts.

1 Jason is an excellent teacher, although _____ I think female teachers are usually better with five-year-olds.

2 **A** Did you buy the shoes in the end?

**B** No, they were too expensive. And _____ I decided that I didn't really like them that much.

3 I really think you ought to apply for the post of Head of Department. _____ you've got nothing to lose.

4 **A** I've just read a brilliant book that Simon lent me.

**B** _____ Simon, did you know he's moving to New York?

5 **A** How was your day?

**B** Fine. I finished work earlier than usual. _____, did you remember to get a birthday present for your mum?

6 _____ salary, you will be paid on the last day of each month, with a bonus in December.

7 It was a very overcast day, but _____ it didn't rain.

8 **A** Do your wife's parents live near you, then?

**B** _____, they live in the flat below us. It's not ideal, but it does have some advantages.

9 They've employed me as a kind of troubleshooter – _____, somebody who sorts out any problems.

10 The food was delicious and the service was excellent. _____, the meal was a great success.

11 You'd better hurry up with your homework, _____ you won't be able to watch TV tonight.

12 I'm not sure what the best solution is. _____, buying our own place would mean not paying rent, but _____, I'm not sure we can afford a mortgage.

◄ *p.31*

# 4A speculation and deduction

## modal verbs: *must, may, might, can't, should, ought*

> 1 They **must be** very well off – they've got a huge house.
>   You **must have seen** him – he was standing right in front of you!
> 2 They **can't be playing** very well – they're losing 0–3.
>   You **can't / couldn't have spent** very long on this essay – you've only written 100 words.
> 3 I haven't seen the Sales Manager today. He **may / might / could be** off sick.
>   The keys of the store cupboard have disappeared. Do you think someone **may / might / could have taken** them?
>   He **may / might not have heard** the message I left.
> 4 If I post the letter today, it **should / ought to arrive** on Friday.
>   I posted the letter a week ago. It **should / ought to have arrived** by now.

1 As well as using *must* for obligation, we also use *must* + infinitive to say that we are almost sure something is true about the present and *must have* + past participle to say that we are almost sure something was true or happened in the past.

2 We use *can't* + infinitive to say that we are almost sure that something isn't true in the present and *can't have / couldn't have* + past participle to say that we are almost sure that something didn't happen / wasn't true in the past.
   • We don't use *mustn't / mustn't have* with this meaning.

3 We use *may / might / could* + infinitive and *may have / might have / could have* + past participle to say that we think it's possible that something is true in the present, or was true / happened in the past.
   • We only use *may not* or *might not* to talk about a negative possibility. NOT *couldn't*

4 We use *should / ought to* + infinitive to describe a situation we expect to happen. We use *should have / ought to have* + past participle to describe a situation we would expect to have happened in the past.

> 🔍 **Infinitive or continuous infinitive after modals?**
> He **must work** really hard. He never gets home before 9.00 p.m.
> (= deduction about a habitual action)
> There's a light on in his office. He **must** still **be working**.
> (= deduction about an action in progress at the moment of speaking)

## adjectives and adverbs for speculation

> 1 He's **bound / sure to** be here in a minute. He left an hour ago.
>   She's **sure / bound to** know. She's an expert on the subject.
> 2 I think she's **likely / unlikely to** agree to our proposal.
>   **It is likely / unlikely that** the government will raise interest rates this year.
> 3 She'**ll definitely pass** the exam. She's worked really hard.
>   She **definitely won't** pass the exam. She hasn't done any work at all.
>   He'**ll probably be** here around 8.00. He usually leaves work at 7.30.
>   He **probably won't be** here until about 8.15. He's stuck in a traffic jam.

1 *bound* and *sure* are adjectives. We use *be bound* or *be sure* + *to* + infinitive to say that we think something is certain to be true or to happen.

2 *likely* and *unlikely* are also adjectives (not adverbs). We can use subject + *be likely / unlikely* + *to* + infinitive, or *it is likely / unlikely* + *that* + clause.

3 *definitely* and *probably* are adverbs. They go before a main verb and after the auxiliary if there is one in ➕ sentences and before the auxiliary in ➖ sentences.
   • With *be* they go after the verb in ➕ sentences and before the verb in ➖ sentences, e.g. *He's probably British. The painting definitely isn't genuine.*

**a** Right (✔) or wrong (✗)? Correct the mistakes in the highlighted phrases.

   Jim didn't leave work until 6.00, so he won't likely be here before 7.00. ✗
   *Jim didn't leave work until 6.00, so he isn't likely to be here before 7.00.*

1 My glasses aren't in their usual place. Someone must move them.
2 **A** Do you know where Ann is?
   **B** She should be in the library. That's where she said she was going.
3 **A** What's that noise in the garage?
   **B** I think it can be the neighbour's cat.
4 I'm sure Chelsea will win tonight. They're unlikely to lose three times in a row.
5 I think you should delete that photo of Tina. She won't definitely like it.
6 Julian is bound be late – he always is.
7 No one's answering the phone at the shop. I'd say they've probably gone home.
8 I don't think Marta has gone to bed yet. I think she must still study.
9 It's quite likely that the boss will retire in a year or two.

**b** Rewrite the sentences using the **bold** word.

   Perhaps Luke has got lost. He has no sense of direction. **might**
   Luke *might have got lost*. He has no sense of direction.

1 I don't think he'll have time to call in and see us. He has a very tight schedule. **probably**
   He _____. He has a very tight schedule.
2 I'm not sure she'll ever get over the break-up. **may**
   She _____ the break-up.
3 They will probably have heard the news by now. **ought**
   They _____ now.
4 I didn't leave my credit card in the restaurant. I remember putting it in my wallet. **can't**
   I _____. I remember putting it in my wallet.
5 I'm sure your sister will like the scarf – it's just her style. **bound**
   Your sister _____. It's just her style.
6 The company director probably won't resign, despite the disastrous sales figures. **unlikely**
   The company director _____, despite the disastrous sales figures.
7 I'm sure he was in love with her, otherwise he wouldn't have married her. **must**
   He _____, otherwise he wouldn't have married her.
8 Are you sure you locked the back door? **definitely**
   Did _____ lock the back door?
9 According to press reports, the couple will probably get divorced soon. **likely**
   According to press reports, it's _____ soon.

◀ p.36

# 4B adding emphasis (1): inversion

1 **Not only is the plot great,** (but) it's also very well written.
**Not until** you can behave like an adult **will we treat** you like an adult.
**Never have I heard** such a ridiculous argument.
**No sooner had the football match started** than it began to snow heavily.

2 **Not only did you forget** to shut the window, (but) you also forgot to lock the door!
**Not until** you become a parent yourself **do you understand** what it really means.

3 The train began to move. **Only then was I able** to relax.
**Only when** you leave home **do you realize** how expensive everything is.
**Hardly had I sat down** when / before the train began to move.
**Rarely have I met** a more irritating person.

In formal English, especially in writing, we sometimes change the normal word order to make the sentence more emphatic or dramatic.

1 This structure is common with negative adverbial expressions such as *Not only…*, *Not until…*, *Never…*, and *No sooner…* (= a formal way of saying *as soon as*).
 • When we use inversion after the above expressions, we change the order of the subject and (auxiliary) verb. NOT *Not only the plot is great,…*
 Compare:
 *I have never heard such a ridiculous argument.* (= normal word order)
 *Never have I heard such a ridiculous argument.* (= inversion to make the sentence more emphatic)

2 In the present simple and past simple tense, rather than simply inverting the subject and verb, we use *do | does | did* + subject + main verb. NOT *Not only forgot you to shut the window…*

3 Inversion is also used after the expressions *Only then…*, *Only when…*, *Hardly | Scarcely…*, *Rarely…*

> 🔍 **Overuse of inversion**
> Inversion should only be used occasionally for dramatic effect.
> Overusing it will make your English sound unnatural.

Rewrite the sentences to make them more emphatic.
 I had just started reading when all the lights went out.
 No sooner *had I started reading than all the lights went out*.

1 I didn't realize my mistake until years later.
 Not until _____.

2 We had never seen such magnificent scenery.
 Never _____.

3 They not only disliked her, but they also hated her family.
 Not only _____.

4 We only understood what he had really suffered when we read his autobiography.
 Only when _____.

5 We had just started to eat when we heard someone knocking at the door.
 Hardly _____.

6 I have rarely read such a badly written novel.
 Rarely _____.

7 Until you've tried to write a novel yourself, you don't realize how hard it is.
 Not until _____.

8 The hotel room was depressing, and it was cold as well.
 Not only _____.

9 We only light the fire when it is unusually cold.
 Only when _____.

10 Shortly after he had gone to sleep the phone rang.
 No sooner _____.

11 I only realized the full scale of the disaster when I watched the six o'clock news.
 I watched the six o'clock news. Only then _____.

12 He has never regretted the decision he took on that day.
 Never _____.

13 I spoke to the manager and the problem was taken seriously.
 Only when _____.

14 He had scarcely had time to destroy the evidence before the police arrived.
 Scarcely _____.

◀ p.39

# 5A distancing

## seem / appear

> 1 **It seems / appears that** when people multitask, they in fact do one thing after another in quick succession.
> The new Head of Department **seems / appears to be** quite friendly.
> Excuse me. **There seems to be** a mistake with the bill.
> 2 **It would seem / appear that** Mr Young had been using the company's assets to pay off his private debts.

1 We often use *seem* and *appear* to give information without stating that we definitely know it is true, in this way distancing ourselves from the information.
We can use *It seems / appears* + *that* + clause, or subject + *seem / appear* + infinitive.
2 We use *It would seem / appear* + *that* + clause to distance ourselves even further from the information, making it sound even less sure. This is more formal than *It seems / appears…*

## the passive with verbs of saying and reporting

> 1 **It is said that** using a washing machine saves people on average 47 minutes a day.
> **It has been announced** by a White House spokesman **that** the President has been taken to hospital.
> 2 The company director **is expected to resign** in the next few days.
> The missing couple **are understood to have been living** in Panama for the last five years.
> 3 There **are thought to be** over a thousand species in danger of extinction.

Another way of distancing ourselves from the facts, especially in formal written English, is to use the passive form of verbs like *say*, *think*, etc. to introduce them. We can use:
1 *It* + passive verb + *that* + clause.
  • Verbs commonly used in this pattern are: *agree, announce, believe, expect, hope, say, suggest,* and *think.*
2 subject + passive verb + *to* + infinitive.
  • Verbs commonly used in this pattern are: *believe, expect, report, say, think,* and *understand.*
3 *There* can also be used + passive verb + *to* + infinitive. Compare:
**It is said that there are** more than five million people living in poverty in this country.
**There are said to be** more than five million people living in poverty in this country.

## other distancing expressions: apparently, according to, may / might

> 1 **Apparently**, Jeff and Katie have separated.
> 2 **According to** new research, the idea that we have to drink two litres of water a day is a myth.
> 3 Dinosaurs **may have died out** due to extremely rapid climate change.
> There are rumours that the band, who broke up ten years ago, **might be planning** to reform and record a new album.

1 We use *apparently* (usually either at the beginning or the end of a phrase) to mean that we have heard / read something, but that it may not be true. This is very common in informal conversation.
2 We use *according to* to specify where information has come from. We use it to attribute opinions to somebody else. NOT ~~According to me…~~
3 Using *may / might* also suggests that something is a possibility, but not necessarily true.

---

**a** Complete the sentences with <u>one</u> word to distance the speaker from the information. Sometimes more than one answer may be possible.

> *Apparently*, people who multitask often have concentration problems.

1 It _____ that the less children sleep, the more likely they are to behave badly.
2 It _____ appear that someone has been stealing personal items from the changing rooms.
3 Mark _____ to have aged a lot over the last year.
4 He may not look it, but he is _____ to be one of the wealthiest people in the country.
5 _____ to some sources, the latest research is seriously flawed.
6 Despite the fact that there will be an autopsy, his death is _____ to have been from natural causes.
7 _____ are thought to be several reasons why the species died out.
8 The missing couple are believed _____ have had financial difficulties.
9 It is understood _____ the minister will be resigning in the near future.

**b** Rewrite the second sentence so that it means the same as the first.

> People say that mindfulness helps people to deal with stressful work environments.
> It is *said that mindfulness helps people to deal with stressful work environments*.

1 Apparently, people who work night shifts die younger.
It would _____
2 It is possible that the prisoners escaped to France.
The prisoners may _____
3 We expect that the Prime Minister will make a statement this afternoon.
The Prime Minister is _____
4 The company has announced that the new drug will go on sale shortly.
It _____
5 People believe that stress is responsible for many common skin complaints.
Stress _____
6 The instructions say you have to charge the phone for at least 12 hours.
According _____
7 It appears that the government are intending to lower the top rate of income tax.
The government _____
8 People have suggested that birth order has a strong influence on children's personality.
It _____
9 It seems that there are more cyclists on the road than there used to be.
There _____

◀ p.45

# 5B unreal uses of past tenses

1 It's so expensive! **I wish I could** afford it!
  I **wish** (that) you **hadn't spoken** to Jane like that – you know how sensitive she is.
2 **If only** he **were** a bit less stubborn! Then we wouldn't have so many arguments!
  **If only** you **hadn't forgotten** the map, we'd be there by now.
3 **I wish** she **were** a bit more generous.
  **If only** the weather **were** a bit warmer, we could walk there.
4 **I'd rather** you **left** your dog outside – I'm allergic to animals.
  Are you sure this is a good time to talk? **Would you rather** I **called** back later?
5 Don't you think **it's time** you **found** a job? It's six months since you finished university!

We use *wish* + past simple to talk about things we would like to be different in the present / future (but which are impossible or unlikely).
We use *wish* + past perfect to talk about things which happened / didn't happen in the past and which we now regret.
• We sometimes use *that* after *wish*.

2 You can also use *If only…* instead of *wish* with the past simple and past perfect. This can be used by itself (*If only I knew!*) or with another clause.
• *If only* is slightly more emphatic than *wish*.
• When we want to talk about things we want to happen or stop happening because they annoy us, we use *wish* or *If only* + person / thing + *would* + infinitive, e.g. *I wish the bus would come! If only he wouldn't keep whistling when I'm working!*

3 We can use *were* instead of *was* for *I | he | she | it* after *wish* and *if only*.

4 We use *would rather* + subject + past tense to express a preference.
• We can also use *would rather* + infinitive without *to* when there is no change of subject, e.g. *I'd rather not talk* about it. However, we cannot use this structure when the subject changes after *would rather*, e.g. *I'd rather you didn't talk* about it. NOT *I'd rather you not talk about it.*

5 We use the past simple after *It's (high) time* + subject to say that something has to be done now or in the near future.
• We can also use *It's time + to + infinitive* when we don't want to specify the subject, e.g. *It's time to go now.*

It's high time we thought about going down!

---

a Complete with the right form of the verb in brackets.
  I wish I *hadn't lent* Gary that money now. Who knows when he'll pay it back? (not lend)
1 It's high time the government _____ that most people disagree with their education policy. (realize)
2 My wife would rather we _____ a flat nearer the city centre, but it was too expensive. (buy)
3 I wish you _____ to stay a bit longer last night – we were having such a good time! (be able)
4 Would you rather we _____ the subject now? (not discuss)
5 I think it's time the company _____ expecting us to do overtime for no extra pay. (stop)
6 If only I _____ a bit more when I was earning a salary, I wouldn't be so hard up now. (save)
7 I'd rather you _____ me in cash, please. (pay)
8 If only we _____ the name of the shop, we could Google it and see where it is. (know)
9 Do you wish you _____ to university or are you glad you left school and started work? (go)

b Rewrite the sentences using the **bold** word or phrase.
  The children ought to go to bed. It's nearly nine o'clock. **time**
  *It's time the children went to bed.* It's nearly nine o'clock.
1 I'd prefer you not to wear shoes in the living room, if you don't mind. **rather**
  _____, if you don't mind.
2 I would like to be able to afford to travel more. **wish**
  _____ travel more.
3 We shouldn't have painted the room blue – it looks awful. **if only**
  _____ – it looks awful.
4 Don't you think you should start looking for a job? **time**
  Don't you think _____ for a job?
5 He should be more positive, then he'd enjoy life more. **if only**
  _____, he'd enjoy life more.
6 Would you prefer us to come another day? **rather**
  _____ another day?
7 I should have bought the tickets last week. They would have been cheaper then. **wish**
  _____ last week. They would have been cheaper then.

◀ p.49

# Personality

# Personality

# Personality

## 1 ADJECTIVES

**a** Complete the sentences with the adjectives in the list.

> bright /braɪt/ conscientious /ˌkɒnʃiˈenʃəs/
> determined /dɪˈtɜːmɪnd/ gentle /ˈdʒentl/
> resourceful /rɪˈsɔːsfl/ sarcastic /sɑːˈkæstɪk/
> self-sufficient /ˌself-səˈfɪʃnt/
> spontaneous /spɒnˈteɪniəs/ steady /ˈstedi/
> straightforward /ˌstreɪtˈfɔːwəd/
> sympathetic /ˌsɪmpəˈθetɪk/ thorough /ˈθʌrə/

1 He is very _thorough_. Whatever part of a job he's doing, he does it with great attention to detail.
2 He's quite _____. He can usually work out how to solve a problem.
3 He's very _____. He never needs anyone else's help.
4 Her boyfriend is a _____ guy. He's sensible and she can really rely on him – just what she needs!
5 She's very _____. Once she's decided to do something, nothing will stop her.
6 My nieces are both really _____. They get very good marks at school in all their subjects.
7 He's not very _____. When I was ill last week he didn't even phone me.
8 She is so _____! She worked all weekend to make sure she got everything done.
9 My sister's a very _____ person. She's calm and kind and she never gets angry.
10 She's such a _____ person. She's honest and open and says just what she thinks.
11 He's very _____. He can suddenly decide to go to Paris in the morning and in the evening he's there!
12 Our maths teacher used to be so _____. She loved making comments that made us feel small.

**b** (1 6)) Listen and check.

> 🔍 **False friends**
> Be careful with *sympathetic*. Many languages have a similar adjective – *sympathique* (French), *simpatico* (Italian), *sympatyczny* (Polish) – which means *friendly*. The same is true of *gentle*; this is not the same as, e.g. *gentil* (French), *gentile* (Italian), which mean *kind* or *polite*.

## 2 PHRASES

**a** Complete the phrases with the verbs from the list in the right form

> change refuse seem take ( x2) tend

1 My father _tends_ **to** avoid conflict. He never argues with my mother – he just leaves the room.
2 I don't really like _____ **risks**, especially with money.
3 She makes life hard for herself because she _____ **to compromise**. Everything has to be perfect.
4 She's quite stubborn. She rarely _____ **her mind** even when she knows she's probably wrong.
5 I worry about my grandmother. She's so trusting that it would be easy for people to _____ **advantage of** her.
6 **On the surface he** _____ self-confident, **but deep down** he's quite insecure.

**b** (1 7)) Listen and check.

## 3 IDIOMS

**a** Match the **bold** idioms 1–6 to their meanings A–F.

1 _F_ My brother-in-law is very **down to earth**.
2 ☐ Mum's got **a heart of gold**.
3 ☐ My boss is a bit of **a cold fish**.
4 ☐ My brother's **a real pain in the neck**.
5 ☐ Dad's **a soft touch**.
6 ☐ My uncle has **a very quick temper**.

A He's unfriendly and he never shows his emotions.
B She's incredibly kind to everyone she meets.
C He's so annoying – he's always taking my things.
D I can always persuade him to give me extra pocket money.
E He gets angry very easily.
F He's very sensible and practical.

**b** (1 8)) Listen and check.

> 🔍 **Being negative about people**
> We often use *a bit / a bit of a* before negative adjectives or idioms to 'soften' them, e.g. *She can be a bit sarcastic. He's a bit of a pain in the neck.* We also often use *not very* + positive adjectives rather than using negative ones, e.g. *He's not very bright.* rather than *He's stupid.*

**activation** Think of people you know for two adjectives from **1**, a phrase from **2**, and an idiom from **3**. Tell your partner about them and why they suit the description.

◄ *p.6*

# Work

## 1 ADJECTIVES DESCRIBING A JOB

**a** Match sentences 1–6 with A–F.

1  C  My job as a divorce lawyer is very **challenging** /'tʃælɪndʒɪŋ/.

2     I'm a checkout assistant in a supermarket. I really enjoy my job, but it can be a bit **monotonous** /mə'nɒtənəs/ and **repetitive** /rɪ'petətɪv/.

3     I'm a primary school teacher. I find working with young children very **rewarding** /rɪ'wɔːdɪŋ/.

4     I work in a small graphic design company and my job's really **motivating** /'məʊtɪveɪtɪŋ/.

5     Being a surgeon is very **demanding** /dɪ'mɑːndɪŋ/.

6     I work at an accounting firm. My job is incredibly **tedious** /'tiːdiəs/.

A I have to do exactly the same thing every day.

B It makes me happy because it's useful and important.

C It tests my abilities in a way that keeps me interested.

D It's very high pressure and you have to work long hours.

E It's really boring and it makes me feel impatient all the time.

F The kind of work I do and the people I work with make me want to work harder (do better).

**b** (1 10)) Listen and check.

**activation** Think of a job you could describe with each adjective in **1**.

IKEA JOB INTERVIEW

Please take a seat.

CANARY PETE

## 2 COLLOCATIONS

**a** Complete the text with the words in the list.

career   clocking   experience   for   full   job   management
permanent   positions   qualifications   unpaid

### What I'm really thinking – THE INTERN

I've just started my third internship. At the end of it, I will have been **working** [1] _unpaid_ for a year. It feels as though I'm not in control of my own life, that I'm helpless. [2]**Academic** _____ and [3]**work** _____ are almost irrelevant when you're competing against people who have years of experience, many of whom are taking a step down the [4]_____ **ladder**. I'm not choosy – I've spent time in a children's charity, [5]**events** _____, a press office – but they haven't got me a [6]_____ **contract**. It's demoralizing. And exhausting – [7]_____-**hunting** is a [8]_____-**time occupation**. After [9]_____ **off**, most people can be free for the night. For the intern, it's time to go home and look for work. I have no idea how many [10]_____ I've [11]**applied** _____ since graduating, but it's more than 100.

**b** (1 11)) Listen and check.

**c** Complete the two words which collocate with the groups below. What do the phrases mean?

| maternity<br>paternity<br>sick<br>compassionate<br>unpaid | l_____ | freelance<br>permanent (opp temporary /<br>    fixed-term )<br>full-time (opp part-time) | c_____ |

## 3 THE SAME OR DIFFERENT?

**a** Look at the pairs of words or phrases. Write **S** if they have the same or a very similar meaning and **D** if they are different.

| | | |
|---|---|---|
| 1 colleagues | co-workers | S |
| 2 quit (a job) | resign | |
| 3 staff | workforce | |
| 4 be laid off | be made redundant | |
| 5 be out of work | be off work | |
| 6 be sacked | be fired | |
| 7 get promoted | get a rise | |
| 8 skills | qualifications | |
| 9 hire sb | employ sb | |
| 10 perks | benefits | |

**b** (1 12)) Listen and check.

**activation** Can you explain the difference between the **D** words in meaning or register?

◄ p.9

# Phrases with *get*

## 1 EXPRESSIONS WITH *GET*

**a** Complete the sentences with the expressions in the list.

> a shock   hold of   into <u>trouble</u> with   out of the way   rid of   the chance
> ~~the impression~~   the joke   to know   (my / your, etc.) own back on

1  I get _the impression_ you're a bit annoyed with me.
2  You'll get _____ when you see him. He looks awful.
3  Since we stopped working together, we hardly ever get _____ to see each other.
4  Everyone else laughed, but I didn't get _____ .
5  When you get _____ him, I think you'll really like him.
6  I need to speak to Martina urgently, but I just can't get _____ her.
7  I want to get _____ that awful painting, but I can't because it was a wedding present from my mother-in-law.
8  I'm going to get _____ my brother for telling my parents I got home late. Now I won't lend him my bike.
9  He's going to get _____ his wife if he's late again.
10  I tried to walk past him, but he wouldn't get _____ .

**b** ❨2 4❩⟫ Listen and check. What do the expressions mean?

## 2 IDIOMS WITH *GET*

**a** Match sentences 1–10 to A–J.

1  | *I* | **Get real!**
2  ☐ **Get a life!**
3  ☐ I'm **not getting anywhere** with this crossword.
4  ☐ She really **gets on my nerves**.
5  ☐ She really needs to **get her act together**.
6  ☐ They **get on like a house on fire**.
7  ☐ You should **get a move on**.
8  ☐ Your grandfather must be **getting on** a bit.
9  ☐ My boyfriend just never **gets the message**.
10  ☐ She always **gets her own way**.

A  It's just too difficult for me.
B  Is he in his eighties now?
C  They have exactly the same tastes and interests.
D  Her exam is in two weeks and she hasn't even started studying.
E  If you don't leave soon, you'll miss the train.
F  Everything about her irritates me, her voice, her smile – everything!
G  He just does whatever she tells him to.
H  I keep dropping hints about us getting engaged, but he takes no notice.
I  There's no way you can afford that car!
J  You're 40 and you're still living with your parents!

**b** ❨2 5❩⟫ Listen and check. What do the idioms mean?

**activation** Make personal sentences with two expressions from **1** and two idioms from **2**, and tell a partner.

## 3 PHRASAL VERBS WITH *GET*

**a** Match the **bold** phrasal verbs to A–L.

1  | J | How often do you **get to<u>get</u>her with** your extended family?
2  ☐ How long do you think it usually takes people to **get over** a break-up?
3  ☐ How do you react if somebody interrupts you when you're trying to **get on with** some work?
4  ☐ Do you have any friends who you find it difficult to **get through to** in spite of trying to talk to them honestly?
5  ☐ What are the best subjects to study in your country if you want to **get into** politics?
6  ☐ What's the best way to **get a<u>round</u>** your city, on foot or by public transport?
7  ☐ Have you ever cheated in an exam but **got a<u>way</u> with** it?
8  ☐ What's the minimum amount of money you would need to **get by** if you were living alone in your town?
9  ☐ If you **get** a bit **behind** with your work or studies during the week, do you make up for it at the weekend?
10  ☐ Does bad weather ever **get you down**?
11  ☐ In your family, who is best at **getting out of** doing their share of the housework?
12  ☐ If you leave people a message, does it annoy you if they don't **get back to** you immediately?

A  recover from
B  start a career or profession
C  move from place to place
D  make sb understand
E  manage with what you have
F  fail to make enough progress
G  depress you
H  respond to sb by speaking or writing
I  avoid a responsibility or obligation
J  meet socially
K  continue doing
L  do sth wrong without getting caught

**b** ❨2 6❩⟫ Listen and check.

**activation** Ask and answer the questions in **3** with a partner.

◀ p.25

# Conflict and warfare

## 1 WEAPONS

**a** Match the words and pictures.

| | |
|---|---|
| ☐ <u>a</u>rrow /ˈærəʊ/ | ☐ ma<u>ch</u>ine gun /məˈʃiːn gʌn/ |
| ☐ bow /bəʊ/ | ☐ <u>mi</u>ssile /ˈmɪsaɪl/ |
| ☐ <u>bu</u>llet /ˈbʊlɪt/ | ☐ shield /ʃiːld/ |
| 1 <u>ca</u>nnon /ˈkænən/ | ☐ spear /spɪə/ |
| ☐ <u>hel</u>met /ˈhelmɪt/ | ☐ sword /sɔːd/ |

**b** (2 10)) Listen and check.

## 2 PEOPLE & EVENTS

**a** Match the people and definitions.

<u>a</u>lly /ˈælaɪ/  <s><u>ca</u>sualties</s> /ˈkæʒʊəltiz/  civilians /səˈvɪliənz/
co<u>mma</u>nder /kəˈmɑːndə/  <u>for</u>ces /fɔːsz/  refugees /ˌrefjuˈdʒiːz/
<u>sni</u>pers /ˈsnaɪpəz/  sur<u>vi</u>vors /səˈvaɪvəz/  troops /truːpz/
the <u>wound</u>ed /ˈwuːndɪd/

1 <u>casualties</u> : people who have been killed or injured in a war
2 _____: people who are forced to leave their country or home because there is a war, or for political or religious reasons
3 _____: a group of people who have been trained to protect others, usually with weapons, e.g. *armed ~, security ~, peace-keeping ~.*
4 _____: soldiers in large groups
5 _____: an officer in charge of a group of soldiers
6 _____: people who have been injured by weapons
7 _____: people who are not members of the armed forces
8 _____: people who shoot at others from a hidden position
9 _____: people who have managed to stay alive in a war
10 _____: in time of war, a country that has agreed to help and support another country

**b** Match the events and definitions.

<u>cea</u>sefire /ˈsiːsfaɪə/  civil war /ˈsɪvl wɔː/  coup /kuː/
<s>re<u>be</u>llion</s> /rɪˈbeljən/  revo<u>lu</u>tion /ˌrevəˈluːʃn/  siege /siːdʒ/  <u>trea</u>ty /ˈtriːti/

1 <u>rebellion</u> : an attempt by some of the people in a country to change their government, using violence
2 _____: a sudden change of government that is illegal and often violent
3 _____: an attempt by a large number of people in a country to change their government
4 _____: when two armies agree to stop fighting temporarily
5 _____: a war between groups of people in the same country
6 _____: when an army tries to take a city or building by surrounding it and stopping the food supply
7 _____: a formal agreement between two or more countries.

**c** (2 11)) Listen and check your answers to **a** and **b**.

## 3 VERBS

**a** Complete the sentences with the verbs in the list in the correct form.

blow up  break out  <u>cap</u>ture  de<u>clare</u>  de<u>feat</u>
<u>exe</u>cute  loot  <s>over<u>throw</u></s>  re<u>lease</u>  re<u>treat</u>
shell  su<u>rren</u>der

1 The rebels <u>overthrew</u> the government. (= removed them from power using force)
2 Fighting _____ between the rebels and the army. (= started)
3 The army _____ the rebel positions. (= fired missiles)
4 The rebels _____ . (= moved back, away from the army)
5 Some of the rebels _____ . (= admitted they had lost and wanted to stop fighting)
6 The rebels _____ the airport runway. (= made it explode)
7 The government _____ war on the rebels. (= announced their intention to go to war with them)
8 Some rebels _____ the city. (= stole things from shops and buildings)
9 The army _____ over 300 rebels. (= took them prisoner)
10 They finally _____ the rebels. (= beat them)
11 The army _____ most of the rebel prisoners. (= let them go)
12 They _____ the rebel leader. (= killed him as a punishment)

**b** (2 12)) Listen and check.

**activation**  Are there any current news stories related to conflict or warfare? What are they about?

◄ p.29

# Sounds and the human voice

## 1 SOUNDS

**a** (2 22)》 All the words in the list can be both nouns and regular verbs. Many of them are onomatopoeic (they sound like the sound they describe). Listen to the sounds and the words.

> bang /bæŋ/    buzz /bʌz/    click /klɪk/    crash /kræʃ/    creak /kriːk/
> crunch /krʌntʃ/    drip /drɪp/    hiss /hɪs/    hoot /huːt/    hum /hʌm/
> rattle /'rætl/    roar /rɔː/    screech /skriːtʃ/    slam /slæm/
> slurp /slɜːp/    sniff /snɪf/    snore /snɔː/    splash /splæʃ/
> tap /tæp/    ~~tick /tɪk/~~    whistle /'wɪsl/

**b** Now complete the **Sounds** column with the words in the list.

| | | Sounds |
|---|---|---|
| 1 | This clock has a very loud [ ]. | _tick_ |
| 2 | Don't [ ]! Get a tissue and blow your nose. | |
| 3 | To get the new software, just [ ] on the 'download' icon. | |
| 4 | There was a [ ] as he jumped into the swimming pool. | |
| 5 | Did you hear that [ ]? It sounded like a gun. | |
| 6 | I heard a floorboard [ ] and I knew somebody had come into the room. | |
| 7 | I could hear the [ ] of a fly, but I couldn't see it anywhere. | |
| 8 | I hate people who [ ] at me when I slow down at an amber light. | |
| 9 | When I'm nervous, I often [ ] my fingers on the table. | |
| 10 | Don't [ ] your soup! Eat it quietly. | |
| 11 | The snake reared its head and gave an angry [ ]. | |
| 12 | Please turn the tap off properly, otherwise it'll [ ]. | |
| 13 | We could hear the [ ] of the crowd in the football stadium from our hotel. | |
| 14 | Some of the players carried on playing because they hadn't heard the [ ]. | |
| 15 | I don't remember the words of the song, but I can [ ] the tune. | |
| 16 | Please don't [ ] the door. Close it gently. | |
| 17 | I heard the [ ] of their feet walking through the crisp snow. | |
| 18 | I can't share a room with you if you [ ] – I won't be able to sleep. | |
| 19 | Every time a bus or lorry goes by, the windows [ ]. | |
| 20 | I heard the [ ] of brakes as the driver tried to stop and then a loud [ ]. | |

**c** (2 23)》 Listen and check.

## 2 THE HUMAN VOICE

**a** Match the verbs and definitions.

> giggle /'gɪgl/    groan /grəʊn/    mumble /'mʌmbl/
> ~~scream~~ /skriːm/    sigh /saɪ/    sob /sɒb/
> stammer /'stæmə/    whisper /'wɪspə/    yell /jel/

1 _scream_ to make a loud, high cry because you are hurt, frightened, or excited
2 _____ (*at sb*) to shout loudly, e.g. because you are angry
3 _____ (*at sth*) to laugh in a silly way
4 _____ (*to sb*) to speak very quietly, so that other people can't hear what you're saying
5 _____ to speak or say sth in a quiet voice in a way that is not clear
6 _____ to make a long deep sound because you are in pain or annoyed
7 _____ (or stutter) to speak with difficulty, often repeating sounds or words
8 _____ to cry noisily, taking sudden sharp breaths
9 _____ to take in and then let out a long deep breath, e.g. to show that you are disappointed or tired

**b** (2 24)》 Listen and check.

**c** Answer the questions using one of the verbs in

What do people do…?
- when they are nervous
- when they are terrified
- when they lose their temper
- when they are not supposed to be making an noise
- when they are amused or embarrassed
- when they speak without opening their mouth enough
- when they are relieved
- when their team misses a penalty
- when they are very unhappy about somethin

**activation** Choose five sounds from **1** and two verbs from **2**. Make the sounds for your partner to identify.

◀ *p.34*

# Expressions with *time*

## 1 VERBS

**a** Complete the sentences with the verbs in the list.

give  have  kill  make up for  run out of  save  spare
spend  take (x2)  take up  ~~waste~~

1 I _waste_ **a lot of time** playing games and messaging on my computer instead of studying.
2 If you take the motorway, you'll _____ time – it's much quicker than the local roads.
3 I had three hours to wait for my flight, so I sat there doing sudoku puzzles to _____ time.
4 There's no hurry, so _____ **your time**.
5 When my mother was young, she never had the chance to travel. Now she's retired and wants to _____ **lost time**, so she's booked a trip around the world.
6 The novel is 700 pages long and I'm a slow reader. It's going to _____ **me a long time** to finish it.
7 I'd better go home now. If I'm late again, Dad will _____ **me a hard time**.
8 I would like to go camping this weekend, but my final exams are next week, so I can't _____ **the time**.
9 My children _____ **all my time** – I never seem to get to read a book or watch a film!
10 New York's such a fantastic city! You're going to _____ **the time of your life** there.
11 Let's not _____ **too long** at the museum or we'll _____ time.

**b** (3 5)) Listen and check.

## 2 PREPOSITIONAL PHRASES

**a** Complete the **Prepositions** column with the prepositions in the list.

at (x3)  before  behind  by  from (x2)  in  off  ~~on~~  to (x2)

|  | Prepositions |
|---|---|
| 1 I'm really punctual, so I hate it when other people aren't ___ time. | *on* |
| 2 I've never heard of that singer. He must have been ___ my time. | _____ |
| 3 ___ the time we got to our hotel, it was nearly midnight. | _____ |
| 4 I missed the birth of my first child. I was on a plane ___ **the time**. | _____ |
| 5 He's been working too hard recently. He needs some **time** ___. | _____ |
| 6 If we don't take a taxi, we won't get to the airport ___ **time** for the flight. | _____ |
| 7 I don't eat out very often, but I do get a takeaway ___ **time** ___ **time**. | _____ |

8 He suffers from back pain and it makes him a little irritable ___ **times**. _____
9 You can come **any time** ___ **10.00** ___ **2.00**. _____
10 He's a bit ___ **the times** – he still thinks men should wear a suit and tie at work. _____
11 Don't try to multitask. Just do **one** thing ___ **a time**. _____

**b** (3 6)) Listen and check.

## 3 EXPRESSIONS

**a** Match sentences 1–12 to A–L.

1 | *I* The referee's looking at his watch.
2 | He hardly spoke to me at lunch.
3 | I'm really looking forward to my holiday.
4 | I'm sorry, I can't help you this week.
5 | I can't afford a new computer.
6 | She's sure to find a job eventually.
7 | I think I need to take up a hobby.
8 | Stop writing, please.
9 | I really thought I was going to be late.
10 | Why not spend a morning at our spa?
11 | I hate having to fill in my tax return.
12 | You've had that computer for ages.

A But in the end I got to the airport **with time to spare**.
B He spent **the whole time** talking on his mobile.
C **Time's up.** The exam is over.
D **I'm** a little **short of time**.
E **I've got time on my hands** since I retired.
F I'll have to carry on with this one **for the time being**.
G It's only **a matter of time**.
H It's very popular with women who want a bit of **me time**.
I **There isn't much time left.**
J **This time next week** I'll be lying on the beach.
K **It's about time** you got a new one.
L It's incredibly tedious and **time-consuming**.

**b** (3 7)) Listen and check.

**activation** Choose six of the **bold** time expressions and write a synonym or a phrase with the same meaning, e.g. *save time* = spend less time, *on time* = punctual.

◀ *p.46*

# Money

## 1 NOUNS

**a** Match the nouns and definitions.

> ~~budget~~ deposit do<u>na</u>tion fare fee fine grant
> ins<u>tal</u>ment loan lump sum <u>sav</u>ings will

1 _budget_ the money that is available to a person or organization and a plan of how it will be spent over a period of time, *have a limited ~*
2 _____ money that is given by the government or another organization for a particular purpose, e.g. education, *give | receive a ~*
3 _____ money that a bank lends and sb borrows, *take out a ~*
4 _____ an amount of money that you pay for professional advice or services, e.g. to a lawyer, *charge | pay a ~*
5 _____ the money you pay to travel by bus, plane, taxi, etc., *pay a ~*
6 _____ money that you keep, e.g. in the bank, and don't spend, *have a ~ account*
7 _____ money that you give to an organization such as a charity in order to help them, *make a ~*
8 _____ money paid as punishment for breaking a law, *pay a ~*
9 _____ one of a number of payments that are made regularly until sth has been paid for, *pay an ~*
10 _____ the first part of a larger payment, *make | pay a ~*
11 _____ a legal document that says what is to happen to sb's money and property after they die, *make a ~*
12 _____ an amount of money that is paid at one time and not on separate occasions, *pay a ~*

**b** **3 11 )))** Listen and check.

## 2 MONEY IN TODAY'S SOCIETY

**a** **3 12 )))** Listen to the sentences. With a partner, say what you think the **bold** phrases mean.

1 We live in **a con<u>su</u>mer so<u>ci</u>ety**, which is dominated by spending money on material possessions.
2 The **<u>stan</u>dard of <u>li</u>ving** in many European countries is lower than it was ten years ago.
3 People's **<u>in</u>come** has gone up, but **in<u>fla</u>tion** is high, so the **cost of <u>li</u>ving** has also risen.
4 House prices are rising and people **can't af<u>ford</u>** to buy a home.
5 Online banking allows people to **<u>man</u>age their a<u>ccounts</u>**, e.g. check their **<u>ba</u>lance** and **make <u>trans</u>fers** and **<u>pay</u>ments**.
6 People who have loans have to pay high **<u>in</u>terest rates**.
7 A lot of people are **in debt** and have problems getting a **<u>mort</u>gage** to buy their first home.
8 Some people make money by buying and selling **shares** on the **stock <u>mar</u>ket**.
9 Our **<u>cu</u>rrency** is unstable and **ex<u>change</u> rates** fluctuate a lot.
10 A lot of small businesses **went <u>bank</u>rupt** during **the re<u>cession</u>**.

**b** Which aspects of the sentences above are true in your country?

## 3 ADJECTIVES

**a** Look at the *Oxford Learner's Thesaurus* entries for *rich* and *poor*. Match the synonyms and definitions.

> **rich** *adj.* rich, <u>a</u>ffluent, <u>load</u>ed, <u>weal</u>thy, well-off
>
> 1 _rich_ / _____ having a lot of money, property, or valuable possessions
> 2 _____ (rather formal) rich and with a good standard of living: The ~ Western countries are better equipped to face the problems of global warming.
> 3 _____ (often used in negative sentences) rich: His parents are not very ~ .
> 4 _____ *[not before noun]* (very informal) very rich: Let her pay. She's ~ .
>
> **poor** *adj.* poor, broke, hard up, <u>penni</u>less
>
> 5 _____ having very little money; not having enough money for basic needs
> 6 _____ (literary) having no money, very poor: She arrived in 1978 as a virtually ~ refugee.
> 7 _____ (informal) having very little money, especially for a short period of time: After he lost his job, he was so ~ he couldn't afford to eat out at all.
> 8 _____ *[not before noun]* (informal) having no money: I'm always ~ by the end of the month.

**b** **3 13 )))** Listen and check.

## 4 SLANG WORDS

> 🔍 **Slang**
> Slang refers to very informal words and expressions that are more common in spoken language. Some slang words (though none of the ones below) can be offensive or taboo.

**3 14 )))** Read and listen to the dialogues. What do you think the **bold** slang words mean?

1 **A** Nice car! How much are you going to ask for it?
  **B** **Five grand**. What do you think?

2 **A** I need **five bucks** for the subway.
  **B** Sure, here you are.

3 **A** Great hat! Was it expensive?
  **B** No, only **five quid**. I got it in a charity shop.

4 **A** What's the building work going to cost you?
  **B** About **50K**. We're redoing the kitchen as wel

 **activation** Make sentences about your country or people from your country with two words from each section **1**, **2**, and **3**.

◀ p.50

# Appendix – dependent prepositions

## adjectives + preposition

A lot of young people are **addicted to** social networking.

I can't eat prawns because I'm **allergic to** seafood.

He always seems to be **angry about** something.

There's no need to get **angry with** me.

We weren't **aware of** the problem with our ticket until we got to the airport.

The film, which is set in Sweden, is **based on** a best-selling novel.

She may be old, but she's quite **capable of** looking after herself.

Frida Kahlo was very **close to** her sister.

Many 30-year-olds are still **dependent on** their parents.

The architecture is very **different from** my city.

We're very **dissatisfied with** the service we received at the hotel.

I'm very **excited about** his new film.

Are you **familiar with** the computer software we use?

The city is **famous for** its university.

I'm **fed up with** waiting for the electrician to come. I'm going out.

Are you **frightened of** insects?

I get very **frustrated with** waiting for my brother.

My children are all **good at** sport.

They say taking half an hour's exercise a day can be very **good for** you.

People are usually very **helpful to** foreign tourists.

We're **hooked on** that new TV series – we never miss it.

Her daughter isn't **interested in** music.

My wife isn't very **keen on** moving to London.

She was very **kind to** me when I was going through a bad time.

A lot of people are **obsessed with** celebrities and their lifestyles.

Older people aren't as **open to** new ideas as younger people are.

I was very **pleased with** my presentation. I thought it went very well.

As a nation, we are very **proud of** our sporting achievements.

As marketing manager I am **responsible for** all our publicity campaigns.

I'm **sick of** listening to her complain about how many hours she has to work.

The staff felt very **sorry for** us and gave us a free cup of tea.

I'm **tired of** being told what to do all the time.

## verb + preposition

The police have **accused** her **of** stealing from her employer.

I think the film is definitely **aimed at** people under 25. I didn't enjoy it at all.

We're still waiting for Laura to **apologize for** her awful behaviour last night.

I've **applied for** more than ten jobs since graduating.

Everyone **blamed** me **for** the mistake, even though it wasn't my fault.

I'm so hard up I'm going to have to **borrow** some money **from** my sister.

I'm going to **complain** to the manager **about** this.

I can't **concentrate on** what I'm doing with all that noise outside.

The exam **consists of** speaking, writing, listening, reading, and use of English papers.

I'm getting much better at **coping with** stress than I used to be.

The government was heavily **criticized for** not acting faster.

My children have had to **deal with** a number of challenges.

I was **faced with** a huge pile of work when I got to the office this morning.

I want to **focus on** my work for the next few weeks.

Which historical figure do you most **identify with**?

When I visit a country, I like to **immerse** myself **in** culture.

Simon **insisted on** paying for everything when we went out.

It's rarely a good idea to **lend** money **to** a friend.

I was **named after** my grandmother, who died before I was born.

Eating tomatoes are said to **protect** the body **against** certain diseases.

I know I can **rely on** you to keep a secret.

My brother is a lawyer who **specializes in** criminal law.

His ex-wife **took revenge on** him by cutting up all his suits.

I need to **translate** this document **into** German. Can you help me?

I was **vaccinated against** yellow fever before visiting Ecuador.

## noun + preposition

I worry about my grandmother. She's so trusting that it would be easy for people to take **advantage of** her.

We don't have the same **attitude to / towards** animals.

The sea always has a calming **effect on** me.

He doesn't have enough **faith in** his own ability.

The police have reported a sharp **increase in** crimes involving identity theft.

I have absolutely no **intention of** resigning.

The **lack of** water is becoming a very serious problem in some countries.

There is an urgent **need for** qualified teachers to work in developing nations.

They've organized a **protest against** the new law.

The **reason for** the delay was the late arrival of the incoming flight.

My boss has asked me to write a **report on / about** the new computer system.

The new managing director has a **reputation for** being completely ruthless.

Jack has a lot of **respect for** his grandfather's achievements.

There doesn't seem to be an easy **solution to** the problem.

# Irregular verbs

| Infinitive | Past simple | Past participle |
|---|---|---|
| beat /biːt/ | beat | beaten /ˈbiːtn/ |
| become /bɪˈkʌm/ | became /bɪˈkeɪm/ | become |
| begin /bɪˈgɪn/ | began /bɪˈgæn/ | begun /bɪˈgʌn/ |
| bend /bend/ | bent /bent/ | bent |
| bite /baɪt/ | bit /bɪt/ | bitten /ˈbɪtn/ |
| bleed /bliːd/ | bled /bled/ | bled |
| break /breɪk/ | broke /brəʊk/ | broken /ˈbrəʊkən/ |
| breed /briːd/ | bred /bred/ | bred |
| bring /brɪŋ/ | brought /brɔːt/ | brought |
| build /bɪld/ | built /bɪlt/ | built |
| burn /bɜːn/ | burnt /bɜːnt/ (burned) /bɜːnd/ | burnt (burned) |
| burst /bɜːst/ | burst | burst |
| buy /baɪ/ | bought /bɔːt/ | bought |
| catch /kætʃ/ | caught /kɔːt/ | caught |
| choose /tʃuːz/ | chose /tʃəʊz/ | chosen /ˈtʃəʊzn/ |
| come /kʌm/ | came /keɪm/ | come |
| cost /kɒst/ | cost | cost |
| cut /kʌt/ | cut | cut |
| deal /diːl/ | dealt /delt/ | dealt |
| draw /drɔː/ | drew /druː/ | drawn /drɔːn/ |
| dream /driːm/ | dreamt /dremt/ (dreamed) /driːmd/ | dreamt (dreamed) |
| drink /drɪŋk/ | drank /dræŋk/ | drunk /drʌŋk/ |
| drive /draɪv/ | drove /drəʊv/ | driven /ˈdrɪvn/ |
| eat /iːt/ | ate /eɪt/ | eaten /ˈiːtn/ |
| fall /fɔːl/ | fell /fel/ | fallen /ˈfɔːlən/ |
| feed /fiːd/ | fed /fed/ | fed |
| feel /fiːl/ | felt /felt/ | felt |
| find /faɪnd/ | found /faʊnd/ | found |
| fly /flaɪ/ | flew /fluː/ | flown /fləʊn/ |
| forget /fəˈget/ | forgot /fəˈgɒt/ | forgotten /fəˈgɒtn/ |
| get /get/ | got /gɒt/ | got |
| give /gɪv/ | gave /geɪv/ | given /ˈgɪvn/ |
| go /gəʊ/ | went /went/ | gone /gɒn/ |
| grow /grəʊ/ | grew /gruː/ | grown /grəʊn/ |
| hang /hæŋ/ | hung /hʌŋ/ | hung |
| hear /hɪə/ | heard /hɜːd/ | heard |
| hit /hɪt/ | hit | hit |
| hold /həʊld/ | held /held/ | held |
| hurt /hɜːt/ | hurt | hurt |
| keep /kiːp/ | kept /kept/ | kept |
| know /nəʊ/ | knew /njuː/ | known /nəʊn/ |

| Infinitive | Past simple | Past participle |
|---|---|---|
| lay /leɪ/ | laid /leɪd/ | laid |
| learn /lɜːn/ | learnt /lɜːnt/ | learnt |
| leave /liːv/ | left /left/ | left |
| lend /lend/ | lent /lent/ | lent |
| let /let/ | let | let |
| lie /laɪ/ | lay /leɪ/ | lain /leɪn/ |
| lose /luːz/ | lost /lɒst/ | lost |
| make /meɪk/ | made /meɪd/ | made |
| mean /miːn/ | meant /ment/ | meant |
| meet /miːt/ | met /met/ | met |
| pay /peɪ/ | paid /peɪd/ | paid |
| put /pʊt/ | put | put |
| read /riːd/ | read /red/ | read /red/ |
| ride /raɪd/ | rode /rəʊd/ | ridden /ˈrɪdn/ |
| ring /rɪŋ/ | rang /ræŋ/ | rung /rʌŋ/ |
| rise /raɪz/ | rose /rəʊz/ | risen /ˈrɪzn/ |
| run /rʌn/ | ran /ræn/ | run |
| say /seɪ/ | said /sed/ | said |
| see /siː/ | saw /sɔː/ | seen /siːn/ |
| seek /siːk/ | sought /sɔːt/ | sought |
| sell /sel/ | sold /səʊld/ | sold |
| send /send/ | sent /sent/ | sent |
| set /set/ | set | set |
| shut /ʃʌt/ | shut | shut |
| sing /sɪŋ/ | sang /sæŋ/ | sung /sʌŋ/ |
| sit /sɪt/ | sat /sæt/ | sat |
| sleep /sliːp/ | slept /slept/ | slept |
| speak /spiːk/ | spoke /spəʊk/ | spoken /ˈspəʊkən/ |
| spend /spend/ | spent /spent/ | spent |
| stand /stænd/ | stood /stʊd/ | stood |
| steal /stiːl/ | stole /stəʊl/ | stolen /ˈstəʊlən/ |
| stick /stɪk/ | stuck /stʌk/ | stuck |
| swim /swɪm/ | swam /swæm/ | swum /swʌm/ |
| take /teɪk/ | took /tʊk/ | taken /ˈteɪkən/ |
| teach /tiːtʃ/ | taught /tɔːt/ | taught |
| tear /teə/ | tore /tɔː/ | torn /tɔːn/ |
| tell /tel/ | told /təʊld/ | told |
| think /θɪŋk/ | thought /θɔːt/ | thought |
| throw /θrəʊ/ | threw /θruː/ | thrown /θrəʊn/ |
| understand /ʌndəˈstænd/ | understood /ʌndəˈstʊd/ | understood |
| wake /weɪk/ | woke /wəʊk/ | woken /ˈwəʊkən/ |
| wear /weə/ | wore /wɔː/ | worn /wɔːn/ |
| win /wɪn/ | won /wʌn/ | won |
| write /raɪt/ | wrote /rəʊt/ | written /ˈrɪtn/ |

| | usual spelling | | ! but also |
|---|---|---|---|
| fish | **i** | kill drip<br>risk idiom<br>stick quit | message rewarding<br>repetitive business<br>building synonym |
| tree | **ee**<br>**ea**<br>**e** | screech fee<br>creak treaty<br>even tedious | routine suite siege<br>key receipt people |
| cat | **a** | bang crash<br>slam tap<br>balance salary | |
| car | **ar**<br><br>**a** | bark smart<br>sarcastic<br>chance grant<br>staff advantage | calf calm<br>laugh draught<br>heart |
| clock | **o** | occupation<br>obviously<br>shock sob<br>contract deposit | squash sausages<br>cough knowledge |
| horse | **(o)or**<br><br>**al (+l, +ll)**<br><br>**aw**<br>**au** | forces snore<br>outdoor<br>although<br>instalment call<br>paw claws<br>long-haul cautious | caught fought<br>war roar pour |
| bull | **u**<br>**oo** | bullet pushed<br>cooking goodness<br>stood wood | should would<br>woman |
| boot | **oo**<br>**u***<br>**ew** | loot troops<br>due flu<br>view blew | moving coup<br>wounded through<br>bruise suit beauty<br>queue shoe |
| computer | Many different spellings – always unstressed.<br>a<u>sser</u>tive <u>re</u>lative <u>practi</u>cal <u>challeng</u>ing<br><u>mem</u>ber <u>opin</u>ion pro<u>fess</u>ion <u>stubborn</u><br>suc<u>cess</u>ful | | |
| bird | **er**<br>**ir**<br>**ur** | herbs nerves<br>circuit birth<br>slurp fur | earth learner<br>world worse<br>journey |
| egg | **e** | gentle debt<br>neck tense<br>benefit temporary<br>surrender | wealthy breathtaking<br>steady friendly<br>many said says |

| | usual spelling | | ! but also |
|---|---|---|---|
| up | **u**<br><br><br>**o** | hum hunt<br>gun gut stuck<br>mussels discuss<br>above oven | blood flood<br>tough enough<br>couple trouble |
| train | **a***<br>**ai**<br>**ay** | wages hatred<br>tail training<br>away tray | great steak<br>neighbour weight<br>survey obey |
| phone | **o***<br><br>**oa**<br>**ow** | totally joke<br>bonus post<br>groan loaded<br>arrow below | soulmate doughnut<br>aubergine |
| bike | **i***<br><br>**y**<br>**igh** | sniper wild<br>Wi-fi<br>deny ally<br>sigh bright | eye neither<br>aisle guy |
| owl | **ou**<br><br>**ow** | around amount<br>profoundly<br>powerful<br>overcrowded<br>meow | plough drought |
| boy | **oi**<br><br>**oy** | point spoilt<br>voice choice<br>loyal employer | |
| ear | **eer**<br>**ere**<br><br>**ear** | career beer<br>adhere<br>atmosphere<br>fear spear | period ideal<br>weird |
| chair | **air**<br><br>**are** | aircraft fair<br>repair<br>fare spare | scary bear<br>wherever<br>there their |
| tourist | **ur (+r)**<br><br>**ure**<br><br>**eur (+r)** | curious<br>during plural<br>mature endure<br>secure<br>Euro Europe | |
| /i/ | A sound between /ɪ/ and /iː/. Consonant + y at the end of words is pronounced /i/.<br>happy angry thirsty | | |
| /u/ | An unusual sound between /ʊ/ and /uː/.<br>education usually situation | | |

# Consonant sounds

| | usual spelling | ! but also |
|---|---|---|
| parrot | **p** perks poached<br>recipe deep<br>**pp** apparently gripping | |
| bag | **b** breed bite<br>tablet grab<br>**bb** scribble bubble | |
| key | **c** screen economic<br>**k** skill bankrupt<br>**ck** click tick<br>**qu** quick picturesque | chorus<br>chiropractic<br>technician<br>accurate |
| girl | **g** grunt guided<br>arguably drug<br>**gg** giggle aggressive | ghost colleague |
| flower | **f** fire refugee<br>**ph** photography metaphor<br>**ff** affluent sniff | laugh rough |
| vase | **v** vast voicemail<br>survive review<br>government hive | of |
| tie | **t** track touristy<br>strength retreat<br>**tt** rattle settings | mashed chopped<br>debt doubt<br>receipt |
| dog | **d** defeat declare<br>update crowd<br>**dd** add middle | steamed bored |
| snake | **s** stranger responsible<br>**ss** hiss across<br>**c** (+ **e**, **i**) ceasefire civilians | scenery<br>psychoanalyst<br>fancy |
| zebra | **z** zip zone<br>**zz** buzz dizzy drizzle<br>**s** misery refuses<br>trousers avoids | dessert |
| shower | **sh** shocked sheet<br>shellfish rash<br>**ti** (+ **vowel**) addiction operation<br>**ci** (+ **vowel**) species crucial | sugar sure<br>chef cliché<br>anxious pressure |
| television | An unusual sound.<br>invasion conclusion pleasure casualties massage | |

| | usual spelling | ! but also |
|---|---|---|
| thumb | **th** thorough thriller<br>thick sympathetic<br>breath death | |
| mother | **th** though therefore<br>either nevertheless<br>smooth | |
| chess | **ch** charge crunch<br>**tch** switched match<br>**t** (+ **ure**) capture sculpture | |
| jazz | **j** juggle enjoyable<br>**g** cage besiege<br>**dge** edgy gadget | soldier<br>suggest |
| leg | **l** legal lively<br>landline deal<br>**ll** colleague scroll | |
| right | **r** revolution ribs<br>grand scrambled<br>**rr** surrender overrated | wrist wrinkle |
| witch | **w** wings waist<br>willing towards<br>**wh** whistle whisper | one once |
| yacht | **y** yell yoga<br>yoghurt yourselves<br>before **u** mule consumer | |
| monkey | **m** mumble motivated<br>temper consumer<br>**mm** stammer recommend | limb dumb |
| nose | **n** nightmare internet<br>monotonous<br>**nn** penniless cannon | knowledge<br>knight<br>design foreign |
| singer | **ng** length strong<br>wing sting<br>before **k** ankle blink | |
| house | **h** heat horns<br>history inherit<br>behave unhelpful | whoever who<br>whole |

○ voiced   ○ unvoiced

Christina Latham-Koenig
Clive Oxenden
Jerry Lambert

with Jane Hudson

# ENGLISH FILE

Advanced  **Workbook A** with key

Paul Seligson and Clive Oxenden are the original co-authors of
*English File 1* and *English File 2*

# Contents

The other night I ate at a real nice family restaurant.
Every table had an argument going.

*George Carlin, American comedian*

# 1A Self-portrait

## 1 GRAMMAR *have*: auxiliary or main verb?

**a** (Circle) the correct words or phrases. In some sentences two answers are correct.

1 Some friends of ours (had) | had got | have had a nasty car accident last night.
2 She can't call her husband because she *doesn't have | hasn't | hasn't got* her mobile.
3 *Did you have | Had you | Have you got* a good time at your nephew's wedding?
4 Why are you going to be late? *Have you | Do you have | Have you got* to go to the doctor's?
5 We *had | had got | have got* our TV repaired last week, but it still doesn't work.
6 If she *had | have | had had* a coffee, she wouldn't have fallen asleep in the meeting!
7 I *didn't have to | hadn't got to | hadn't to* wear a uniform when I went to school.
8 The boss *didn't have | hadn't | won't have* heard the news yet because he's been off sick.

**b** Complete the sentences with the correct form of *have*. Sometimes more than one answer is possible.

1 They couldn't go to the concert because they ___didn't have___ tickets.
2 Jessica doesn't need a company car because she _____ travel for her job.
3 This is a great car, Alex. How long _____ you _____ it?
4 Let's take a taxi. We _____ time to walk.
5 I can't lend you my bike. I _____ it repaired at the moment.
6 Ben doesn't know everyone yet. He _____ working in our office for very long.
7 Welcome to the UK. _____ you _____ a good flight?
8 I'll give you a lift. What time _____ you _____ to be at the airport?

## 2 VOCABULARY personality

**a** (Circle) the correct word.

1 Emily doesn't need any help – she's very *conscientious | gentle |* (self-sufficient).
2 I don't like my boss much. He can be very *bright | sarcastic | steady*.
3 She's a really *conscientious | spontaneous | sympathetic* student, so she attends all her lectures.
4 My father is great at household repairs because he's very *resourceful | sarcastic | straightforward*.
5 The doctor was quite *self-sufficient | spontaneous | thorough* and examined the patient carefully.
6 I had a terrible day at work, but my husband wasn't very *determined | steady | sympathetic*.
7 My grandmother was a *bright | gentle | thorough* woman who was kind to everyone.
8 My best friend is very *determined | resourceful | straightforward*; there's nothing complicated about her.

**b** Complete the verbs in the sentences.

1 Ann's very indecisive. She's always **ch**___anging___ her mind.
2 On the surface, she **s**_____ not to care, but deep down I'm sure she's terribly upset.
3 He's so innocent, he often gets **t**_____ advantage of.
4 She's very spontaneous, but her boyfriend **t**_____ to plan ahead.
5 We agreed to some of their demands, but they still **r**_____ to compromise.
6 I'm not adventurous, so I don't **t**_____ risks.

**c** Replace the words in **bold** with a personality idiom using the word in brackets.

1 My aunt can be a bit impatient, but she's got **a very kind personality**. (heart) ___a heart of gold___
2 That customer is **really annoying** – he's always calling to complain. (neck) _____
3 My friend's dad **gets angry very easily**, so we try to keep out of his way. (quick) _____
4 Our new neighbour is **very reserved and unfriendly** (fish) _____
5 My parents are very **sensible and practical**. They're full of good advice. (earth) _____
6 My brother is **very easily persuaded**. I can get him to do whatever I want. (soft) _____

4

## 3 PRONUNCIATION using a dictionary

**a** Underline the stressed syllable in the words below.

1 straight|for|ward
2 con|sci|en|tious
3 cu|ri|ous
4 de|ter|mined
5 gen|tle
6 self-|suf|fi|cient
7 stea|dy
8 re|source|ful
9 sar|cas|tic
10 spon|ta|ne|ous
11 sym|pa|the|tic
12 tho|rough

**b** **iChecker** Listen and check. Practise saying the words.

## 4 LEXIS IN CONTEXT
### What's your personality?

Look at the Lexis in Context on Student's Book p.6. Then complete the sentences.

1 We followed your directions **to the l***etter*___, so we didn't get lost.
2 Maria **got st**_____ on a question, so she couldn't finish her homework.
3 It's best to **put t**_____ a list of points for discussion before you hold a meeting.
4 The jacket in the window **caught my e**_____, so I went into the shop to try it on.
5 It wasn't easy to **go r**_____ the exhibition because there were so many people.
6 The gambler went with his **g**_____ **feeling** and put all his money on the same horse.
7 A good manager faces problems **h**_____ **on** in order to solve them as quickly as possible.
8 My flatmate always **puts o**_____ doing the washing up until there aren't any clean plates left.
9 I didn't want to hurt my sister's feelings, so I told her a **wh**_____ **lie** about her new dress.

## 5 LISTENING

**a** **iChecker** Listen to four people comparing having brothers and sisters and being an only child. Do they mention more advantages or disadvantages of having siblings?

**b** Listen again. Which speaker mentions these advantages of having brothers and sisters?

A ☐ learning to interact with other children
B ☐ not being spoilt
C ☐ not being the sole centre of your parents' expectations
D ☐ being able to share the responsibility of caring for elderly parents

**c** Listen again with the audio script on p.69 and try to guess the meaning of any words that you don't know. Then check in your dictionary.

## 6 READING

**a** Read the article once and choose the sentence that best describes Ang Lee.

1 He is more content now than he was as a child.

2 He is as content now as he was as a child.

3 He was more content as a child than he is now.

**b** Read the text again and choose **a**, **b**, **c**, or **d**.

1 How did Ang Lee regard his father as a child?

  a He admired him.

  b He was fond of him.

  c He was in awe of him.

  d He hated him.

2 What is Ang Lee's greatest criticism of his father?

  a He had too many children.

  b He lacked a sense of humour.

  c He forced his children to study art.

  d He never took them to the cinema.

3 What was Sheng Lee's opinion of his son's choice of career?

  a He had no faith in Ang's ability to make films.

  b He hoped that Ang would be successful.

  c He regarded it as a respectable profession.

  d He didn't think it was a proper job.

4 What does Ang Lee say about his mother?

  a She brought up her children well.

  b She was a soft touch.

  c She should have been more rebellious.

  d She stood out from all his friends' mothers.

5 Why didn't Ang Lee do very well at school?

  a Because he wasn't very bright.

  b Because he never did his homework.

  c Because he didn't focus on what he had to study.

  d Because he often played truant.

6 Why were the first years of Ang Lee's marriage difficult?

  a Because his wife didn't approve of his career choice.

  b Because he didn't have any paid employment.

  c Because he had been brought up in a different way from his wife.

  d Because his children needed special attention.

**c** Look at the highlighted adjectives. What do you think they mean? Check in your dictionary.

### Glossary
**tiger mother** a demanding mother who pushes her children to high levels of achievement

# Ang Lee: my family values

The film director on moving out of his father's shadow and being determined to make life fun for his own children.

**My late father, Sheng Lee,** was a traditional Chinese authority figure. He represented the traditional Chinese patriarchal society. I was always living in his shadow; that was my big thing. I was shy and docile and never rebellious. But he taught me how to survive and how to be useful. He was a very pragmatic man, the headmaster of a high school – I don't know if that was a good or a bad thing.

**When I was growing up** [as one of four children] he made me study all the time; studying was all that was important to him. He was not much fun and he was kind of disappointed with me in some ways. Artistically, I was very repressed. I never really got to express myself and wasn't exposed to much art other than watching movies once a week.

**My father wanted me to have** a respectable profession. Teaching was respectable to him. He said, 'Get a degree and teach in university.' When I wasn't working he would say, 'What are you going to do? Are you going to set an example for your kids?' But I just wanted to make movies, so I never fulfilled the hopes he had for me. Even when I was successful, he would say, 'Now it's time to do something real.'

**My mother, Se-Tsung,** was very submissive with my father and obedient. I don't have many issues with her: she was a very good mother to me and my siblings. When I was growing up, women didn't matter as much. It was patriarchal, all about the father. Everyone tried to please my father.

**As a kid I could not really concentrate** on books or homework. I did OK to poorly at school because I would fantasize all the time, having a lot of fun in my head because I didn't have a lot of fun. It took 35 years to release all that energy. I was repressed and then that repression was released when I became a filmmaker.

**When I had my own family** I was different because I didn't want to do that to my own kids, so I am fun. My wife [Jane Lin, a microbiologist] is the tiger mother in the home, the wise one in the family. I am like the third kid at home. She makes all the rules. We [our two sons, Mason, an actor, and Haan, an artist] obey. Before I got work as a director, my wife worked. I was lucky, my wife provided for the family herself and never asked me to find a job. I was picking up the kids from school and doing the cooking and writing. Most of the time I didn't do anything – there was a lot of anxiety because I couldn't invest in anything apart from filmmaking.

A professional is one who does his best work
when he feels the least like working.

*Frank Lloyd Wright, American architect*

# 1B Nice work!

## 1 LEXIS IN CONTEXT
### What I'm really thinking

Look at the Lexis in Context on Student's Book p.8.
Then complete the expressions.

1 I wouldn't worry about the interview – it's not a matter
of l*ife or death*.
2 Turn that music off! It's **doing my h_____ in**.
3 If you paid attention, you might be able to **k_____
up with** the lesson.
4 My father is an intellectual snob. He **l_____ down
on** people who haven't been to university.
5 My mind's **gone bl_____**! I can't remember my own
phone number!
6 The traffic begins to **b_____ up** at around 7 o'clock
on weekdays.
7 It **breaks my h_____** when I see pictures of
malnourished children on the TV.
8 I don't mind dealing with the public, but it **gets
w_____** answering the same questions all day.

## 2 VOCABULARY work

a (Circle) the correct word.

1 My company offers considerable benefits to the
*colleagues | co-workers | (staff.)*
2 It's so *repetitive | challenging | rewarding* when you see
your students really start to improve.
3 My girlfriend's job is quite *rewarding | demanding |
tedious*, so she gets very stressed.
4 I'm hoping to get *a rise | promoted | raised* to Head of
Department by the end of the year.
5 He wants to *quit | employ | resign* a new assistant to deal
with his mail.
6 Over 2,000 workers will be *fired | made redundant |
sacked* when the car factory closes down.
7 Working on a production line can be *challenging |
motivating | monotonous* because you do the same thing
all day every day.
8 My husband is *off work | out of work | laid off* with a bad
back at the moment.
9 I'm really jealous of my sister because she gets so many
*skills | qualifications | perks* in her job.
10 We're looking to *hire | fire | lay off* somebody with a
positive, can-do attitude.

b Match the words in **A** to the words in **B** and complete
the sentences below.

| A | academic | apply for | career | clocking |
| | events | full | job | permanent | ~~work~~ |

| B | contract | ~~experience~~ | hunting | ladder |
| | management | off | a position | qualifications | time |

1 The company is offering _work experience_ to
students in their final year of school.
2 Looking after small children is a
_____-_____ occupation.
3 I've spent six months _____-_____,
but I'm still out of work.
4 She never went to university so she doesn't have many
_____ _____.
5 He's very ambitious, so he's hoping to climb the
_____ _____ as quickly as possible.
6 If you're good at organizing parties, you could work
in _____ _____.
7 I'm hoping they'll give me a _____ _____
when I finish my three-month trial period.
8 She cleared her desk and locked the drawers before
_____ _____.
9 I'm going to _____ _____ _____
_____ as a sales assistant at the new shopping
centre, which is opening soon.

## 3 GRAMMAR discourse markers (1): linkers

a ~~Cross out~~ the linker that is NOT possible in the sentences.

1 We set off at dawn ~~owing to~~ | *in order to* | *so as to* avoid
the rush-hour traffic.
2 Laila's mother-in-law was a very difficult woman.
*However | Nevertheless | Consequently* Laila couldn't
help liking her.
3 *In spite of | Even though | Despite* being the better
player, Richard lost the match.
4 Sales figures have fallen drastically *due to | because |
owing to* the recession.
5 The workers covered the furniture with sheets *so as not
to | not to | in order not to* splash it with paint.
6 After his accident, my brother sold his car *as | since |
due to* he couldn't afford the insurance.
7 We accept full responsibility for the error and *nevertheless |
consequently | therefore* wish to offer you a full refund.
8 I agreed to help *although | in case | even though* I didn't
feel like it.

**b** Rewrite the sentences using the word(s) in brackets.

1  We have not received payment for your last bill. Consequently, you are being sent a reminder. (since)
   You are being sent a reminder _since we have not received payment for your last bill_ .

2  She wrote down the appointment so that she wouldn't forget the time. (so as)
   She wrote down the appointment _____
   _____ .

3  The motorway is being resurfaced and so it will be closed until further notice. (result)
   The motorway is being resurfaced, and _____
   _____ .

4  The flight is delayed because the incoming plane arrived late. (due)
   The flight is delayed _____
   _____ .

5  He decided to apply for the job although he didn't meet all the requirements. (despite)
   He decided to apply for the job _____
   _____ .

6  They had an early night in order to be ready for the exam the next day. (so that)
   They had an early night _____
   _____ .

7  She was offered a job even though she wasn't able to go to the interview. (spite)
   She was offered the job _____
   _____ .

8  He was unable to attend the conference because he was ill. (owing)
   He was unable to attend the conference _____
   _____ .

## 4 LEXIS IN CONTEXT  Skyscanner

Look at the Lexis in Context on Student's Book p.11. Then complete the sentences.

1  When you live near an airport, the noise of the planes eventually becomes the **n** _orm_ .

2  Her sickness was just a **pl**_____ so she could stay at home.

3  Please don't let the fact that I got the promotion over you become an **i**_____ between us.

4  He wanted a job that was **tr**_____**-f**_____, so he became a flight attendant.

5  I can handle a fairly heavy **w**_____. I'm used to doing lots of things at once.

6  How do we **t**_____ the problem of unemployment?

## 5 PRONUNCIATION  word stress

**a**  Underline the stressed syllable in the words below.

1  re|<u>war</u>|ding
2  free|lance
3  tem|po|ra|ry
4  vo|lun|tary
5  com|pas|sio|nate
6  ma|ter|ni|ty

7  per|ma|nent
8  mo|ti|va|ting
9  mo|no|to|nous
10  a|ca|de|mic
11  ma|nage|ment
12  qua|li|fi|ca|tions

**b**  **iChecker**  Listen and check. Practise saying the words.

**c**  Circle the word with a different sound.

| 1 | tree | tedious | colleague | event |
| 2 | bike | quit | resign | fire |
| 3 | ear | career | perks | experience |
| 4 | fish | redundant | demanding | benefits |

**d**  **iChecker**  Listen and check. Practise saying the words.

8

# 6 READING

a Read the article once. How would the writer answer the question in the title?

## 'BEST JOB IN THE WORLD': FACT OR FICTION?

Who wouldn't jump at the chance of 'working' for six months as the caretaker of an idyllic holiday island off the coast of Queensland, Australia? For Ben Southall, winner of the 'Best Job in the World' contest, the prospect seemed like a dream come true. The 34-year-old former charity worker, from Petersfield, UK, beat 34,000 other competitors for the job, which also came with a £2.5 million beachside mansion boasting magnificent ocean views. ¹ _____

Alas, at the end of his posting, Mr Southall admitted that being a tourist ambassador for paradise was not all plain sailing. In fact, there was very little time for sailing at all – or sunbathing, or simply relaxing and enjoying those fine ocean views.

² _____ 'It has been very busy, busier than most people would have imagined, and certainly busier than I had imagined,' Mr Southall told the press, adding that he had been 'too busy' to sit back and reflect on it all very much. ³ _____

True, somewhere along the line he did also learn to sail, play golf, and kayak. But even those activities were limited by the need to keep a running web commentary about what he was up to. He posted more than 75,000 words in 60 separate blogs – the equivalent of a small novel – uploaded more than 2,000 photos, and 'tweeted more than 730 times,' according to Peter Lawlor, Queensland's Tourism Minister.

⁴ _____ Readers of the website complained that the jam-packed itineraries organized by Tourism Queensland left Mr Southall no time to explore the reef privately and deliver detailed accounts of his experiences. They also said that the blogs were too sanitized and promotional, without any critical or personal angle.

⁵ _____ Nevertheless, in what is perhaps the ultimate proof of his new skills as a PR man, he still insists he enjoyed himself thoroughly. And his demanding taskmasters at Tourism Queensland are also pleased, so much so that they have offered him a new 18-month, six-figure contract to promote their state worldwide.

In his spare time, if he gets any, he will also start on a book about his experiences over the last six months. Whether it will prove a best-selling beachside read is another matter.

b Five sentences and paragraphs have been removed from the article. Read it again and match A–F to the gaps 1–5. There is one sentence or paragraph you do not need to use.

A Indeed, in the view of his online audience, he spent so much time blogging about having a good time that he didn't really have much of a time at all.

B Instead, he found himself working seven days a week, slave to a gruelling schedule of promotional events, press conferences, and administration.

C Soon after he started, Ben had a brush with death after being stung by a jellyfish. The incident did not deter him, however, and he got on with his job.

D Either way, Mr Southall admits that he is now tired out – and in need of a holiday. 'It was a job that needed 18 to 19 hours' work every day,' he said. 'Not just the interviews and the social side of it, but also blogging and uploading pictures – it's very time consuming.'

E Other perks in the contest included a £74,000 salary, a private pool, and a courtesy golf buggy.

F A snapshot of just how demanding the Best Job in the World could be is provided by Tourism Queensland's official report on Mr Southall's posting. It announced that he had visited 90 'exotic locations', made 47 video diaries, and given more than 250 media interviews.

c Look at the highlighted idioms and match them to the definitions.

1 very full _____
2 at some point during an activity _____
3 simple and free from trouble _____
4 was doing _____
5 is very different _____
6 accept an opportunity with enthusiasm
_____

# 7 LISTENING

a **iChecker** Listen to a man talking about a kind of job he would love to do and one he would hate. What are the jobs?

b Listen again. Answer the questions.

1 Why does the man think he would be good at the first job?
2 What does he think might be the downside?
3 Why does he think he would hate the second job?
4 Has he done this kind of work? If so, did he like it?

c Listen again with the audio script on p.69 and try to guess the meaning of any words that you don't know. Then check in your dictionary.

## 1 LOOKING AT LANGUAGE

### discourse markers

Complete the sentences with a discourse marker from the list.

| anyway | apparently | as to | basically |
|--------|------------|-------|-----------|
| I mean | in a way | of course | really |

1 My sister gets quite lonely in the evenings. _Of course_ her husband's around, but he's always falling asleep in front of the TV.

2 I can't remember much about my childhood. _____, I spent most of the time running wild with the other kids in the village. That's what my mum tells me, anyway.

3 My nephew's such a lovely boy. But _____ what he wants to do in the future, he hasn't got a clue.

4 We've had a great holiday but _____, I'm glad to be going home. I've missed the cat!

5 If I have to take my daughter to work, I _____ do the same as I would on a normal day.

6 That woman isn't _____ her mother; she's her stepmother.

7 I'm hoping to move out soon. _____, I love my parents, but I'd like a place of my own.

8 I'm not going to apply for that job. It's too far away and _____, the pay is too low.

## 2 READING

a Read the article. Five sentences have been removed from it. Match the sentences A–F to the gaps 1–5. There is one sentence you do not need to use.

A This gives them the chance to learn from each others' experiences, and also to reflect more profoundly on their own.

B The idea is that all daughters and sons should be able to participate.

C Each year, a theme is chosen for the event, and a new logo is designed for the T-shirts worn by participants.

D The success of the event is reflected in the well over twenty years in which it has been running.

E After that, they should spend the rest of the day shadowing their mother or father in all that they do.

F Too often, this led to them dropping out of school early.

b Underline five words or phrases you don't know. Use your dictionary to look up their meaning and pronunciation.

# Take Our Daughters and Sons to Work Day

Many parents would probably agree that work and family life are not always easy to balance. Not so the 37 million US employees who take part each year in the *Take Our Daughters and Sons to Work Day*. On this day, the fourth Thursday in April, parents in over 3.5 million companies take their children into work to give them a taste of just what it is their parents get up to all day. [1]____ Today, it is now regarded as a kind of national institution.

The scheme has not always catered for both boys and girls. It was originally conceived in 1993 by the non-profit organization *Ms. Foundation for Women* as the *Take Our Daughters to Work Day*. In the early 1990s, research had revealed that schoolgirls were often lacking the confidence they needed to succeed. [2]____ It was hoped that the event would show them the importance of finishing their education and what they could achieve if they did so. By 2003, it had become apparent that boys were suffering a similar lack of self-esteem, and so they were also incorporated into the scheme, which changed its name accordingly.

The *Take Our Daughters and Sons to Work Day* takes place on a school day, because it is a valuable educational experience. In class the next day, pupils are expected to share news from their day at the office with their classmates. [3]____ Older students taking part in the scheme, aimed primarily at eight- to 18-year-olds, can get a good idea of the attitude and behaviour common to the workplace, which helps prepare them for any part-time jobs they might do in the future.

Parents are encouraged to enhance their child's experience by preparing carefully for the day beforehand. The organizers recommend discussing the day before and after the child is brought to work so that they get as much as possible out of their visit. According to employees who have already taken part in the programme, children should be introduced to their parent's colleagues to get an insight into how the team works. [4]____ In some cases, companies plan special activities, which make the day more interactive and memorable for the children, and give parents a chance to catch up on any urgent work alone.

It is not only the children of employees that the scheme is aimed at, hence its name: *Take Our Daughters and Sons to Work*. [5]____ This means that workers may invite the children of friends, relatives, neighbours, or even children from residential homes to accompany them. The main aim is to expose as many schoolchildren as possible to the world of work in the hope that it will give them a goal in life to work towards and help them land their dream job.

# 2A Changing language

## LEXIS IN CONTEXT Spell it out

Look at the Lexis in Context on Student's Book p.14. Then complete the sentences.

1 Today there is no st*igma*___ attached to speaking with a regional accent.
2 Even today, languages are more fl_____ than we suppose.
3 Loan words have played as big a p_____ in English as they have in other European languages.
4 Students are sometimes bewildered by the r_____ nature of irregular verbs.
5 Most nationalities have an authority they look to for g_____ on correct grammar.

## PRONUNCIATION
### sound–spelling relationships

Say the words aloud. Write **S** if the **bold** letters are pronounced the same or **D** if the pronunciation is different.

| 1 snake | 2 bike | 3 horse |
|---|---|---|
| **s**ympathetic **s**ynonym _S_ | de**s**pite **s**ince _D_ | th**aw** j**aw** ___ |
| 4 bird | 5 witch | 6 jazz |
| b**ir**th f**ir**m ___ | **wh**irl **wh**ose ___ | **j**ealous **j**ournalist ___ |
| 7 house | 8 chess | 9 bird | 10 phone |
| dis**h**onest in**h**erit | **ch**ime **ch**orus | w**or**m w**or**th | l**ow**er p**ow**er |

**iChecker** Listen and check. Practise saying the words.

## 3 GRAMMAR pronouns

**a** Right (✓) or wrong (✗)? Correct the mistakes in the highlighted phrases.

1 One need to listen to both sides of the story in order to find out the truth.   ✗ *One needs to listen*_____
2 Two of my friends aren't talking to themselves because they've had a big argument.   _____
3 As soon as he woke up, Brad washed and dressed and left the house.   _____
4 The receptionist accompanied us to the meeting room and said we should help us to tea and coffee.
   _____
5 When a guest leaves his room, we recommend locking the door.   _____
6 I much prefer travelling by my own.
   _____
7 She felt dizzy when she looked out of the window and saw the land so far below herself.   _____
8 This is a delicious cake. Did you make it yourself?
   _____

**b** Complete the mini-dialogues with a suitable pronoun.

1 **A** Who hasn't handed in _their_ homework?
  **B** Me. Sorry. Here it is.
2 **A** What a gorgeous dress! Where did you get it?
  **B** Well, actually, I made it _____.
3 **A** Why isn't Judy with Pete tonight?
  **B** They're not going out with _____ any more.
4 **A** I think CD players are completely out of date.
  **B** Yes. _____ doesn't see many of them these days.
5 **A** I've just been promoted!
  **B** Well done! You must be really proud of _____!
6 **A** Why don't you join the army?
  **B** I don't know. _____ say it's really tough.
7 **A** Who's Grace going round Europe with?
  **B** No one. She's going by _____.
8 **A** People say _____ shouldn't sit in a draught.
  **B** Rubbish! There's nothing wrong with fresh air.

**c** Complete the text with *it* or *there*.

¹ *It*_____ takes me ages to get to work, although ²_____'s only a few miles from my house to the office. ³_____ isn't too much traffic on the roads when I leave home, but ⁴_____'s impossible to park by the time I reach the city centre. ⁵_____ are always loads of cars driving around looking for a space and these days ⁶_____ are parking meters, so you have to pay. ⁷_____ used to be a company bus, but they stopped it because ⁸_____ were only a few of us that used it. ⁹_____'s all right for those people with a motorbike, but ¹⁰_____'s really tedious for us car drivers!

## 4 VOCABULARY learning languages

**a** Circle the correct word(s).

1 You have to *say* | *speak* | *talk* a number of languages to be a flight attendant.
2 The speaker went too fast, so it was impossible to *pass for* | *pick up* | *take in* all the information.
3 Bear in mind that children don't always *say* | *talk* | *tell* the truth.
4 Did you manage to *brush up* | *get by* | *pick up* any Portuguese while you were in Lisbon?
5 Sorry, I didn't get that. Can you *say* | *speak* | *tell* it again, please?
6 How will you *pick up* | *get by* | *pass for* in Kyoto if you don't speak any Japanese?
7 He wants to have a few days off, so he needs to *say* | *talk* | *tell* to his boss.
8 She needs to *brush up* | *pick up* | *take in* her French before she takes up her new job in Paris.

**b** Replace the **bold** words in sentences 1–5 with a more formal word or expression.

1 Students will be tested on **vocabulary** and grammar in this part of the test. l*exis*____
2 Candidates are **asked** to switch off their mobile phones before the exam. **r**_____
3 A serious **mistake** has been found in the manuscript. **e**_____
4 This is an automatically generated email. Please do not attempt to **answer** it. **r**_____ _____
5 Children brought up in a bilingual environment may have more than one native **language**. **t**_____

**c** Complete the sentences with an idiom containing the word in brackets.

1 She told me her name, but I can't _get my tongue round_ it. (tongue)
2 He got_____ and thought Anna was being sarcastic when she was trying to be nice. (stick)
3 Wait, give me a minute. Oh, it's_____ _____, but I just can't think of the word! (tip)
4 I didn't mean that at all – I think we're talking _____ . (cross)
5 This instruction manual is so confusing. I can't _____ it. (head)

## 5 READING

**a** Read the article once. Which three features of a language may cause it to affect our personality?

**b** Read the text again and match the missing sentences A–H to the gaps 1–6. There are two sentences you do not need to use.

A French has an unusually large vocabulary, allowing the speaker to find extremely precise words with specific meanings.

B In Russian, however, the emphasis is on the shape, not the material, so all of these would merely be 'little glasses' or 'stakanchiki'.

C Speaking it will force you to think longer and harder, and you may feel like you played a five-set tennis match after a conversation.

D And yet, his personality seemed to vary.

E After the first ad, they referred to her with positive words, such as 'self-sufficient' and 'strong', suggesting that they looked up to her.

F A comparative analysis between languages shows that languages may well rewire our minds.

G He and his mentor, Edward Sapir, compared this with English and noticed how the two languages had a completely different system for forming words.

H He claims that it is thoughts that lead to language, and not the other way round.

**c** Look at the highlighted words and match them to a neutral equivalent.

1 insulting _____
2 work out _____
3 agree _____
4 against _____
5 decide _____
6 spoke to _____
7 showing _____

# New language, new personality?

When Jacques was 12 years old, his mother began speaking to him only in French, his father addressed him only in Greek, and he was sent to an English-speaking day school in Paris. Of course, the child was the same person no matter which of the three languages he was using. [1]____ 'I felt probably ruder and more aggressive in Greek, clear and concise in French, and creative and long-winded in English,' he said.

Jacques' experience of languages seems to concur with a theory developed back in 1931 in the linguistics department of Yale University. A student by the name of Benjamin Whorf was carrying out some research into the Algonquian language, Shawnee, which was spoken by only 200 people at the time. [2]____ Their findings led them to develop the 'Sapir-Whorf hypothesis' which claims that the language we speak shapes our experience of the world.

But how is it possible for a language to determine our understanding of the world and therefore affect our personality? The answer may lie in the way that different languages are constructed. In Greek, for example, the verb usually comes first, its conjugation revealing the tone and meaning of the rest of the sentence, making it easier for the listener to interrupt. [3]____ And in English, words tend to be more adaptable and easier to rhyme.

Yet construction of a language is not the only determining factor. A study at Baruch College, New York, suggests that culture may also play a part. Researchers showed a group of bilingual Hispanic-American women the same commercial about a woman doing housework, first in Spanish and then in English. [4]____ But when the women watched the English version, they used the derogatory terms 'traditional' and 'dependent'. Despite the striking contrast between the adjectives, it is not clear whether it was the language itself that influenced the volunteers' choices or the cultural habits associated with that language.

A third determining factor may be the way in which objects are classified in a language. Let's take Russian as an example. A Russian speaker learning English would associate 'glass' and 'cup' with their translations, 'stakan' and 'chashka'. Yet, in English we call all sorts of things 'cups': coffee to-go cups, Styrofoam™ cups, plastic cups, paper cups. [5]____ Therefore, in order for the Russian speaker to correctly learn English (or vice versa), he must pay attention to not just direct translations but also to categorizations, in this case shape versus material.

Although there seems to be a great deal of evidence supporting the argument that language influences personality, there are obviously those who do not agree. One of the greatest opponents is Stephen Pinker of Harvard University. [6]____ Consequently, he believes that as long as we can think about something, then we can formulate a way to say it. And so the debate rages on. But as Jacques himself points out: it makes a big difference which language to choose when it comes to discussing a subject like economics!

## 6 LISTENING

**a** You're going to listen to two people talking about their experiences of being non-native speakers of English. Before you listen, check the meaning of the words in the glossary.

> ### Glossary
> **Glasgow** a large city in Scotland
> **BBC English / Standard English** English as spoken with a 'standard' pronunciation which corresponds to the pronunciation given in a dictionary
> **General American** US English as spoken with a 'standard' pronunciation which corresponds to the pronunciation given in a dictionary
> **Scots** a way of speaking English found in Scotland
> **Geordie** a way of speaking English typically from the area in and around Newcastle, in the north-east of England
> **University of Michigan** a university in the mid-west of the USA
> **The Simpsons** a very well-known US cartoon series

**b** **iChecker** Listen once. What four questions do they answer?

1 _____
2 _____
3 _____
4 _____

**c** Listen again and mark the sentences **W** (woman), **M** (man), or **B** (both).

1 They think that native speakers don't spell as well as some non-native speakers. ____
2 They feel comfortable about being corrected. ____
3 They usually get what non-native speakers say because there is no hidden meaning. ____
4 They notice a gap in their knowledge of English because they were born elsewhere. ____
5 They could have had an awkward conversation, but, thankfully, it never occurred. ____
6 They find some native speakers easier to understand than others. ____

**d** Listen again with the audio script on p.69 and try to guess the meaning of any words that you don't know. Then check in your dictionary.

My childhood was endless –
from eight to 18 felt like hundreds of years.

*Karl Lagerfeld, German designer*

# 2B  Do you remember...?

## 1  LEXIS IN CONTEXT  *Boy*

Look at the Lexis in Context on Student's Book p.18.
Then complete the words.

1  When I was little, I used to **gr**_ab___ my mother's hand if
we came across a big dog on the street.

2  At lunchtime, everybody would go **r**_____ to the
canteen to be first in the queue.

3  Dinner would be **b**_____ **a**_____ in a pot
on the stove when we used to get home from school.

4  'Well done!' my father said, as he **sl**_____ me on
the back for scoring the winning goal.

5  My mother was always **c**_____ different kinds of
soup out of whatever she could find in the fridge.

6  I can still **p**_____ the first teacher I ever had – she
seemed ancient to me, but she was extremely kind.

7  When the bell rang, we would all **l**_____ from
our seats before the teacher could set any homework.

## 2  GRAMMAR  the past:
### habitual events and specific incidents

**a**  Right (✓) or wrong (✗)? Correct any mistakes in the
highlighted phrases.

1  As a child, Tom was always knocking off my glasses
when my parents weren't looking.  ✓ ____

2  My brother climbed a tree when he slipped and
fell.  ✗  *was climbing*_____

3  My mum had been forgetting to turn off the oven, so
there was a terrible smell of gas in the kitchen.
_____

4  Most days we rode our bikes to school, but sometimes
we were catching the bus. _____

5  One day, our car used to break down in the fast lane of
the motorway. _____

6  When we were kids, our dad would give us a packed
lunch and send us out to play for the day.
_____

7  Emily's grandparents would live in an old farmhouse in
the heart of the countryside. _____

8  I'd hidden in the bushes for over an hour before I
realized that everyone else had gone home.
_____

9  When we got home from school that evening, our
parents still worked. _____

10  I burst into tears when I saw what my brother had done
to my favourite doll. _____

**b**  Complete the text with the correct form of the verbs
in brackets. Use a narrative tense or *would / used to.*

When I ¹ _was___ (be) little, I ² _____ (share) a bedroom
with my sister Catherine. As I was eight years her junior,
I obviously ³_____ (go) to bed earlier than her.
As soon as I ⁴_____ (clean) my teeth, my mum
⁵ _____ (lie) on my sister's bed and sing me nursery
rhymes until I ⁶_____ (fall) asleep.
   One night when my mum ⁷_____ (sing) for about
five minutes, she suddenly ⁸_____ (stop) and
⁹ _____ (stand) up. I ¹⁰_____ (look) over at her
and saw that she ¹¹_____ (stare) at something on
the wall above my head. Without raising her voice, she
¹² _____ (tell) me to go downstairs where my dad
¹³ _____ (watch) TV. Later she told me she ¹⁴ _____
(see) a big, hairy spider climb out of the air grille and make its
way up the wall. I ¹⁵_____ (not sleep) much that night,
as you can imagine!

14

# 3 VOCABULARY
word building: abstract nouns

**a** Complete the sentences with the abstract nouns of the **bold** words.

1 When my aunt **lost** her husband, she was driven to despair. She never got over her _loss_.

2 I'm **afraid** of flying. I've never been abroad because of my _____ of crashing.

3 My dad's health has **improved** a lot. We've noticed a great _____.

4 We **hated** our physics teacher with a vengeance. I'm fairly sure our _____ was returned as well.

5 The **dead** statesman was buried immediately. The whole country mourned his _____.

6 For medicine to work, you have to **believe** in it. It is often this _____ that makes you well again.

7 Rosie was so **ashamed** of her behaviour that her face burned with _____.

**b** Complete the sentences with the correct form of the words in brackets.

1 I am truly grateful to my cousin for her _friendship_ during these difficult times. (friend)

2 In some societies, the _____ of the older generation must never be questioned. (wise)

3 Despite a very traumatic _____, Adam grew up to be quite a sensible young man. (child)

4 Ruth tried to hide the _____ in her eyes as she left the house for ever. (sad)

5 We had a big family _____ for my dad's 80th birthday. (celebrate)

6 I remembered to renew my _____ at the golf club before the tournament started. (member)

7 My grandmother will be staying in a nursing home until she has fully recovered from her _____. (ill)

8 We dread our history lectures because every week we nearly die of _____. (bored)

# 4 PRONUNCIATION
word stress with suffixes

**a** Look at the word pairs. Circle the abstract nouns where the stress is different.

1 compete      competition

2 neighbour    neighbourhood

3 partner      partnership

4 happy        happiness

5 celebrate    celebration

6 relation     relationship

7 imagine      imagination

8 believe      belief

9 curious      curiosity

**b** iChecker Listen and check. Practise saying the words.

# 5 LISTENING

**a** iChecker Listen to five people talking about their earliest memories. Which speaker doubts whether they can actually remember experiencing the incident?

**b** Listen again and answer the questions with speakers 1–5. Use each speaker twice. Who talks about…?

A ☐ a significant day in many people's lives

B ☐ an everyday occurrence

C ☐ a moment just before or after a flight

D ☐ some dramatic weather

E ☐ finding something beautiful

F ☐ something that others may find quite boring

G ☐ receiving advice from a parent

H ☐ seeing a photo of themselves

I ☐ damage to a property

J ☐ feeling anxious on this day

**c** Listen again with the audio script on p.70 and try to guess the meaning of any words that you don't know. Then check in your dictionary.

## 6 READING

**a** Read the article once. What year do childhood memories need to survive until to stand a chance of making it into adulthood?

**b** Read the article again and mark the sentences **T** (true) or **F** (false).

1 At the age of five or six, children tend to still remember events that happened when they were two.

2 From the age of seven, early memories don't feature key details like location.

3 Children recalled six different life events at their later sessions with the psychologist.

4 The events discussed with the psychologist included day-to-day school life and the context of lessons.

5 By the age of eight or nine, children could only recall approximately a third of their early memories.

6 The researchers found out that the kind of details which stayed in the mind didn't alter much over the years.

**c** Look at the highlighted verbs and try to work out their meaning. Check in your dictionary.

# When childhood memories fade

**M**ost adults struggle to recall events from their first few years of life and now scientists have identified exactly when these childhood memories are lost forever. A new study into childhood amnesia – the phenomenon where early memories are forgotten – has found that it tends to take effect around the age of seven.

The researchers found that while most three year olds can recall a lot of what happened to them over a year earlier, these memories can persist while they are five and six, by the time they are over seven these memories decline rapidly.

The psychologists behind the research say this is because at around this age the way we form memories begins to change. Before the age of seven, children tend to have an immature form of recall where they do not have a sense of time or place in their memories. In older children, however, the early events they can recall tend to be more adult like in their content and the way they are formed. Children also have a far faster rate of forgetting than adults and so the turnover of memories tends to be higher, meaning early memories are less likely to survive.

Professor Patricia Bauer, a psychologist and associate dean for research at Emory College of Art and Science, studied 83 children over several years for the research, which was published in the scientific journal Memory. The youngsters first visited the laboratory at the age of three years old and discussed six unique events from their past, such as family outings, camping holidays, trips to the zoo, first day of school and birthdays. The children then returned for a second session at the ages between five years old and nine years old to discuss the same events and were asked to recall details they had previously remembered.

The researchers found that between the ages of five and seven, the amount of memories the children could recall remained between 63 and 72 per cent. However, the amount of information the children who were eight and nine years old could remember dropped dramatically to 35 and 36 per cent.

When the researchers looked closely at the kind of details the children were and were not able to remember, they found marked age differences. The memories of the younger children tended to lack autobiographical narrative such as place and time. Their memories also had less narrative, which researchers believe may lead to a process known as 'retrieval induced forgetting' – where the action of remembering causes other information to be forgotten. As the children got older, however, the memories they recalled from early childhood tended to have these features.

Professor Bauer said, 'The fact that the younger children had less complete narratives relative to the older children, likely has consequences for the continued accessibility of early memories beyond the first decade of life. We anticipate that memories that survive into the ninth or tenth year of life, when narrative skills are more developed, would continue to be accessible over time.'

The best revenge is to be
unlike him who performed the injury.

*Marcus Aurelius, Roman Emperor*

# 3A Don't get mad, get even

## 1 PRONUNCIATION

words and phrases of French origin

**a** **iChecker** Listen and write the French words.

1 /ˈkliːʃeɪ/     _cliché_
2 /ˈrɒndeɪvuː/     _____
3 /ˌfəʊ ˈpɑː/     _____
4 /ˌdeɪʒɑː ˈvuː/     _____
5 /ˌɒntrəprəˈnɜː/     _____
6 /ˈbæleɪ/     _____
7 /buˈkeɪ/     _____
8 /fiˈɒnseɪ/     _____
9 /kuː/     _____
10 /ˌfeɪt əˈkɒmpliː/     _____

**b** Practise saying the words in **a**.

## 2 VOCABULARY phrases with *get*

**a** Match the sentence halves.

1 I'm going to get     | *i* |
2 I'll call you back as soon as I get     | |
3 I wanted to get     | |
4 I can't get past. Can you get     | |
5 When I went out, I got     | |
6 The heating isn't working. Can you get     | |
7 Max hit Stevie but Stevie got     | |
8 My colleagues didn't trust me until they got     | |
9 When I met up with my boss, I got     | |

a his own back by kicking him.
b hold of someone in Maintenance?
c to know me better.
d out of the way, please?
e rid of my parents before my boyfriend arrived.
f the chance.
g a shock because my car wasn't on the drive.
h the impression she was angry with me.
i into trouble if I'm late again.

**b** Complete the idioms with these words.

act    anywhere    house    life
message    ~~nerves~~    on    way

1 My sister gets on my _nerves_ . She's always borrowing my clothes without asking me.
2 I've bought my boyfriend an electric shaver in the hope that he'll get the _____ about his beard.
3 Laura's parents don't know how to say no. She always gets her own _____ .
4 I'm not getting _____ with this essay. I don't know where to start.
5 My flatmate needs to get a _____ . He hasn't got any friends and he never goes out.
6 My dad is getting _____ a bit now. He's nearly 80.
7 Luckily, my mum and my girlfriend have got on like a _____ on fire since they first met.
8 I really need to get my _____ together if I'm going to catch the plane. I haven't packed yet!

**c** Complete the sentences with the missing particle.

1 At last, my sister has got _over_ her ex-boyfriend and she's started going out again.
2 It's a tiny island so you can use bikes to get _____ .
3 We got _____ with not doing the homework because the teacher forgot to take it in!
4 They've got really _____ with the project so they'll have to work late until they finish it.
5 Ryan is trying to get _____ of going on holiday with his in-laws by saying he's got too much work.
6 My gran has stopped reading all the bad news in the paper because she says it gets her _____ .
7 Stop chatting to your friends and get _____ with your homework!
8 I've tried to explain to my girlfriend how I feel but I can't get _____ to her.
9 I can't get _____ on what I earn, so I'm looking for some extra work.
10 I got _____ to my friend as soon as I read her text message.

## 3 LEXIS IN CONTEXT  Blind Date

Look at the Lexis in Context on Student's Book p.26. Then complete the sentences.

1 You may as well be honest instead of **dr**_essing_ **u**p the truth.
2 You can't **r**_____ **o**_____ the possibility that he may be seeing somebody else.
3 Pete's girlfriend has such a lovely smile that she can **w**_____ anybody **o**_____ .
4 It's all very well apologizing, but who is going to **f**_____ the **b**_____ for the damage?
5 I've only got ten minutes, so we'll have to make this **sh**_____ and **sw**_____ .
6 I'm going to the party because I don't want to **m**_____ **o**_____ on all the fun.
7 My husband is good at making promises, but he finds it hard to **f**_____ them **th**_____ .
8 I can't **m**_____ **u**_____ my **m**_____ if I want to see him again.

## 4 GRAMMAR  get

Rewrite the **bold** phrases using the correct form of *get*.

1 We **arrived at the theatre** too late to see the show.
   _got to the theatre_
2 Can you **persuade Paul to look** at my computer?
   _____
3 I'll never **become accustomed to** getting up at 5.30 in the morning.
   _____
4 The afternoon shadows **lengthened** as the sun went down.
   _____
5 We're **having our kitchen repainted** next month.
   _____
6 I can't **make the kids eat** their dinner.
   _____
7 I hope **I'm not sent to** Manchester – I want to stay in London.
   _____
8 Public transport in my town is **improving**.
   _____
9 **They fired my boss** for stealing money.
   _____
10 Could you possibly **ask Mike to** pick me up?
   _____

## 5 LISTENING

a Listen to five speakers talking about memorable dates. Which speakers had successful dates? Which dates were unsuccessful?

b Listen again and mark the sentences **T** (true) or **F** (false).

1 Speaker 1 agreed to the date straight away.
2 Speaker 1 went out with someone who was desperately in love with her.
3 Speaker 2 was the victim of an accident during their memorable date.
4 The incident on Speaker 2's date ruined the relationship.
5 Speaker 3 enjoyed herself tremendously.
6 Speaker 3 decided it was best not to meet up again.
7 Speaker 4 organized the date spontaneously.
8 Speaker 4 and their partner often joke about their date.
9 Speaker 5 didn't have the same sense of humour as the person she went out with.
10 Speaker 5 was upset not to get a marriage proposal.

c Listen again with the audio script on p.70 and try to guess the meaning of any words that you don't know. Then check in your dictionary.

## 6 READING

a Read the article once. Which act of revenge caused the most damage?

b Read the article again and match the headings A–H with the stories 1–6. There are two headings you do not need to use.

A That's what friends are for
B Dedicated to the profession
C Welcome home
D Kiss and tell
E Clean plate
F Total shutdown
G Silent witnesses
H His pride and joy

c Look at the highlighted phrasal verbs and idioms. What do you think they mean? Check in your dictionary.

# Revenge is sweet

According to writer Claire Gillman, getting even is becoming increasingly popular as life gets more stressful. In her book *Revenge is Sweet* Claire reveals that men are much more the vengeful sex, except over romantic matters, when it is women who are most likely to take revenge. Here are some of her favourite tales from the book.

**1** \_\_\_\_

The wife of a radio DJ saw red when she heard her husband flirting with a glamorous model on air. She immediately posted an advert for his £30,000 Lotus Esprit Turbo sports car on eBay for 50p and sold the car within five minutes. Later, she told journalists that she didn't care about the money. 'I just wanted to get my own back,' she admitted.

**2** \_\_\_\_

After a long-running dispute between neighbours, one of the parties went on holiday for two weeks in the summer. The other neighbour took advantage of their absence to put two pints of maggots through the neighbour's letter box. The family returned to a house full of flies.

**3** \_\_\_\_

An 80-year-old woman was in front of a judge, charged with shoplifting. He asked her what she had stolen. 'A can of peaches,' replied the woman. 'How many peaches were in the can?' asked the judge. She replied that there were six. 'Then I'll give you six days in jail,' said the judge. Before he had time to speak further, the woman's husband added, 'She also stole a tin of peas.'

**4** \_\_\_\_

Rude customers tend to drive staff in restaurants crazy. One chef confessed that after a customer had demanded that the sauce be removed from his burger, she licked the sauce off it with her tongue and then sent it back via the waiter.

**5** \_\_\_\_

A computer technician was angered when his temporary position was terminated so he deliberately brought down five of eight network servers. All the data in the servers was deleted and none was recoverable. As a result, the company was forced to shut its New York office for two days and sustained losses of more than $100,000.

**6** \_\_\_\_

A doctor was called out at 2 a.m. one night to visit a patient who lived some distance away. On his arrival, he discovered that it was, in fact, a non-urgent case, and the patient could perfectly well have waited until the next day to visit him in his surgery. Imagine the patient's surprise when the doctor popped by in the early hours of the following morning to check he was OK!

---

**Glossary**

**pint**  a unit for measuring liquids. 1 pint = 0.568 litres
**maggot**  a creature like a short worm which is the young form of a fly

> War is what happens when language fails.
> *Margaret Atwood, Canadian author*

# 3B History in the making

## 1 VOCABULARY conflict and warfare

**a** Complete the crossword.

**Clues across →**

| ¹H | E | L | ²M | E | T |

**Clues down ↓**

**b** Circle the correct word.

1 During the coup, the military tried to (overthrow) | *release* the government.
2 There were very few *casualties* | *wounded* from the fighting – only two people were killed.
3 The country *declared* | *broke out* war on its neighbour because there were troops on the border.
4 The city was *blown up* | *shelled* all night.
5 The two armies agreed to a *treaty* | *ceasefire* to give them a chance to tend to the wounded.
6 The troops saw they could not win so they held up a white flag indicating that they wanted to *capture* | *surrender*.
7 The government forces *retreated* | *defeated* the rebels during the night.
8 During the siege, civilians were shot at by isolated *snipers* | *troops* hiding in the hills.
9 Soldiers *looted* | *executed* shops in their search for food.
10 The new *ally* | *commander* of the armed forces will be meeting the President later today.

## 2 PRONUNCIATION stress in word families

**a** Underline the stressed syllable in the following words.

1 ca|sual|ties
2 ci|vil
3 re|fu|gee
4 sur|vi|vor
5 com|man|der
6 cease|fire
7 vic|to|ry
8 re|lease
9 cap|ture
10 re|treat
11 ex|e|cute
12 sur|ren|der

**b** iChecker Listen and check. Practise saying the words.

**c** Circle the word with a different sound.

| 1 aɪ bike | 2 uː boot | 3 iː tree | 4 ɔː horse |
|---|---|---|---|
| ally | troops | besiege | war |
| sniper | bullet | treaty | sword |
| shield | wounded | weapon | declare |

**d** iChecker Listen and check. Practise saying the words.

## 3 GRAMMAR discourse markers (2): adverbs and adverbial expressions

**a** Complete the mini-dialogues with a discourse marker.

1  A  Have you got your tickets for the concert yet?
   B  Yes, I have. T_alking_ of the concert, have you heard their new album yet?

2  A  How did your interview go?
   B  It was brilliant. In other w_____, I got the job!

3  A  Could you tell us about our board and lodging?
   B  As far as meals are c_____, breakfast and dinner will be provided by the hotel.

4  A  Are you going to Jay's party on Saturday?
   B  No, I'm not. As a m_____ of fact, I haven't been invited.

5  A  So, let's decide. The beach or the mountains?
   B  On the wh_____ I'd rather go to the beach, so that we can have a swim.

6  A  Thanks for filling me in on what I missed.
   B  No problem. By the w_____, there's another meeting on Wednesday. Did you know?

7  A  Can we inform our families of our destination?
   B  No. This is top secret. That is to s_____, you are not to reveal your whereabouts to anyone.

8  A  Did you buy anything while you were in town?
   B  No, I didn't take any money with me. In any c_____, there wasn't anything I liked.

9  A  How does it feel to be famous at last?
   B  The attention is incredible. On the other h_____, I miss my privacy.

10 A  We're going to my mum's for dinner on Saturday.
   B  OK. At l_____ we won't have to cook.

**b** (Circle) the correct discourse marker.

1  (In conclusion) | As far as, I think the company should invest in new machinery to update the factory.

2  Basically | At least, Sam and Ella aren't very well-off because they're both unemployed.

3  Ask your boss if you can take the day off. In other words | I mean, he can't say no.

4  I don't feel like cooking tonight. On the whole | Besides, there's nothing in the fridge.

5  Obviously | Regarding, I'm going to study Maths because there's nothing else I'm good at.

6  I've read all the applications and by the way | all in all, I think Adam is the best person for the job.

7  You might want to dress up for dinner. After all | To sum up, everyone will be wearing a suit.

8  As I was saying | Talking of before I got cut off, we need to make a decision.

9  To sum up | As regards, we recommend accepting the pay deal in case management decide to withdraw the offer.

10 You'll need a jacket, that is | otherwise you might get cold.

## 4 LISTENING

The Last Emperor

Elizabeth

**a**  **iChecker**  Try to match the historical films 1–5 with the periods in which they are set a–e. Then listen to five speakers talking about the films and check your answers.

1  *Elizabeth*  ☐
2  *Argo*  ☐
3  *The Last Emperor*  ☐
4  *Invictus*  ☐
5  *Agora*  ☐

a  early 20th century China
b  16th century England
c  Roman Empire
d  1979–81 Iran hostage crisis
e  late 20th century South Africa

**b**  Listen again and match the speakers 1–5 to the reasons why these films are the speakers' favourites A–G. There are two reasons that you do not need.

Speaker 1 ☐       A  the acting
Speaker 2 ☐       B  the director
                  C  the plot
Speaker 3 ☐       D  the main character
                  E  the costumes
Speaker 4 ☐       F  the ending
Speaker 5 ☐       G  the photography

**c**  Listen again with the audio script on p.71 and try to guess the meaning of any words that you don't know. Then check in your dictionary.

## 5 READING

**a** Match the opponents a–e to the battles 1–5, then read the article once to check your answers.

1 The Battle of Plataea ☐
2 The Battle of Waterloo ☐
3 The Battle of Cannae ☐
4 The Battle of Thermopylae ☐
5 The Battle of Gettysburg ☐

a Carthage versus Rome
b Greece versus Persia
c The Union versus the Confederacy
d France versus Britain and Prussia
e Sparta versus Persia

**b** Read the article again and choose the correct answer from the battles A–E. The battles may be chosen more than once.

In which battle…?

1 did reinforcements arrive once the battle had started _____

2 was one of the armies tiny _____
3 was one of the armies more confident than the other _____

4 did both sides lose almost the same number of soldiers _____

5 did the army catch their enemy by surprise _____
6 did the losing army contain three times as many soldiers as the victors _____
7 was one side defeated through treachery _____
8 had one army previously had to make a perilous journey _____
9 did the commanders' mistakes contribute to their defeat _____
10 did a group of soldiers attack a certain part of the other army _____

**c** Look at the highlighted words and phrases and match them to the definitions below.

1 bad luck *noun* _____
2 rushed forward and attacked *verb* _____
3 strongly influencing the way something develops *verb* _____
4 killed a large number of people violently *verb* _____
5 showing no kindness or pity *adverb* _____
6 the amount of confidence and enthusiasm a person has at a particular time *noun* _____
7 a narrow passage through mountains *noun* _____
8 of great importance because other things depend on it *adjective* _____

# Five important battles from history

Every age of human history has experienced battles that have been instrumental in moulding the future. Below are five of the bloodiest and most pivotal battles ever fought.

### A The Battle of Plataea (479 BCE)

This battle occurred during the Greco-Persian Wars. An army of 40,000 Greek soldiers, of which 10,000 were Spartans, faced the invading force of Persia with 120,000 men. Although outnumbered, the Spartans and Athenians were more tactical, heavily armed and had higher morale. The Persian army had just suffered a previous defeat and some inner conflicts and divisions. The Greeks slaughtered the Persians at Plataea and succeeded in driving them out of Greece.

### B The Battle of Waterloo (18 June 1815)

This battle was fought between the French army, led by Napoleon Bonaparte, and the British and Prussian forces led by Wellington and von Blucher respectively. Napoleon took the initiative during the early part of the battle, but things began to go awry later in the day when the army suffered the effects of bad weather, blunders by some of the generals, ill fate, and the timely arrival of the Prussian forces (50,000 men). After suffering heavy casualties, Napoleon was forced to leave Waterloo and surrender.

### C The Battle of Cannae (2 August 216 BCE)

This battle is regarded as one of the greatest tactical military achievements in war history. The Carthaginian commander Hannibal Barca led a massive troop of soldiers, accompanied by hundreds, or possibly thousands, of war elephants, across the mountainous Alps. He took a backdoor entrance into northern Italy and slaughtered the Romans at Cannae, killing 70,000 of the 87,000 soldiers in the Roman army.

### D The Battle of Thermopylae (480 BCE)

This battle occurred on the eve of the Greco-Persian wars when King Leonidas of Sparta faced the invading Persian troops with only 300 Spartan soldiers. The King and his men blocked the only narrow pass through which the Persians could go, killing a total of 20,000 Persians. The Spartans only lost when one of their soldiers betrayed them by showing the Persians a secret passage. Leonidas and his men were all mercilessly slaughtered.

### E The Battle of Gettysburg (July 1863)

This battle was fought during the American Civil War between the Confederate troops from the South, led by General Robert Lee, and the Union troops, led by General George Meade. One of the most dramatic moments was the Pickett's Charge, when 12,500 Confederate infantry charged towards the Union's centre formation. In the end, the Union side won, but lost a total of 23,055 soldiers. The defeated Confederate army lost 23,231 soldiers.

## LOOKING AT LANGUAGE
### collocations

Complete the collocations in the sentences.

1 The problems we **f**ace___ today are quite different from those that troubled our ancestors.
2 We have an **a**_____ lot of revision to do for our History exam.
3 The leader of the opposition seems to be **d**_____ serious about resigning if his party doesn't win the next election.
4 We could talk for hours about the **r**_____ and wrongs of the political system in ancient Rome.
5 Politicians need to concentrate on the big **p**_____ and not get distracted by small details.
6 Manchester Town Hall is a **cl**_____ example of Gothic revival architecture.
7 Freedom of speech and the right to vote are two important **c**_____ rights.
8 In medieval times, life was good for the landowners, but **o**_____ people had a difficult time.

## 2 READING

**a** Read the article. Mark the sentences **T** (true) or **F** (false).

1 The author of *Horrible Histories* used to work on the stage.
2 Deary's *Horrible Histories* books are purely fictional.
3 Deary began writing the stories in the same year as his country celebrated an important occasion.
4 Teachers bought *Blitzed Brits* to teach their classes about World War II.
5 The host of the TV shows is a famous figure from history.
6 In many of the comedy sketches, a parallel is drawn between past and present events.
7 The author did not expect his concept to be so popular.
8 Plans to build a *Horrible Histories* theme park have been announced.

**b** <u>Underline</u> five words or phrases you don't know. Use your dictionary to look up their meaning and pronunciation.

### Why *Horrible Histories* is a hit

Getting an audience interested in history can be a daunting task at the best of times, but it's especially difficult when your medium is the written word. Enter Terry Deary, former actor and full-time author of the best-selling series *Horrible Histories*. Since the publication of *Terrible Tudors* and *Awesome Egyptians* in 1993, readers have been hooked on the series, which now consists of over 60 titles. More than 20 million copies have been sold in around 30 different languages. So just what is the secret behind Deary's success?

The answer lies in the way the subject is presented. For each of his tales, Deary selects an important era from the past and picks out the most unpleasant events: gory killings, juicy scandal and grim tales of revenge. These lesser-known aspects of history are recounted in comic-book fashion, eliciting disbelief in the reader, although the details are completely accurate. And this is what appeals to children about his books: the fact that by reading them, they learn something unbelievable but true.

As well as Deary's writing style, it was also coincidence that contributed to his rise to fame. Two years after the series began, the 50th anniversary of the end of World War II came along. Deary had conveniently just written *Blitzed Brits*, a description of events in wartime Britain. Teachers were looking for something on the subject to grab their students' attention in class and *Blitzed Brits* fitted the bill perfectly. The book shot up the sales charts and made Deary into a bestselling author almost overnight.

Yet *Horrible Histories* is not confined to books. Deary's gruesome tales have also been adapted for television, providing the material for five whole series. The shows are presented by a talking rat called Rattus Rattus, whose job is to introduce comedy sketches portraying a particular historical event and to verify the facts they contain. The sketches often parody current media stories, and each episode contains a song that imitates a particular pop style, which can be anything from boy bands to hard rock. The outrageous costumes and ridiculous humour of the show appeal to both children and grown-ups alike, and the TV series has won numerous awards at both children's and adult ceremonies.

Not even Terry Deary anticipated the huge success of *Horrible Histories*, which has joined the ranks of other children's favourites such as *Harry Potter* and *The Hunger Games*. Along with reading the books and following the TV series, fans can also purchase magazines, listen along to audio books, play video games and watch stage productions. There have even been rumours of a theme park. With a range of products that wide, who would dare claim that history is boring?

No man should live where he can hear
his neighbor's dog bark.

*Nathaniel Macon, American politician*

# 4A Sounds interesting

## 1 VOCABULARY sounds and the human voice

**a** Circle the correct word.

1 The children ran out of the room because of the large bee *hissing | buzzing* around the window.
2 She was *banging | tapping* her finger on the table, waiting for her brother to answer his phone.
3 There was a loud *bang | slam* as the fireworks went off.
4 I can't stand people who *slurp | drip* their soup when they eat it.
5 I had to get up and lock the door because it was *hooting | rattling* in the wind.
6 The cat arched its back and *hissed | whistled* at us as we walked in.
7 The engine *crashed | roared* into life when he switched it on.
8 Johnny's got a cold, so he's been *snoring | sniffing* all day.
9 The little girl liked the way the sweets *splashed | crunched* in her mouth.
10 It was so quiet in the room that you could hear the *ticking | clicking* of the clock.
11 We heard the *screeching | creaking* of tyres as Janet's boyfriend drew up outside her front door.
12 After the argument, Carl stormed out of the room and *slammed | hummed* the door.

**b** Complete the sentences with the verbs in the list.

| | | | | |
|---|---|---|---|---|
| giggled | groaned | mumbled | screamed | sighed |
| sobbed | stammered | whispered | ~~yelled~~ | |

1 'STOP MAKING SO MUCH NOISE!' the old man _yelled_ from an upstairs window.
2 'What have you done *this* time?' _____ Stephen's mother with resignation.
3 'My new doll is broken,' _____ the little girl, tears rolling down her cheeks.
4 'My ankle hurts,' the player _____ as he lay on the ground.
5 'There's a spider in the bath!' my sister _____ in horror.
6 'I didn't have t-t-time to do my h-h-homework,' Phil _____ nervously.
7 Half way through the exam, David _____ to Alison, 'What's the answer to number 5?'
8 'Look at her hat!' the students _____. 'It looks really funny.'
9 'Sorry,' he _____, but nobody could understand what he said.

## 2 PRONUNCIATION
### consonant clusters

**a** **iChecker** Listen and write the missing words with consonant clusters.

1 Some of the pictures on __display__ have been lent by other galleries.
2 It's always a good idea to _____ before and after doing exercise.
3 'What a wonderful surprise,' she _____.
4 My son's just failed his driving test for the _____ time!
5 We're going to IKEA to get some new _____ for my study.
6 The best speech was the one given by the _____.
7 We _____ out the map on the dining room table, and planned our route.
8 The man _____ the burglar on the nose.

**b** Practise saying the sentences in **a**.

## 3 LEXIS IN CONTEXT
### I have a phobia of sound

Look at the Lexis in Context on Student's Book p.34. Then complete the words.

1 The passengers wanted to know why the train had stopped so **a**_bruptly_ .
2 It can be very tiring being with my brothers because they are **c**_____ arguing.
3 He had been revising for months, so he passed his exams **w**_____ **e**_____ .
4 **St**_____, I actually like commuting: it gives me some valuable time to myself.
5 The area has a number of Italian restaurants **i**_____ close **pr**_____ to each other.
6 Her **s**_____ stupid question produced an extremely useful answer.
7 I try to avoid giving my neighbour a lift because she chatters **i**_____ the whole journey.

## 4 GRAMMAR speculation and deduction

**a** Complete the mini-dialogues using *must | might | could | may | can't* or *should* and the correct form of the verbs in brackets.

1   **A** Jessica's looking pleased with herself.
    **B** Yes. She _must have done_ well in her job interview. (do)

2   **A** Where's Eve? She said to meet her just outside the tube station.
    **B** I suppose she _____ at a different entrance. (wait)

3   **A** Harry left work about an hour ago.
    **B** Yes, he _____ here by now. It only takes 20 minutes. (be)

4   **A** How about this dress for your cousin?
    **B** I don't know. I've never seen her in a dress. She _____ it. (not like)

5   **A** My brother's in his room doing his homework.
    **B** Well, he _____ . I can hear him talking on the phone! (study)

6   **A** Jason isn't answering his phone.
    **B** Well, he's gone swimming and _____ it with him to the pool. (not take)

7   **A** My secretary is off sick.
    **B** Well, she _____ anything serious. I've just seen her playing tennis. (have)

8   **A** Tony didn't show up at the party. He _____ about it. (forget)
    **B** Yes, he's very absent-minded.

**b** Complete the second sentence using the **bold** word so that it means the same as the first.

1   I don't think Luke will pass his driving test. **probably**
    Luke _probably won't pass his driving test._

2   I'm sure we'll win the match. **bound**
    We _____

3   I'm sure you'll enjoy the film. **definitely**
    You _____

4   I don't think it'll rain tonight. **likely**
    It _____

5   They probably won't agree to our proposal. **unlikely**
    They _____

6   My father is likely to take early retirement. **probably**
    My father _____

7   Your parents will almost certainly complain about it. **sure**
    Your parents _____

8   The manager is sure not to give us a pay rise. **definitely**
    The manager _____

## 5 LISTENING

**a**  **iChecker** Listen to someone talking about the percussionist Evelyn Glennie. In what way is she an unusual musician?

**b** Listen again and complete the summary.

Dame Evelyn Glennie was born in Aberdeen, Scotland. She studied at the Royal Academy of Music. She has been performing for more than [1]_____ years, and plays over [2]_____ different percussion instruments. She not only plays and records classical and pop music, but has also composed several film [3]_____. Dame Evelyn finds it frustrating that journalists often write about her [4]_____ more than her music. She thinks that there is no real difference between hearing and [5]_____ a vibration. Dame Evelyn never wears [6]_____ when she performs, in order to feel the vibrations of her instruments.

**c** Listen again with the audio script on p.71 and try to guess the meaning of any words that you don't know. Then check in your dictionary.

## 6 READING

**a** Read the article once. What is piped music? According to the writer, in which place might piped music have the most serious consequences?

# Silence is golden

**You hear it everywhere: in pubs, restaurants and hotels, in the plane, on the train, or on the bus. It comes at you unexpectedly down the phone, and it's even on television ruining perfectly decent programmes. This unsolicited noise is, of course, piped music, an incessant jingle that is almost impossible to escape.**

Contrary to popular belief, it appears that more people dislike this kind of music than actually appreciate it. In a poll carried out by a British newspaper, piped music came third in the list of things people most detested about modern life. (The first two most hated things were other forms of noise.) What is more, a recent survey into shopping habits shows that at least 50 per cent of customers would walk out of a store that had piped music. With figures like these, there can be no doubt about the widespread aversion to the noise.

It is people with some kind of hearing impairment who suffer most from the din. This group includes the elderly, who often develop an age-related hearing problem called presbycusis. The condition prevents them distinguishing the individual words of a conversation above the noise of any background music. As time goes by, they find it more and more difficult to interact. In fact, a 2013 survey commissioned by a British bank showed that around 61 per cent of older people consider piped music in shops and banks their biggest bugbear. The reason most of them gave was that it makes them feel alienated.

However, piped music may also be responsible for far more serious health problems. It has long been recognized that unwanted noise produces stress. The listener experiences a rise in blood pressure and a depression of the immune system. A survey of 215 blood donors at Nottingham University Medical School found that playing piped music made donors more nervous before giving blood. They also felt more depressed afterwards. These results suggest that a hospital might not be the right place to play this kind of sound.

Yet a care institution in London has recently announced that it is going to do just that. The hospital plans to introduce piped music into its Accident and Emergency Department to 'calm distressed patients'. The music will be provided by legendary musician Brian Eno, who has been supplying 'ambient music' to airports for nearly four decades. The hospital's objective is to make A & E more patient-friendly, but it is likely to have quite the opposite effect.

Fortunately, help is at hand in the form of Pipedown, a campaign for freedom from piped music. The movement is pushing for legislation to ban its use in public places, especially in hospitals and doctors' surgeries where patients are in no position to argue or go somewhere else. If the campaign is successful, the London hospital will have to drop its plans. But for many, this will not be a bad thing.

**b** Read the article again and mark the sentences **T** (true) or **F** (false).

1 According to the writer, the main problem with piped music is you can't get away from it.
2 The results of the newspaper poll show that the top three annoyances are all noise-related.
3 Piped music encourages the majority of people to shop in a store.
4 Elderly people tend to dislike piped music because it's not their kind of music.
5 Piped music can help blood donors to relax.
6 The writer thinks Brian Eno's music probably won't improve the atmosphere of A & E.
7 The main aim of the Pipedown campaign is to get rid of piped music in all public places.

**c** Find words or phrases in the article which mean:

1 piped music

_____ music
_____ music

2 a recognizable tune that is easy to remember

_____

3 a loud and unpleasant noise

_____

# 4B From cover to cover?

## 1 VOCABULARY
describing books and films

Complete the sentences.

1 The story was really **h**_aunting__. I can't stop thinking about it.
2 The book was extremely **th**_____-**pr**_____ and it made me think seriously about human rights issues.
3 This is the perfect holiday read – a really **e**_____ book.
4 The ending was completely **i**_____ . That would never have happened in real life and it ruined the whole film for me.
5 The plot is **i**_____ . I never know what's going to happen next.
6 The book's focus on the cruel and violent events that occur in a war make for a really **d**_____ read.
7 The plot was absolutely **gr**_____ . I couldn't put the book down.
8 The writer's style is difficult to read. I find his books very **h**_____-**g**_____ .
9 The final scene was incredibly **m**_____ – I cried all the way out of the cinema!
10 His new novel is very **f**_____-**m**_____ – so much happens in each short chapter.

## 2 PRONUNCIATION /ɔː/

**a** Write the words with the /ɔː/ sound.

1 /ˈdrɔːbæk/      _drawback_____
2 /wɔːk/
3 /ɪmˈplɔːzəbl/
4 /rɪˈzɔːsfl/
5 /rɪˈwɔːdɪŋ/
6 /ˈdɔːtə/
7 /ˈθɔːt-prəvəʊkɪŋ/
8 /ˈwɜːkfɔːs/

**b** **iChecker** Listen and check. Practise saying the words.

**c** **iChecker** Listen and write five sentences.

1 _____
2 _____
3 _____
4 _____
5 _____

**d** Practise saying the sentences in **c**.

## 3 GRAMMAR adding emphasis (1): inversion

**a** Complete the sentences with the adverbial expressions in the list. In some sentences more than one answer may be possible.

| ~~Hardly~~ | Never | No sooner | Not only |
|---|---|---|---|
| Not until | Only | Rarely | Scarcely |

1 _Hardly_____ had we set off when the engine started rattling.
2 _____ the clock struck midnight did the musicians start playing.
3 _____ have I heard such a moving speech. The last time was at the funeral of a close relation.
4 _____ had we sat down to eat than the doorbell rang.
5 _____ when you get on the scales do you realize how much weight you've put on over Christmas.
6 _____ had she entered the classroom when the students started to pester her.
7 _____ was my father in pain, but his pride had also been hurt.
8 _____ had the fans witnessed such a resounding victory in the history of the club.

**b** Rewrite the sentences to make them more emphatic.

1 The exam began when all the papers had been given out.
Only _when all the papers had been given out did the_
_exam begin_ .

2 He betrayed my trust and he wrecked my car.
Not only _____
_____ .

3 The sun had only just gone down when the temperature
fell dramatically.
Scarcely _____
_____ .

4 I have never seen such a wonderful sight.
Never _____
_____ .

5 As soon as the teacher turned her back, the children
started whispering.
No sooner _____
_____ .

6 The woman had just sat down when her baby started
crying.
Hardly _____
_____ .

7 You rarely find two people so alike.
Rarely _____
_____ .

8 Classes will not recommence until a replacement teacher
has been found.
Not until _____
_____ .

## 4 LEXIS IN CONTEXT Translation Diary

Look at the Lexis in Context on Student's Book p.41.
Then complete the words.

1 The man turned around and **l**_eft_ when nobody answered
the door.
2 All of the rooms in the hotel were **i**_____ .
3 He **i**_____ the kidnapper not to hurt him.
4 The child sat **m**_____ in the corner of the room.
5 His illness has left him completely **i**_____ , and he
has to remain in bed.
6 Can I borrow that book when you're **d**_____
**w**_____ it?
7 She said nothing and **m**_____ smiled in response
to his question.
8 I tried to give the police an **a**_____ description of
the attacker.
9 Beware! Thieves may try to steal your **b**_____
without you noticing.
10 That shop sells bags of every **c**_____ shape
and size.

## 5 LISTENING

**a** (iChecker) Listen to a radio programme about film
adaptations of books. According to Lindsey, are
these book-to-film adaptations successful or not?

1 *The Lord of the Rings* _____
2 *The Hunger Games* _____

**b** Listen again and mark the sentences
**T** (true) or **F** (false).

1 According to Lindsey, a good film adaptation is
exactly the same as the book.
2 A good adaptation has to get the timing right.
3 Choosing the right cast can make a big difference
to the success of a film adaptation.
4 The main reason for the success of *The Lord of the
Rings* series is its setting.
5 Special effects were used extensively in the creation
of the character Gollum.
6 The main reason why Lindsey doesn't like *The
Hunger Games* films is the casting.

**c** Listen again with the audio script on p.71 and try
to guess the meaning of any words that you don't
know. Then check in your dictionary.

## 6 READING

**a** Read the text once. What advice does the writer give?

**b** Read the text again and choose the best answer.

1 As an adult, the writer regards her childhood ideas about reading as… .
   a extremely resourceful
   b quite thorough
   c rather immature
   d very sophisticated

2 The writer hates Russell Banks' *Book of Jamaica* because… .
   a she didn't understand the plot
   b she made herself finish it
   c she doesn't think much of the author
   d she had an awful summer job at the time

3 The writer's advice to readers who aren't enjoying a particular book is to… .
   a find an alternative
   b take a break
   c try a different book by the same author
   d finish it at all costs

4 According to the writer, the first 50 pages of a book is… .
   a the minimum that her friends suggest reading
   b enough to find out what a book is about
   c what she advises people to read to find out if they will like a book
   d the minimum she needs to read to know if she's going to like a book

5 The writer considers that people may end up reading less if… .
   a they watch a lot of TV adaptations
   b they think reading is a waste of time
   c they persevere with books they aren't enjoying
   d they are given too many bad books to read

**c** Look at the highlighted idioms and phrasal verbs in the text. What do you think they mean? Check in your dictionary, then use them to complete the sentences.

1 If the title doesn't _____, the story surely will.
2 Whenever I _____ an author, I go on to read all of their books.
3 Have you ever read a review that _____ reading a novel?
4 If you've read it, _____ don't tell me what happens in the end!
5 I watched the film _____ although I can't say that I really enjoyed it.
6 All our proposals were dismissed _____.

# Lionel Shriver
# On how not to read

The most stupid childhood vow I ever made was to finish every book I started. Maintained well into adulthood, this policy turned reading the first page of any volume into a miniature death sentence. I imagined my compulsive completion to be a sign of adult seriousness. In truth, it was a vanity – a poorly thought-out and typically adolescent whim.

As a consequence of this inane commitment, I reserve a special loathing for many books that I shouldn't have been reading in the first place. I remember working as a summer camp councillor in my 20s and absolutely despising poor Russell Banks' *Book of Jamaica*. Yet I never allowed myself to read something else because I had already started it. I say 'poor' Russell Banks, because I love his other books, and the fact that I forced myself to keep reading a book for which I was not remotely in the mood was not his fault.

I have occasionally heard from a reader who is furious because he or she did not enjoy one of my novels yet still read to its bitter end. I reject this fury out of hand. For pity's sake, if you don't take a shine to a novel, there are loads more in the world; read something else. Continue suffering and it's not the author's fault. It's yours.

Granted, it's a good idea to give some books a chance even if they don't grab you at first, especially if they come recommended by someone you trust. But 50 pages is plenty. With some books I have an allergic reaction after two or three.

Reading time is precious. Don't waste it. Reading bad books, or books that are wrong for a certain time in your life, can dangerously put you off the activity altogether. The sign that I don't like the book I'm reading is finding myself watching reruns of *Come Dine With Me*.

### Glossary

***Come Dine With Me*** a popular British reality TV show that has been running since 2005.

The bad news is time flies.
The good news is you're the pilot.
*Michael Altshuler, American entrepreneur*

# 5A One thing at a time

## 1 LEXIS IN CONTEXT
### Multitasking and mindfulness

Look at the Lexis in Context on Student's Book p.44. Then complete the sentences with the prepositions.

1  Please stop interrupting me; I can't concentrate _on_ my work.
2  Owing to poor sales during the recession, the company was faced _____ closure.
3  My grandfather is in a home because he is no longer capable _____ looking after himself.
4  While he was walking home, he became aware _____ a figure behind him.
5  She works on the front desk, dealing _____ customer enquiries.
6  The documentary focuses _____ the rise in knife crime in the UK.

## 2 GRAMMAR distancing

a  Complete the sentences with the words in the list.

| according | agreed | apparently | appears |
|---|---|---|---|
| ~~believed~~ | expected | may | seem |

1  There are _believed_ to be many homeless people living on the streets of the capital.
2  It _____ that there is a connection between eating too many carbohydrates and depression.
3  The Prime Minister is _____ to announce his resignation by the end of the day.
4  _____ to local residents, the man had always been a little strange.
5  The thieves _____ have been disturbed while they were going through the rooms upstairs.
6  It would _____ that there is some confusion about our new dress code. Staff are still turning up in jeans.
7  It is _____ that climate change is one of the greatest dangers facing the planet.
8  _____, the footballer was arrested because of an incident at a party last night.

b  Complete the second sentence so that you distance yourself from the information. Use the correct form of the verb in brackets.

1  An employee leaked the information to the press.  (say)
   _It is said that_ an employee leaked the information to the press.
2  Politicians have been falsifying their expenses.  (appear)
   _____ politicians have been falsifying their expenses.
3  The country's largest bank has gone bankrupt.  (announce)
   _____ the country's largest bank has gone bankrupt.
4  The pop star has had another breakdown. (think)
   The pop star _____ had another breakdown.
5  The accused was under the influence of drugs. (may)
   The accused _____ under the influence of drugs.
6  The winner had been chosen before voting commenced. (seem)
   _____ the winner had been chosen before voting commenced.
7  The burglars entered through an open window. (might)
   The burglars _____ through an open window.
8  The economic situation will improve by next year. (hope)
   _____ the economic situation will improve by next year.

## 3 VOCABULARY expressions with *time*

a  Complete the sentences with the correct form of the verbs in the list.

| give | have | make | run | save | spare | take | ~~waste~~ |
|---|---|---|---|---|---|---|---|

1  I spent all morning cleaning the windows and now it's raining. I shouldn't have _wasted_ my time.
2  We _____ a lot of time by getting the direct train to King's Cross instead of changing at Birmingham.
3  Alex has basketball training every day and also at weekends. The sport _____ up all his time.
4  Kate has too much to do. She can't even _____ the time to Skype her friends.
5  My dad had never been to his club's stadium, but now he's bought a season ticket, to _____ up for lost time.

6 Mum _____ me a really hard time for failing my exams.

7 Jenna's enjoying herself a lot at university. She's _____ the time of her life.

8 I only managed to answer half the exam questions before I _____ out of time.

**b** Complete the sentences with a suitable preposition.

1 My manager's been really stressed recently, so she's having some time _off_ .

2 My parents like to go abroad occasionally. _____ time _____ time they visit their friends in Greece.

3 I couldn't answer my phone when you rang. I was in a meeting _____ the time.

4 Karen is very punctual. She's always _____ time.

5 _____ five days' time I'll be on a plane to Hawaii for my holiday.

6 There was a huge traffic jam and _____ the time we arrived home it was dark.

7 You weren't even born when The Police were big. They were way _____ your time.

8 She can be a bit annoying _____ times, but I still love my sister.

**c** Complete the time expressions in the mini-dialogues.

1 A Where are you going?
  B Shopping! I need some _me_ time.

2 A Can you come to my presentation later?
  B Sorry, I can't. I'm a bit _____ of time today.

3 A Was the bride late for the wedding?
  B No, she got to the church with time to _____ .

4 A Why are you so bored these days?
  B I've got too much time on my _____ now I'm retired.

5 A Are you going to look for a new job?
  B No, I'm staying where I am for the time _____ .

6 A Do you think the business is in trouble?
  B Yes, I do. It's just a _____ of time before it closes.

7 A Why can't I stay any longer?
  B Time's _____ . Visitors have to leave at 8 p.m.

8 A Why aren't you going to see Andy again?
  B Because he spends the _____ time talking about himself!

## 4 PRONUNCIATION
### linking in short phrases

**a** Draw a line between the words that are linked.
  1 Oliver's asking for some extra time off.
  2 My cousin Nick is never on time.
  3 I find doing housework takes up a lot of time.
  4 We walked to town as we had plenty of time.
  5 We seem to have run out of time.
  6 It's a question of time before the sports centre opens.

**b** **iChecker** Listen and check. Practise saying the sentences.

**c** **iChecker** Listen and write six sentences.
  1 _____
  2 _____
  3 _____
  4 _____
  5 _____
  6 _____

**d** Listen again and repeat the sentences in **c**.

## 5 LISTENING

**a** **iChecker** Listen to a radio programme about some new research into time. What is the science expert's 'good news'?

**b** Listen again and complete the summary.

**How we perceive time**
The brain takes time to process information from the [1]_____ . The [2]_____ it takes to process the information, the slower time seems to pass.

**How our perception changes with age**
Children receive a lot of [3]_____ information which takes a long time to process. For them, time passes [4]_____ .

Adults receive information which is more [5]_____ , so it doesn't take long to process. For them, time passes more [6]_____ .

**What can we do to slow down time?**
Keep [7]_____ .
Visit [8]_____ .
Meet [9]_____ .
Be [10]_____ .

**c** Listen again with the audio script on p.72 and try to guess the meaning of any words that you don't know. Then check in your dictionary.

## 6 READING

**a** Read the article once. How does the author answer the question in the title?

**b** Read the article again and choose the right answers.

1 How did the writer and the other participants of the meetings react to their colleague's lateness?
   a They spoke to the person about it.
   b They complained to their superiors.
   c They accepted it.
   d They weren't affected by it.

2 According to Irvin Yalom, what is responsible for the way we behave?
   a Our body clock.
   b The way our minds work.
   c Our religious convictions.
   d The pressures of time.

3 What does the writer imply was the reason that Berlusconi made Merkel wait?
   a He received an important phone call.
   b He wasn't ready for their meeting.
   c He wanted to show his importance.
   d He was having his photo taken.

4 How do most people react when their lateness is out of their control?
   a They don't really mind.
   b They get very nervous.
   c They blame someone else.
   d They have different reactions.

5 How does lateness have a 'social value'?
   a It affects other people.
   b It makes us look good.
   c It influences how we feel.
   d It isn't important to us.

**c** Choose the right answers.

What do you think the writer means by…?
1 The whole day lost its shape. (para 1)
   a The day's schedule was ruined.
   b The day was a complete disaster.
   c The day became shorter.

2 …are acting out an inner agenda (para 2)
   a are pretending to be something they're not
   b are trying to hide something
   c are controlling a situation for their own benefit

3 It speaks volumes. (para 2)
   a His phone call was very loud.
   b His behaviour tells you a lot.
   c His phone call goes on for a long time.

4 …the power of their absence. (para 3)
   a the effect they have on the people they're with
   b the effect they have on the people who are waiting for them
   c the effect they have on their own lives

## Is being late fashionable or rude?

Being repeatedly late may just be accidental – or it could show a deep-seated psychological desire to express your own superiority

**1** When I worked in an office, meetings would often start late, usually because of a certain individual. Then they would overrun and the whole day lost its shape. But the individual was high-ranking and self-important: nobody challenged. So what are the ethics of lateness?

**2** There's a psychotherapist called Irvin Yalom who argues that all behaviour reflects psychology. Just as people who like to be on time are motivated by certain deep-seated beliefs, so those who make others wait are acting out an inner agenda, often based on an acute sense of power. There's famous footage in which Silvio Berlusconi keeps Angela Merkel waiting while he makes a call on his mobile. It speaks volumes.

**3** But that suggests all lateness is in one's control. What about when your train is cancelled or your flight is delayed or you had to wait longer for the plumber to arrive? In such cases, there's not a lot of psychology involved. Or is there? Some people will genuinely worry about the impact it will have on those left waiting, while others might secretly enjoy the power of their absence.

**4** The essential fact is that lateness means breaking a convention – you can only be late in respect of a time agreed with other people. Regardless of psychology, it has a social value. And when we treat other people's time as less valuable than our own, we treat them as inferior.

**d** Without looking back at the text, can you remember the nouns from the following verbs and adjectives?

1 superior _____
2 behave _____
3 late _____
4 believe _____
5 absent _____

No woman marries for money; they are all clever enough,
before marrying a millionaire, to fall in love with him first.

*Cesare Pavese, Italian writer*

# 5B A material world

## 1 LEXIS IN CONTEXT

### Do women really want to marry for money?

Look at the Lexis in Context on Student's Book p.49.
Then complete the words.

1 You've got a very **s**_our_ face – what's the matter?
2 Problems occur when important meetings and children's birthdays **c**_____.
3 Who **sh**_____ the responsibility of bringing up the kids in your relationship?
4 The park was **l**_____ **w**_____ plastic cups after the concert.
5 Working mothers have to **j**_____ their jobs with the needs of their children.
6 She's a successful businesswoman with a **h**_____-**fl**_____ career.

## 2 GRAMMAR unreal uses of past tenses

a Complete the mini-dialogues with the correct form of the words in brackets.

1 **A** Your parents will be here in an hour.
  **B** I know. _It's time I tidied up._ (time / I / tidy up)
2 **A** I'll call you in the morning.
  **B** _____ in person.
     (I / rather / you / come round)
3 **A** Our new dishwasher doesn't work very well.
  **B** I know. _____ it.
     (I / wish / we / not buy)
4 **A** It's a shame we can't meet up more often.
  **B** Yes. _____ nearer each other.
     (only / we / live)
5 **A** I won't tell your girlfriend you were here.
  **B** Thank you. _____
     (I / rather / she / not know)
6 **A** Did you get the grades to go to university?
  **B** No. _____ harder for my exams.
     (only / I / work)
7 **A** I'm fed up with working all the time.
  **B** _____ a holiday.
     (time / you / have)
8 **A** We can't afford a holiday this year.
  **B** I know. _____ better off.
     (I / wish / we / be)

b Complete the second sentence so it means the same as the first, using the words in brackets.

1 I should have applied for a grant. (wish)
  _I wish I had applied_ _____ for a grant.
2 We are unhappy because we owe the bank a lot of money. (if only)
  _____ the bank so much money.
3 Sally ought to make up her mind about her job. (time)
  _____ her mind about her job.
4 Would you prefer us to take you home now or later? (rather)
  _____ you home now or later?
5 We regret spending all our savings on our honeymoon. (if only)
  _____ all our savings on our honeymoon.
6 Don't you think you ought to apologize to Anna? (time)
  Isn't _____ to Anna?
7 I would like to be able to see my family more. (wish)
  _____ my family more.
8 We'd prefer you not to bring your dog in here. (rather)
  _____ bring your dog in here.

33

## 3 VOCABULARY money

**a** Complete the missing words.

1 Would you like to pay monthly or in an annual **l**_ump_ **s**_um_?
2 My uncle works in the **st**_____ **m**_____, buying and selling shares all day.
3 You can get a better **e**_____ **r**_____ at some Bureaux de Change than at others.
4 If you are **i**_____ **d**_____, you owe someone money.
5 Despite the recession, many people's **st**_____ of **l**_____ has remained high.
6 Many people are struggling because wages aren't rising at the same rate as **i**_____.
7 We live in a **c**_____ **s**_____ where people are obsessed with money.
8 **I**_____ **r**_____ have been cut to try and encourage people to borrow more money.
9 My sister has managed to get a government **g**_____ to study abroad for a year.
10 I give a **d**_____ to my favourite animal charity every year.

**b** Order the letters to make synonyms of *rich* or *poor*. Write **R** (rich) or **P** (poor) after each one.

1 F L T U F E N A    _affluent_    _R_
2 E S N I L E P N S   _____   ____
3 A D E O D L         _____   ____
4 A D R H  P U        _____   ____
5 L W E Y T A H       _____   ____
6 L E W L - F O F     _____   ____
7 R E B O K           _____   ____

**c** Complete the second sentence so that it means the same as the first. Use an idiom with the **bold** words.

1 Our friends buy many things they can't afford. **means**
Our friends are _living beyond their means_____.
2 We're overdrawn. **red**
We're _____.
3 Don't spend all your money. It's hard work to make more. **grow**
Don't spend all your money. It _____.
4 That yacht must have been really expensive. **arm**
That yacht must have _____.
5 We'll never be able to buy a house unless we start saving. **belt**
We'll never be able to buy a house unless _____.
6 Bill never eats out. He thinks it's too expensive. **robbery**
Bill never eats out. He thinks it's _____.
7 My in-laws are extremely mean. **fist**
My in-laws are very _____.
8 We hardly earn enough to buy what we need. **ends**
We're struggling to _____.

## 4 PRONUNCIATION
### US and UK accents

**iChecker** Can you tell the difference between US and UK accents? Listen and write **US** (US accent) or **UK** (UK accent).

1  _US_         6  _____
2  _____       7  _____
3  _____       8  _____
4  _____       9  _____
5  _____      10  _____

## 5 LISTENING

**a** **iChecker** Listen to a radio phone-in programme about saving money. Answer the questions with the names in the list.

Emily    Jonathan    Mary    Philip    Wendy

Which caller has a tip for saving money…?
1 at meal times
2 at the supermarket
3 for holidays
4 at home
5 on all kinds of purchases

**b** Listen again and answer the questions.

According to the callers, …?
1 at what temperature should your thermostat be set
2 what should you take to work to eat
3 where should you put your small change
4 how should you pay for everything you buy
5 when shouldn't you do your food shopping

**c** Listen again with the audio script on p.72 and try to guess the meaning of any words that you don't know. Then check in your dictionary.

## 6 READING

**a** Read the article once. Choose the sentence which best summarizes the results of the research.

   A If everyone in the country has more money as a result of economic development, then we're all happier.

   B It takes a long time to get used to being rich, so you don't notice if you feel any happier.

   C Money makes us happier if we are richer than those around us, but not if we all have a similar amount of wealth.

**b** Read the article again and match the missing sentences A–F to the gaps 1–5. There is one sentence you do not need to use.

   A 'People's aspirations tend to rise as their incomes rise, so rather quickly they start to think of a lot of additional things that they need to buy. So they end up no happier than they were before.'

   B Or they are more likely to hold jobs in which people defer to them.

   C The apparent contradiction is that people don't seem to be any happier now than they were then despite their enrichment through economic growth, but that people who are richer at any one time are happier on average than people who are poorer.

   D They think it's important to try to make everyone as happy as they possibly can be.

   E Increase the total amount of happiness, which means enabling people to have better human relationships.'

   F Happiness academics do accept that richer people are, by and large, happier than their poorer neighbours.

**c** Look at the highlighted expressions and try to work out their meaning. Check in your dictionary.

# Does money make you happy?

The unhappy answer to whether or not your happiness expands in line with your wealth is 'yes, but - no, but'. It seems it does if your riches rise relative to that of the Joneses, but not if you all rise together. 'What we actually care about is our income compared with other people,' says Lord Layard, one of the founders of 'happiness studies'. 'But if over time everybody is becoming richer, then people don't on average feel any better than they did before.'

Lord Layard bases the conclusion on studies and surveys that have been conducted over the past half a century or so in the world's richer countries. What the studies reveal is a paradox. ¹____

We like to look out at the neighbours' drive and see a smaller car. This is partly because aspirations rise with incomes. 'You rather quickly get adapted to more money so you don't get the pleasure out of it that you expected to get,' explains Derek Bok, a former president of Harvard University and author of *The Politics of Happiness*. ²____

³____ But they are not even certain that it is the money that does it. 'Happier people on the whole tend to be richer, but we're not quite sure why that is so,' says Mr Bok. 'It may not be the money. It may be that richer people command more respect or they have the freedom to do more things. ⁴____ Or they have more autonomy in what they do. So it

doesn't always follow that giving more money if you don't change those other things is really going to improve their happiness.'

So if money is not all it is cracked up to be, then what should people and governments do? For starters, believes Lord Layard, a break-neck chase after economic growth is misplaced. 'This competition to get richer than other people; it can't be achieved at the level of society,' he says. 'What we should do is have a positive sum. ⁵____

Rather than going for high growth, smoother growth might produce more happiness by producing less disruption and the uncertainty that comes with the ups and down of the economy, according to Lord Layard. 'I certainly think that the relief of poverty is an incredibly important objective, but it shouldn't be done at any cost. We shouldn't just go for economic development even if it leads to the complete fragmentation of society...and a decline in happiness.'

## Glossary

**The Joneses** from the idiom 'keep up with the Joneses', which means to try and have all the possessions and social achievements that your friends and neighbours have.

## 1 LOOKING AT LANGUAGE

Match a word in **A** to a word in **B** to make compound nouns. Then complete the sentences.

| A | age | blood | breathing | college |
|---|-----|-------|-----------|---------|
| | life | ~~stress~~ | support | text |

| B | exercises | group | ~~levels~~ | messages |
|---|-----------|-------|------------|----------|
| | network | pressure | saver | students |

1 My _stress_ _levels_ always go through the roof at exam time.

2 Flu can affect anyone, regardless of which _____ _____ they're in.

3 The doctor has given me some tablets because my _____ _____ is too high.

4 You need your _____ _____ around you to help you through challenging times.

5 Which is cheaper, sending _____ _____ or making phone calls?

6 Pregnant women are encouraged to do _____ _____ to prepare for the birth of their child.

7 A mobile phone can be a _____ _____ if you're involved in an accident and need help.

8 Some _____ _____ suffer badly from stress, particularly at exam time.

## 2 READING

Read the article. Choose the right answers.

1 Students at Seton Hall...
    a are not allowed to receive visitors.
    b can attend a special programme designed to reduce stress.
    c are allowed to bring their pets to class.

2 The remarkable thing about William Wynne's dog was...
    a it survived for many years on the battlefield.
    b it brightened the atmosphere in the hospital.
    c it made friends with all of the hospital staff.

3 Therapy Dogs International...
    a ensures that animals used for visits are properly trained.
    b works mainly with German Shepherd dogs.
    c raises funds to purchase dogs to use in the organization.

4 The article describes dog therapy as a 'win-win situation' because...
    a it never fails to work on humans.
    b the handlers benefit as much as the patients.
    c both the patients and the dogs benefit from it.

5 In general, how do students feel about the therapy dogs?
    a They are nervous about touching them.
    b They are eager for them to arrive.
    c They are confident that the dogs will help them.

## De-stressing with dog therapy

Visitors to Seton Hall University, New Jersey, may be forgiven for thinking they have turned up at the wrong place. Instead of encountering students rushing off to lectures or studying diligently in the library, they will see large numbers of them milling around in a hall in the company of several dogs. But these are no ordinary canines. They are therapy dogs, brought in by the Counselling and Psychology Services Department of the university to de-stress students. And by the looks on the students' faces, the therapy seems to be working.

The first recorded instance of a dog having an impact on our mood occurred during World War II. A soldier, William Wynne, had come across a stray dog on the battlefield that he befriended and named Smoky. Later, when Wynne was admitted to hospital suffering from a tropical disease, his friends took Smoky to visit him. Not only did the animal cheer Wynne up, but it became a big hit with all of the other wounded soldiers on the ward. Noting the positive effect that Smoky had on the men, the doctors allowed the dog to continue doing rounds and sleep on Wynne's bed. Thus Smoky became the first therapy dog, although the term had not yet been coined.

It wasn't until some 30 years later that the concept of therapy dogs really took off. In the mid-1970s, nurse Elaine Smith noticed how well patients responded to a golden retriever brought into hospital by a regular visitor. She decided that there should be more dogs like this in places of healing and so in 1976, she founded Therapy Dogs International, an organization that trained dogs to visit institutions. The first TDI visit took place that year, when five German shepherds and a collie accompanied their handlers to a therapy session in New Jersey. The day was a complete success and since then, TDI has grown to include over 24,000 registered teams of dogs and their handlers.

So how is it that these animals can lead to such a marked improvement in our moods? Research has shown that being around dogs affects various chemicals released by the brain. The amount of the feel-good chemicals, oxytocin and dopamine, increases while the level of stress-inducing substances like cortisol goes down. These variations result in a lowering of the blood pressure, a relief of stress and an improvement in the mood. The dogs experience similar chemical changes as well, and so it's a win-win situation.

The lift in spirits is certainly evident among the students of Seton Hall and other universities with a similar scheme. The students generally reach out and touch the animals as soon as the team from TDI gets through the door. Test-weary faces begin to relax as their worries fade away, and soon everyone is smiling. Of course, the therapy dogs are not able to determine the final grades awarded to the students, but the experience is bound to make the revision process much more bearable.

# Listening

## 1 A )))

**Speaker 1** Speaking from my own personal situation, I love the fact that I have a brother. Um, it provided, he provided me with a lot of fun when, when we were growing up um, and um and having, having two kids myself I am very pleased that they, they've got each other to look after. And, er, I think as you go through life and your own parents get older, um and you know, you will one day have to look after them, I think doing that with a, with a sibling would be a lot easier.

**Speaker 2** I'm an only child, and someone said to me, 'Oh that must be so much better to be an only child because you get all your parents' attention and you don't have to share it with your brothers and sisters,' and to an extent I kind of agree because um, you, it is wonderful to have all that attention from your parents. But you can end up becoming, sort of spoilt and um used to having this attention, so when you have to go to school or you have to interact with other people, if you don't get the attention that you've been used to, you can react in a, in a really spoilt way without, sort of, meaning to.

**Speaker 3** I've got two children and although they fight all the time and they, you know, all this sort of thing, there's, I think, I often, well when they are fighting, try and look at the positives of it and think, well, I suppose it's a good thing that they are sort of, you know, learning to do all those things within a safe family environment, which I suppose if you are, I mean, if you are an only child, perhaps then it has to be at school or, you know, it's like practising.

**Speaker 4** I'd hate to have been an only child, I mean I had three brothers and sisters, and I think only, there was, the girl next door was an only child and she was under so much pressure from her parents to succeed and all their hopes were focused on this one girl … I thought, I wouldn't want all that pressure on me.

## 1 B )))

1 Well, one job I've always rather fancied is being a travel writer, I mean, basically because I like travelling and I like going round the world and I'd like to have an excuse to do it and someone to pay me to do it if possible, um, and I think I would be quite good at it because, well, I am quite sociable and I like to think I can write and er, and I'm quite good at living out of a suitcase and living cheap, um and it just seems to be a wonderful way of seeing the world. I mean, I don't actually know anybody who does it, but I've always sort of envied people like Michael Palin who do these television series going all round the world and they seem to have such a wonderful time.

But I have occasionally had to read travel books and some of them are brilliant and some you definitely get the impression that they've been sent there by their publisher to do a travel book about Patagonia or whatever it is and nothing much has happened, but they've still got to write the book. So you get rather a boring drudgy book sometimes, and I suppose that might be a drawback that you'd feel you had to write a book even if you'd got nothing to say.

2 Well, what I'd really hate to do is any sort of job on a production line, any sort of real drudgery where there's really no, sort of, mental input at all, but you're just repeating the same task again and again and again and I think that would probably drive me insane.

I have done something a bit like it when I was about 18, I worked in a plastics factory to earn some money for a couple of months and I remember I went in, in the dark and I came out in the dark, because it was winter, so I never saw the light of day, it was about a ten-hour day, paid almost nothing, we had half an hour for lunch and the noise of the machines was so loud that you could, you could shout at the top of your voice and the person next to you couldn't hear you, and the smell of plastics filled the air and it was absolutely hideous. The only, the only advantage was that it was so loud that you could actually sing at the top of your voice and nobody could hear, so I spent a lot of my day singing to myself, which, which I quite enjoyed.

## 2 A )))

**Interviewer** Do you find it easier to understand native or non-native speakers of English?

**Zoltan** It depends what you mean. As far as pronunciation goes, it's a lot easier to understand native speakers with a standard accent like BBC English or General American. And for me, some of the regional dialects are quite easy to understand as well. Um, other dialects are a lot harder to decipher, like Scots, or Geordie, or New Zealand are really hard to understand. As far as content is concerned, it's a lot easier to understand non-native speakers. Because they don't use idiomatic expressions or obscure cultural references; they don't use regional slang. They also use the Latin, er, verb instead of a phrasal verb, for example like 'continue' rather than 'carry on', which is less easy to confuse. And the other thing about non-native speakers is that they are a lot more direct. When they speak in English, they say what they mean. There are no… allusions and metaphors and references to other things.

**Interviewer** How do you feel about having your English corrected?

**Zoltan** I don't mind. Er, I'm sometimes annoyed with myself for making a recurring mistake again like mixing up 'he' and 'she' and I find it a bit weird when a non-native speaker who is less fluent than me corrects my English. And … I also think that non-native speakers, good non-native speakers, are often better at spelling than native speakers, because we learn words with their spelling whereas native speakers learn the word first and learn the spelling years later. And just recently an English friend of mine corrected my spelling of 'accommodation', which I'd spelt with double 'c' and double 'm', and he insisted that it was spelled with a single 'm' and in fact I was right.

**Interviewer** Do you have any funny or embarrassing stories related to misunderstanding someone?

**Zoltan** Hungarians aren't generally interested in bird watching, and most Hungarians I know can't tell one bird from another. And recently a friend of mine told me about seeing some kites over, over the fields near their house the previous weekend. And I said that flying kites is really popular in Budapest too, meaning that people go in to the hills at the weekend to fly their home-made paper kites. It never occurred to me for a second that she may be talking about a bird. I don't think a Hungarian would ever tell someone else about seeing some bird several days before.

**Interviewer** Is there anything you still find difficult about English?

**Zoltan** Not really. I've been learning English for 26 years. If I had to say anything, I would say counting, numbers. If I have to count anything, I have to switch back to Hungarian, even if the person I'm speaking to will need the English sum.

**Interviewer** Do you find it easier to understand native or non-native speakers of English?

**Cristina** Well, it all depends where they come from. I suppose it's more or less the same. Some non-natives are more difficult than others if you're not used to the accent. For instance, I used to find some Japanese and Chinese speakers difficult to understand, but then because of work I went to the Far East lots of times and then it became OK. Natives, again it all depends. I was taught RP and one assumes that everybody speaks that, and of course I had friends from lots of parts of Britain who did not speak RP. In fact, it is a pretty rare thing these days. So we have a good friend from, from Glasgow and it was always embarrassing for me because I could not understand most of what he was saying. I still don't.

**Interviewer** How do you feel about having your English corrected?

**Cristina** I don't mind. My children used to love correcting me. They still say I speak very funny English, but usually adults in this country do not correct you. I would like to be corrected.

**Interviewer** Do you have any funny or embarrassing stories related to misunderstanding someone?

**Cristina** Um yes, misunderstanding and being misunderstood. Several! Some I don't think I would like to tell you about, but I'll tell you one. I was a student at the University of Michigan in the United States and my phonetics professor was very handsome and therefore I did extremely well, not in all subjects, but it was worth studying that one. But I remember my first tutorial when he said 'See you later' and I thought, 'Hmm, interesting. Where?' And in class he'd said, I'd asked a question and

he'd said, 'Interesting question' so I thought, 'Great! He thinks I'm clever, and maybe he thinks I'm interesting to meet somewhere else, but I couldn't understand how I was going to find out where or when. I luckily didn't ask. It would have been very embarrassing.

**Interviewer** Is there anything you still find difficult about English?

**Cristina** Yes, I think there are things that have especially to do with cultural aspects. I used to find when my children were little that I didn't know the same nursery rhymes that you know here. I didn't know the actions, and I still don't know lots of things. It's, I don't know to give an example, say I had learnt American English, but I still didn't know who the Simpsons were.

## 2 B ))

**Speaker 1** My earliest memory is from when I was about three years old and I was at home with my mum and I was playing with my red plastic hoover, which I really liked as a toy when I was little. Um, it might have seemed a bit dull but I really enjoyed playing with it.

**Speaker 2** My earliest memory is of, er, living in Malta when I was young and looking out of the window to see, um, the grapevine and the veranda outside my bedroom window having been destroyed by a whirlwind that had just gone through the, gone through the garden of the house. It hadn't touched the house itself just taken out the veranda and the grapevine.

**Speaker 3** My earliest memory is my first day of school when I was about five because I was really nervous and I forgot to tell the other people my name so people were kind of confused.

**Speaker 4** My earliest memory is probably at the local airport, but um I've got a feeling that it's a memory of looking at a photograph of myself in a basket at the local airport. So it's a bit hard to distinguish whether that's a real memory or a perceived one.

**Speaker 5** Um, my earliest memory is walking on a beach with my family collecting shells. I somehow remember finding a piece of blue glass which had been worn smooth by the waves. When I showed it to my mum, she told me to keep it because it was such a pretty colour.

## 3 A ))

**Speaker 1** My best friend kept insisting that I met up with a cute, single male friend of hers. Finally, I gave in and went on a date. My friend was right: he really was cute and single. But he was totally obsessed with my friend – all he did was talk about her. I finally made an excuse to go home early after he asked me if I thought my friend was happy with her boyfriend!

**Speaker 2** I was on my first date with this beautiful young lady, and we went to a nice restaurant. The waitress was bringing our drinks to us when one of the other waitresses asked her a question. And as she turned around, she tipped our drinks all over me – I mean, I was drenched from head to toe. Other than that, though, the date went really well. We got married after six months and well, now, fifteen years later, we still laugh about our first date.

**Speaker 3** This is one of my more memorable dates, but for quite the wrong reason. What we did was this: he took me for a loooooong drive in his truck – I had absolutely no idea where we were. Then he stopped at a gas station and bought me an ice cream. And then he drove me back home again. That was it. As you can imagine, I didn't bother to find out what would happen the second time round.

**Speaker 4** My most memorable first date was at a fast food restaurant! I'd been trying to get together with this girl for weeks, but our schedules just didn't coincide. So, when I was going out for a burger one evening, I just texted her and asked her to come. And amazingly, she did! And we ended up talking about everything from work to family. We've been together for eight months now, and she often pulls my leg about it.

**Speaker 5** When my current boyfriend asked me out, we went out for dinner and then back to my place for coffee. And at some point he got down on his knees, you know, like he was going to propose, or something – and he got me really worried, then he got a ring pull out of his pocket – you know, the ones that come off the top of a drinks can – and he said, 'Will you be my girlfriend?' And after that, we couldn't stop laughing.

## 3 B )))

**Speaker 1** Erm, as far as historical films go, my personal favourite is *Elizabeth*. Um, as the title suggests, it's about one of the most famous queens of England, Elizabeth I, who ruled the country in the second half of the sixteenth century. The plot is based on the early years of her reign, when she is on the lookout for a suitable husband. Cate Blanchett plays the role of Elizabeth, and she looks wonderful in the flowing gowns typical of that era. In fact, all the actors look the part, because of the great attention paid to what each of the characters is wearing.

**Speaker 2** I think my favourite historical film is Ben Affleck's thriller *Argo*. The film tells the story of the rescue of six American diplomats in Iran when relations between the two countries were starting to break down in the late 1970s. Erm, it's got to be one of the most exciting films I've ever seen – I spent the whole time sitting on the edge of my seat. Some of the events may be a bit exaggerated, but it's a true story all the same.

**Speaker 3** Erm, my favourite historical film has got to be *The Last Emperor*. It's based on the autobiography of the last emperor of China, Puyi, who died in 1967. Puyi grew up in the Forbidden City in Beijing, and the film's director, Bernardo Bertolucci, was lucky enough – he got permission to film inside this amazing palace in Beijing. I mean, visually, the film is absolutely stunning, so it's not surprising that it won nine Oscars.

**Speaker 4** Erm, I thoroughly enjoyed the historical film *Invictus* when it came out. Um, it's about the events that occurred in South Africa before and during the Rugby World Cup in 1995, I think. And there are two great actors in it: Morgan Freeman, he plays Nelson Mandela, the President of South Africa at the time, and Matt Damon. He plays the captain of the rugby team. They're both brilliant in the parts. I like it because at first they're hostile to each other and then they become friends. That's why I like the film.

**Speaker 5** This film isn't particularly well-known, er, but it's definitely my favourite historical film. It's a drama called *Agora*, and it's based on the life of a Greek philosopher called Hypatia, who lived in Roman Egypt in the fourth century. Hypatia was also a mathematician and an astronomer and she taught at a school in Alexandria. Hypatia is admired by many, including myself, for giving her life trying to protect the library of Alexandria when it was attacked.

## 4 A )))

Our composer of the week this week is Aberdeen-born percussionist, Dame Evelyn Glennie. She studied at the Royal Academy of Music. In a career spanning more than 20 years, she has performed with almost all of the world's leading orchestras, playing up to 60 different percussion instruments, from the xylophone to the timpani. In that time, she has won over 80 international music awards, including two Grammies. Outside classical music, she has achieved crossover success in the worlds of pop and rock, having recorded with artists such as Sting and Björk as well as composing and performing a number of soundtracks for film and television.

Glennie began studying music at the age of 12, by which time she was profoundly deaf. However, she has never been deterred by her loss of hearing and doesn't see it as an obstacle to composing and performing music. In fact, she is frustrated by the fact that despite all her achievements as a musician, it's her deafness that always makes the headlines. As she writes on her website in her essay about hearing, 'If you are standing by the road and a large truck goes by you, do you hear or feel the vibration? The answer is both. For some reason we tend to make a distinction between hearing a sound and feeling a vibration, in reality they are the same thing.' She goes on to point out that this distinction doesn't exist in all languages. For example, in Italian, the verb 'sentire' means 'to hear' while the same verb in the reflexive form means 'to feel'.

In concert and in the studio, Glennie performs barefoot in order to feel the sounds of her instruments vibrating through the floor, and the title of her best-selling autobiography is *Good Vibrations*. But let's get on to the music. Glennie released her first album in…

## 4 B )))

**Presenter** If you're a regular cinema-goer, you may have noticed the long list of films that have been shown recently which are based on books. Yet it can't be easy to turn literature into cinema successfully. Today, we're going to take a look at the subject of film adaptations and we've invited film buff Lindsey Wallace into the studio to share her views with us. Hello, Lindsey.

**Lindsey** Hi there.

**Presenter** Lindsey, what is it that makes a good film adaptation?

**Lindsey** Basically, it's finding the right balance between telling the original story while at the same time adding something new to it. If there are too many changes to the plot, the fans will get upset, but if the film is too faithful to the original, they'll go away wondering why they bothered to see it in the first place.

**Presenter** Are you suggesting that the film adaptation doesn't have to be 100% faithful to the book?

**Lindsey** It isn't really a question of being faithful to the book; it's more a question of capturing the spirit of the original story. A good screenplay writer is one who understands the material and is able to pick out the themes, characters and scenes that are most important. After that, it's a question of timing – deciding how much or how little emphasis to place on each of these things.

**Presenter** Hmm. Apart from the balance and the timing, is there anything else that contributes to a good film adaptation?

**Lindsey** Well, once you've got the screenplay right, you obviously have to find the right actors for all the different roles. Casting is fundamental when it comes to film adaptations, as readers will already have an idea in their minds of what the characters are like.

**Presenter** Lindsey, now that we've established what makes a good film adaptation, can you give us an example?

**Lindsey** Um, actually, I can give you more: the three films that make up *The Lord of the Rings* series. All of them have an exceptional cast including renowned actors such as Elijah Wood, Ian McKellen, Liv Tyler, and Cate Blanchett. And the makers have been faithful to the J.R.R. Tolkien novels; at times parts of the original narrative are read over the images that appear on the screen. At the same time, the timing is impeccable as the film focuses on what is truly important in the story. But the key to the film's success is Peter Jackson's use of special effects, some of which had never been seen in the cinema before.

**Presenter** What kind of special effects?

**Lindsey** Take, for example, the character of Gollum, a creature created almost entirely by computer-generated images. You believe he's really there next to the real actors on the screen.

**Presenter** That's very true. How about giving us an example of a bad film adaptation, Lindsey?

**Lindsey** Again, I'm going to give you another film series: *The Hunger Games*. The films are hugely popular and have won several different awards. I think the casting is certainly excellent, and

Jennifer Lawrence is superb as the central character, Katniss Everdeen. But I feel that the filmmakers have been a bit too faithful to the books. Each film tells the story in the exact order that it happens in the original, which, to me, makes the plot seem a bit flat. There is little use of timing, so the key scenes aren't given enough emphasis. On top of this, I don't think there's really anything new for the readers – even the colour and flamboyance of the Capitol comes as no surprise as it is depicted just as it is in the book, which I found a bit disappointing.

**Presenter** That's a shame because all three of the books were excellent. Lindsey Wallace, thank you for joining us today.

**Lindsey** My pleasure.

## 5 A ))

**Presenter** Time flies, as the saying goes, and it's quite true. Gone are the lazy days of childhood when the summer holidays seemed to crawl by – once you become an adult, the weeks pass by in a whirl of activity. An American neuroscientist has recently published a paper exploring this phenomenon. Our science expert, Stephen, is here with us to explain the theory. Stephen, why does time seem to go so slowly when we're children and so fast when we grow up?

**Stephen** First of all, it's important to understand how we perceive time. Essentially, our brains take in a whole lot of information from our senses and organize it in a way that makes sense to us before we ever perceive it. When we receive lots of new information, it takes our brains a while to process it all. The longer this processing takes, the longer that period of time feels. Conversely, if your brain doesn't have to process lots of new information, time seems to go much faster.

**Presenter** Well how does that explain why our perception of time changes as we get older?

**Stephen** When we're younger, most of the information we receive is brand new – and there's lots of it. The new information takes longer to process, which is why time seems to pass more slowly. Whereas when we are older, the world is much more familiar to us, so there is less new information to process. It doesn't take long to process anything that's new, which explains why time seems to pass more quickly.

**Presenter** Uh-uh. Stephen, is there anything we can do to slow time down?

**Stephen** The good news is that there is, yes. The first thing you can do is to keep learning. If you're constantly reading, trying new activities or taking courses to learn new skills, you'll be feeding your brain with loads of new information that will make time pass more slowly.

**Presenter** Hmm. That sounds easy. What else?

**Stephen** The second thing you can do is to visit new places. A new environment can send a mass of information rushing to your brain: smells, sounds, people, colours, textures. Your brain has to interpret all of this, which will give it plenty of work to do.

**Presenter** I suppose meeting new people might help as well?

**Stephen** That's right. Meeting new people is a good workout for our brains because it takes a lot of time and effort to process and understand details about them.

**Presenter** Hmm. Is there anything else we can do, Stephen?

**Stephen** Yes, being spontaneous can help a lot. Surprises are like new activities: they make us pay attention and heighten our senses.

**Presenter** Well, so, now you know. All you have to do if you want to slow down time is to follow Stephen's advice. Stephen Carter, thank you for joining us.

**Stephen** My pleasure.

## 5 B ))

**Presenter** Hello and welcome to the show. Today we're looking at different ways of saving money, and we're asking you, the listeners, to phone in with any ideas you've experimented with. The number you need to call is 081 272 272 and the lines are already open. And it looks as if we have a caller on line 1. Can you tell us your name, please?

**Caller 1** Yes, I'm Mary.

**Presenter** Hello, Mary. What's your money-saving idea, please?

**Caller 1** Well, when I noticed that my energy bill kept creeping up and up, I decided to turn down the thermostat on my heating. Instead of having it at 21°, I've put it down to 18°, and it's made a big difference. I pay about fifty pounds less on my heating bill than I did before, and if I feel a bit cold, I put an extra jumper on.

**Presenter** That sounds like a great idea, Mary. Most of us have our heating on too high, so it makes sense to turn it down to pay less – and save energy at the same time. OK, thanks Mary. There's another caller on line 2 – Philip, is that right?

**Caller 2** Yes, it is.

**Presenter** What do you do to save money, Philip?

**Caller 2** Um, I always take a packed lunch to work. We've got a small kitchen on my floor with a microwave, so we can bring our food in a plastic box and heat it up. I usually take what's left from dinner the night before, but if there isn't anything hot, I make a salad. It's certainly a lot cheaper than having to pay for a meal every day.

**Presenter** Thanks for that, Philip. Yeah, taking a packed lunch is an excellent way of saving money when you need to have lunch at work. OK, our next caller is Emily. How do you try to save money, Emily?

**Caller 3** Um, yes, um, a couple of years ago, I decided to start putting all my change in a coin jar at the end of the day. I've got one of those big sweet jars, so it takes quite a long time to fill it up. It's my way of saving up to go away in the summer – I wouldn't be able to afford it, otherwise.

**Presenter** Those sweet jars are great for saving money in, aren't they, Emily? OK, back to line 2 for our next caller. What's your name, please?

**Caller 4** Jonathan.

**Presenter** Jonathan, tell us your money-saving idea.

**Caller 4** Well, it might sound a bit radical, but I cut up all of my credit cards last year. Now, I only use cash. Paying in cash really makes you think about how much you're spending – if you use a credit card, you tend to lose control, to some extent. It's worked for me, anyway, and I've cut my spending by about 20%.

**Presenter** Jonathan, that's certainly the bravest solution we've had so far. OK, we've just got time for one more call, Wendy on line 1. What's your money-saving idea?

**Caller 5** Um, it might sound a bit weird, but I've found that it's a really bad idea to go shopping on an empty stomach. When I'm hungry, I end up buying loads of snacks on impulse – it's such a waste of money. So now I do my shopping straight after I've had a meal and I don't spend half as much.

**Presenter** That makes sense, Wendy, thank you for calling. Well, I hope that the rest of our listeners have found those ideas useful. And now it's time for the news…

# Answer key

**1A**

## 1 GRAMMAR

a 2 doesn't have / hasn't got
  3 Did you have
  4 Do you have / Have you got
  5 had
  6 had had
  7 didn't have to
  8 won't have

b 2 doesn't have to
  3 have, had
  4 haven't got / don't have / haven't
  5 'm having
  6 hasn't been
  7 Did, have
  8 do, have / have, got

## 2 VOCABULARY

a 2 sarcastic
  3 conscientious
  4 resourceful
  5 thorough
  6 sympathetic
  7 gentle
  8 straightforward

b 2 seems
  3 taken
  4 tends / tries
  5 refused
  6 take

c 2 a pain in the neck
  3 has a (very) quick temper
  4 a cold fish
  5 down to earth
  6 a soft touch

## 3 PRONUNCIATION

a 2 conscie̲ntious
  3 cu̲rious
  4 dete̲rmined
  5 ge̲ntle
  6 self-suffi̲cient
  7 ste̲ady
  8 reso̲urceful
  9 sarca̲stic
  10 sponta̲neous
  11 sympa̲thetic
  12 tho̲rough

## 4 LEXIS IN CONTEXT

  2 stuck
  3 together
  4 eye
  5 round
  6 gut
  7 head
  8 off
  9 white

## 5 LISTENING

a They mention more advantages.

b A 3  B 2  C 4  D 1

## 6 READING

a Sentence 1 is the best.

b 1 c  2 b  3 d  4 a  5 c  6 b

**1B**

## 1 LEXIS IN CONTEXT

  2 head
  3 keep
  4 looks
  5 blank
  6 build
  7 heart
  8 wearing

## 2 VOCABULARY

a 2 rewarding
  3 demanding
  4 promoted
  5 employ
  6 made redundant
  7 monotonous
  8 off work
  9 perks
  10 hire

b 2 full-time
  3 job-hunting
  4 academic qualifications
  5 career ladder
  6 events management
  7 permanent contract
  8 clocking off
  9 apply for a position

## 3 GRAMMAR

a 2 Consequently
  3 Even though
  4 because
  5 not to
  6 due to
  7 nevertheless
  8 in case

b 2 so as not to forget the time
  3 as a result, it will be closed until further
    notice
  4 due to the late arrival of the incoming plane
  5 despite not meeting all the requirements
  6 so that they would be ready for the exam
    the next day
  7 in spite of not being able to go to the
    interview / in spite of the fact that she
    wasn't able to go to the interview
  8 owing to his illness / owing to the fact
    that he was ill

## 4 LEXIS IN CONTEXT

  2 ploy
  3 issue
  4 travel-focused
  5 workload
  6 tackle

## 5 PRONUNCIATION

a 2 free̲lance
  3 te̲mporary
  4 vo̲luntary
  5 compa̲ssionate
  6 mate̲rnity
  7 pe̲rmanent
  8 mo̲tivating
  9 mono̲tonous
  10 acade̲mic
  11 ma̲nagement
  12 qualifica̲tions

c 1 event
  2 quit
  3 perks
  4 benefits

## 6 READING

a He would say it was fiction.

b 1 E  2 B  3 F  4 A  5 D

c 1 jam-packed
  2 somewhere along the line
  3 plain sailing
  4 was up to
  5 is another matter
  6 jump at the chance

## 7 LISTENING

a The man would love to be a travel writer
  and would hate a job on a production line.

b 1 The man thinks he would be good at the
    first job because he thinks he is quite
    sociable, is a good writer, he doesn't
    mind living out of a suitcase, he can live
    cheap, and it would be a wonderful way
    to see the world.
  2 A downside might be that you would
    have to write a book, even if you had
    nothing to say.
  3 He thinks he would hate the second job
    because he wouldn't have to think and it
    would be very repetitive.
  4 He did a job of this kind when he was 18,
    but he didn't like it.

## Colloquial English
### Talking about...work and family

### 1 LOOKING AT LANGUAGE
2 Apparently
3 as to
4 in a way
5 basically
6 really
7 I mean
8 anyway

### 2 READING
a 1 D  2 F  3 A  4 E  5 B

## 2A

### 1 LEXIS IN CONTEXT
2 fluid
3 part
4 random
5 guidance

### 2 PRONUNCIATION
a 3 S
  4 S
  5 D
  6 S
  7 D
  8 D
  9 S
  10 D

### 3 GRAMMAR
a 2 ✗ talking to each other / one another
  3 ✓
  4 ✗ we should help ourselves
  5 ✗ When a guest leaves their room
  6 ✗ by myself / on my own
  7 ✗ so far below her
  8 ✓
b 2 myself
  3 each other / one another
  4 One
  5 yourself
  6 They
  7 herself
  8 you / one
  2 it
  3 There
  4 it
  5 There
  6 there
  7 There
  8 there
  9 It
  10 it

### 4 VOCABULARY
a 2 take in
  3 tell
  4 pick up
  5 say
  6 get by
  7 talk
  8 brush up
b 2 requested
  3 error
  4 respond to
  5 tongue
c 2 the wrong end of the stick
  3 on the tip of my tongue
  4 at cross purposes
  5 get my head round

### 5 READING
a How the language is constructed, culture, and the way in which objects are classified

b 1 D  2 G  3 A  4 E  5 B  6 H

c 1 derogatory
  2 formulate
  3 concur
  4 versus
  5 determine
  6 addressed
  7 revealing

### 6 LISTENING
b 1 Do you find it easier to understand native or non-native speakers of English?
  2 How do you feel about having your English corrected?
  3 Do you have any funny or embarrassing stories related to misunderstanding someone?
  4 Is there anything you still find difficult about English?

c 1 M  2 B  3 M  4 W  5 W  6 B

## 2B

### 1 LEXIS IN CONTEXT
2 rushing
3 bubbling away
4 slapped
5 concocting
6 picture
7 leap

### 2 GRAMMAR
a 3 ✗ had forgotten to
  4 ✗ would catch / used to catch / caught
  5 ✗ broke down
  6 ✓
  7 ✗ lived / used to live
  8 ✗ I'd been hiding
  9 ✗ were still working
  10 ✓

b 2 shared / used to share
  3 went / used to go
  4 had cleaned
  5 would lie / used to lie
  6 fell
  7 had been singing
  8 stopped
  9 stood
  10 looked
  11 was staring
  12 told
  13 was watching
  14 had seen
  15 didn't sleep

### 3 VOCABULARY
a 2 fear
  3 improvement
  4 hatred
  5 death
  6 belief
  7 shame
b 2 wisdom
  3 childhood
  4 sadness
  5 celebration
  6 membership
  7 illness
  8 boredom

### 4 PRONUNCIATION
a Circle *celebration*, *imagination*, and *curiosity*

### 5 LISTENING
a Speaker 4

b A 3  B 1  C 4  D 2  E 5
  F 1  G 5  H 4  I 2  J 3

### 6 READING
a 9/10

b 1 T  2 F  3 F  4 F  5 T  6 F

## 3A

### 1 PRONUNCIATION
a 2 rendezvous
  3 faux pas
  4 déjà vu
  5 entrepreneur
  6 ballet
  7 bouquet
  8 fiancé(e)
  9 coup
  10 fait accompli

### 2 VOCABULARY
a 2 f
  3 e
  4 d
  5 g
  6 b
  7 a
  8 c
  9 h

b  2  message
3  way
4  anywhere
5  life
6  on
7  house
8  act

c  2  around
3  away
4  behind
5  out
6  down
7  on
8  through
9  by
10  back

## 3 LEXIS IN CONTEXT

2  rule out
3  win, over
4  foot, bill
5  short, sweet
6  miss out
7  follow, through
8  make up, mind

## 4 GRAMMAR

2  Can you get Paul to look at my computer?
3  I'll never get used to getting up at 5.30 in the morning.
4  The afternoon shadows got longer as the sun went down.
5  We're getting our kitchen repainted next month.
6  I can't get the kids to eat their dinner.
7  I hope I don't get sent to Manchester – I want to stay in London.
8  Public transport in my town is getting better.
9  My boss got fired for stealing money.
10  Could you possibly get Mike to pick me up?

## 5 LISTENING

a  Speakers 2, 4 and 5 had successful dates. Speakers 1 and 3 had unsuccessful dates.

b  1 F  2 F  3 T  4 F  5 F  6 T
7 T  8 T  9 F  10 F

## 6 READING

a  Number 5 caused the most damage.

b  1 H  2 C  3 D  4 E  5 F  6 B

## 1 VOCABULARY

a  Across:  3  spear
5  cannon
6  bow
8  shield
9  bullet

Down:  2  machine gun
3  sword
4  arrow
7  missile

b  2  casualties
3  declared
4  shelled
5  ceasefire
6  surrender
7  defeated
8  snipers
9  looted
10  commander

## 2 PRONUNCIATION

a  2  civil
3  refugee
4  survivor
5  commander
6  ceasefire
7  victory
8  release
9  capture
10  retreat
11  execute
12  surrender

c  1  shield
2  bullet
3  weapon
4  declare

## 3 GRAMMAR

a  2  words
3  concerned
4  matter
5  whole
6  way
7  say
8  case
9  hand
10  least

b  2  Basically
3  I mean
4  Besides
5  Obviously
6  all in all
7  After all
8  As I was saying
9  To sum up
10  otherwise

## 4 LISTENING

a  1 b  2 d  3 a  4 e  5 c

b  1 E  2 C  3 G  4 A  5 D

## 5 READING

a  1 b  2 d  3 a  4 e  5 c

b  2  D
3  A
4  E
5  C
6  A
7  D
8  C
9  B
10  E

c  1  ill fate
2  charged
3  moulding
4  slaughtered
5  mercilessly
6  morale
7  pass
8  pivotal

Talking about...history

## 1 LOOKING AT LANGUAGE

2  awful
3  deadly
4  rights
5  picture
6  classic
7  civil
8  ordinary

## 2 READING

a  1  T
2  F
3  F
4  T
5  F
6  T
7  T
8  F

**4A**

## 1 VOCABULARY

a  2  tapping
3  bang
4  slurp
5  rattling
6  hissed
7  roared
8  sniffing
9  crunched
10  ticking
11  screeching
12  slammed

b  2  sighed
3  sobbed
4  groaned
5  screamed
6  stammered
7  whispered
8  giggled
9  mumbled

## 2 PRONUNCIATION

a  2  stretch
3  exclaimed
4  sixth
5  shelves
6  bridegroom
7  spread
8  punched

## 3 LEXIS IN CONTEXT

2 continually
3 with ease
4 Strangely
5 in, proximity
6 seemingly
7 incessantly

## 4 GRAMMAR

a 2 could / might / may be waiting
3 should have been
4 might / may not like
5 can't be studying
6 might / may not have taken
7 can't have
8 must have forgotten

b 2 're bound to win the match
3 'll definitely enjoy the film
4 's not likely to rain tonight
5 're unlikely to agree to our proposal
6 will probably take early retirement
7 are sure to complain about it
8 definitely won't give us a pay rise

## 5 LISTENING

a She is deaf.

b 1 20
2 60
3 soundtracks
4 hearing / deafness
5 feeling
6 shoes

## 6 READING

a In a hospital.

b 1 T
2 T
3 F
4 F
5 F
6 T
7 T

c 1 background, ambient
2 jingle
3 din

## 1 VOCABULARY

2 thought-provoking
3 entertaining
4 implausible
5 intriguing
6 depressing
7 gripping
8 heavy-going
9 moving
10 fast-moving

## 2 PRONUNCIATION

a 2 walk
3 implausible
4 resourceful
5 rewarding
6 daughter
7 thought-provoking
8 workforce

c 1 I bought his autobiography from the store.
2 The crowd roared when the captain scored.
3 Your lawyer talks more when he's in court.
4 He was caught by enemy forces in the war.
5 That story is awfully boring.

## 3 GRAMMAR

a 2 Not until
3 Rarely
4 No sooner
5 Only
6 Scarcely
7 Not only
8 Never

b 2 did he betray my trust, but he also wrecked my car.
3 had the sun gone down when / before the temperature fell dramatically.
4 have I seen such a wonderful sight.
5 had the teacher turned her back than the children started whispering.
6 had the woman sat down when / before her baby started crying.
7 do you find two people so alike.
8 a replacement teacher has been found will classes recommence.

## 4 LEXIS IN CONTEXT

2 identical
3 implored
4 mute
5 immobile
6 done with
7 merely
8 accurate
9 backpacks
10 conceivable

## 5 LISTENING

a 1 successful
2 not successful

b 1 F  2 T  3 T  4 F  5 T  6 F

## 6 READING

a The author advises not to try to finish a book if you're really not enjoying it.

b 1 c  2 b  3 a  4 c  5 c

c 1 grab you
2 take a shine to
3 put you off
4 for pity's sake
5 to its bitter end
6 out of hand

## 1 LEXIS IN CONTEXT

2 with
3 of
4 of
5 with
6 on

## 2 GRAMMAR

a 2 appears
3 expected
4 According
5 may
6 seem
7 agreed
8 Apparently

b 2 It appears / It would appear that
3 It has been announced / It was announced that
4 is thought to have
5 may have been
6 It seems / It would seem that
7 might have entered
8 It is hoped that

## 3 VOCABULARY

a 2 saved
3 takes
4 spare
5 make
6 gave
7 having
8 ran

b 2 From, to
3 at
4 on
5 In
6 by
7 before
8 at

c 2 short
3 spare
4 hands
5 being
6 matter
7 up
8 whole

## 4 PRONUNCIATION

a 2 My cousin‿Nick‿is never‿on time.
3 I find‿doing housework takes‿up‿a lot‿of time.
4 We walked‿to town‿as we had plenty‿of time.
5 We seem to have run‿out‿of time.
6 It's‿a question‿of time before the sports‿centre opens.

c 1 I always freak out if the bus arrives late.
2 He's a bit impatient at times.
3 We stood in the queue for over an hour.
4 You'll have to wait a moment until I'm ready.
5 The performance starts at 8 o'clock.
6 She's awfully insecure about their relationship.

81

## 5 LISTENING

a The good news is that it's possible to slow time down.

b 1 senses
  2 longer
  3 new
  4 slowly
  5 familiar
  6 quickly
  7 learning
  8 new places
  9 new people
  10 spontaneous

## 6 READING

a The writer thinks that being late is rude.

b 1 c  2 b  3 c  4 d  5 a

c 1 a  2 c  3 b  4 b

d 1 superiority
  2 behaviour
  3 lateness
  4 belief
  5 absence

## 1 LEXIS IN CONTEXT

  2 collide
  3 shoulders
  4 littered with
  5 juggle
  6 high-flying

## 2 GRAMMAR

a 2 I'd rather you came round
  3 I wish we hadn't bought
  4 If only we lived
  5 I'd rather she didn't know.
  6 If only I'd worked
  7 It's time you had
  8 I wish we were

b 2 If only we didn't owe
  3 It's time Sally made up
  4 Would you rather we took
  5 If only we hadn't spent
  6 it time you apologized
  7 I wish I were able to see
  8 We'd rather you didn't

## 3 VOCABULARY

a 2 stock market
  3 exchange rate
  4 in debt
  5 standard, living
  6 inflation
  7 consumer society
  8 Interest rates
  9 grant
  10 donation

b 2 penniless, P
  3 loaded, R
  4 hard up, P
  5 wealthy, R
  6 well-off, R
  7 broke, P

c 2 in the red
  3 doesn't grow on trees
  4 cost an arm and a leg
  5 we tighten our belts
  6 daylight robbery
  7 tight-fisted
  8 make ends meet

## 4 PRONUNCIATION

a 2 US
  3 UK
  4 US
  5 UK
  6 UK
  7 US
  8 UK
  9 UK
  10 US

## 5 LISTENING

a 1 Philip
  2 Wendy
  3 Emily
  4 Mary
  5 Jonathan

b 1 18°C
  2 a packed lunch
  3 in a jar
  4 in cash
  5 when you're hungry / on an empty stomach

## 6 READING

a C

b 1 C  2 A  3 F  4 B  5 E

### Colloquial English

## Talking about...stress and relaxation

## 1 LOOKING AT LANGUAGE

  2 age group
  3 blood pressure
  4 support network
  5 text messages
  6 breathing exercises
  7 life saver
  8 college students

## 2 READING

a 1 b  2 b  3 a  4 c  5 b

# OXFORD
## UNIVERSITY PRESS

Great Clarendon Street, Oxford, OX2 6DP,
United Kingdom

Oxford University Press is a department of the
University of Oxford. It furthers the University's
objective of excellence in research, scholarship,
and education by publishing worldwide. Oxford
is a registered trade mark of Oxford University
Press in the UK and in certain other countries

ACKNOWLEDGEMENTS

*The authors would like to thank all the teachers and students round the
world whose feedback has helped us to shape* English File.

*The authors would also like to thank*: all those at Oxford University
Press (both in Oxford and around the world) and the design team
who have contributed their skills and ideas to producing this
course.

A very special thanks from Clive to Maria Angeles, Lucia, and
Eric, and from Christina to Cristina, for all their support and
encouragement. Christina would also like to thank her children
Joaquin, Marco, and Krysia for their constant inspiration.

*The publisher and authors would also like to thank the following for their
invaluable feedback on the materials*: Adam Szynal, Beatriz Martin
Garcia, Brian Brennan, Danny Fernandez, Elif Barbaros, Federico
Alonso, Freia Layfield, Isidrio Almendarez, Jane Hudson, Joanna
Sosnowska, John Bolton, Juliana Stucker, Katarzyna Bielawska,
Lesley Pouland, Magda Miszczak-Berbeć, Magda Muszyńska,
Morgan Ormond Pavlina Zoss, Philip Drury, Rachael Smith,
Robert Anderson, Sandy Millin, Sinead O'Dea, Tim Weatherhead,
Wayne Rimmer.

*The Publisher and Authors are very grateful to the following who have
provided information, personal stories, and/or photographs*: Ghislaine
Kenyon, Lisa Imlach (and Skyscanner), Joanna Borysiak, Polly
Akhurst (and 'Talk to me London'), Daniel Hahn (and Free Word,
who published his blog), Beverly Johnson, Matt Cutts, David
and Emma Illsley, Kamila Shamsie, Eliza Carthy, Professor Mary
Beard, Jordan Friedman, Quentin Blake, George McGavin.

STUDENT'S BOOK ACKNOWLEDGEMENTS

*The authors and publisher are grateful to those who have given permission
to reproduce the following extracts and adaptations of copyright material*:
p.7 Adapted extracts from the Myers Briggs Test included in the
BBC programme "What's your personality type?". Reproduced
courtesy of Mentorn Media; p.8 Extract from "What I'm really
thinking: the checkout girl", www.theguardian.com, 1 February
2014. Copyright Guardian News & Media Ltd 2014. Reproduced
by permission; pp.8–9 Extract from "What I'm really thinking:
the university lecturer", www.theguardian.com, 21 December
2012. Copyright Guardian News & Media Ltd 2012. Reproduced
by permission; p.9 Extract from "What I'm really thinking:
the 999 operator", www.theguardian.com, 24 August 2013.

Copyright Guardian News & Media Ltd 2013. Reproduced by
permission; p.10 Adapted extract from "The Sunday Times 100
Best Companies", www.thesundaytimes.co.uk, 2014. Reproduced
by permission of News Syndication; p.15 Adapted extract from
"Spell It Out: The Singular Story of English Spelling by David
Crystal" by Daisy Goodwin, www.thesundaytimes.co.uk, 19
August 2012. Reproduced by permission of News Syndication;
pp.18–19 Extract from *Boy: Tales of Childhood* by Roald Dahl,
published by Penguin Books Ltd (2008) and Jonathan Cape Ltd
(2012). © 1984 by Roald Dahl. Reproduced by permission of David
Higham and Farrar Straus and Giroux. All rights reserved; p.23
Adapted extract from "Learning a second language in adulthood
can slow brain ageing" by Lucy Kinder, www.telegraph.co.uk,
2 June 2014. © Telegraph Media Group Limited. Reproduced by
permission; p.24–25 Extracts from *Take Care of Yourself* by Sophie
Calle, (Actes Sud, 2007). © ADAGP, Paris 2015. Reproduced
by permission; p.24–25 Adapted extract from "Blind date",
*The Guardian*, 19 December 2009. Copyright Guardian News
& Media Ltd 2009. Reproduced by permission; p.26 Adapted
extract from "The Inside Out Dating Guide 2 – 10 tips for a
first date" by Sarah Abell, www.telegraph.co.uk, 23 July 2010.
© Telegraph Media Group Limited. Reproduced by permission;
p.35 Adapted extract from "Experience: I have a phobia of
sound" by Vicky Rhodes, www.theguardian.com, 22 February
2014. Copyright Guardian News & Media Ltd 2014. Reproduced
by permission; p.36 Extracts from www.talktome.global.
Reproduced by permission; p.37 Adapted extracts from the
comments under "Yes, London is an unfriendly city – and long
may it stay that way" by Stuart Heritage, www.theguardian.com,
6 April 2014. Copyright Guardian News & Media Ltd 2014.
Reproduced by permission; p.38 Adapted extracts from "Time
to Rename the Spoiler: Knowing How Something Ends May
Actually Make It More Enjoyable" by Maria Konnikova, http://
bigthink.com, 8 September 2011. Reproduced by permission
of The Big Think Inc.; p.38 Adapted extract from "Do Not
Read This Post: The 10 Biggest Book Spoilers, Ever" by Lauren
Passell, barnesandnoble.com, 22 August 2013. Reproduced by
permission of barnesandnoble.com LLC; p.40 Adapted extracts
from "Translation diary: 1 – An Introduction" (28 October 2013)
and "Translation diary: 7 – Try, try again" (10 December 2013)
by Daniel Hahn, www.freewordcentre.com. Copyright © Daniel
Hahn 2013. Reproduced by permission; p.43 Adapted extract
from "Experience: I've been to the quietest place on Earth" by
George Michelson Foy, www.theguardian.com, 18 May 2012.
Copyright Guardian News & Media Ltd 2012. Reproduced by
permission; p.45 "The Chocolate Meditation" by Dr. Danny
Penman and Professor Mark Williams from http://franticworld.
com/. © 2015 Danny Penman. Reproduced by permission;
p.45 Adapted extract from "Working With Mindfulness:
Overcoming the Drive to Multitask" by Jacqueline Carter,
www.huffingtonpost.com, 26 February 2014. Reproduced by
permission of Jacqueline Carter.

*Illustrations by*: Agnes Bicocchi pp.44, 45; Lo Cole: pp.8, 9, 48;
Atsushi Hara pp.140, 143, 144, 147, 149; Olivier Latyk p.16; Tim
Marrs pp.26/7; The Project Twins pp.7, 160.

*The Publishers would like to thank the following for their kind permission
to reproduce photographs and other copyright material*: Polly Akhurst
p.36 (Talk to me London); Alamy Images p.12 (Martin & Eliza
Carthy/Lebrecht Music and Arts Photo Library), 13 (Eliza Carthy/
WENN Ltd), 14 (letterpress alphabet/Tetra Images), 21 (Victorian
governess with baby/The Keasbury-Gordon Photograph
Archive), 24 (modern art gallery/Forray Didier/Sagaphoto.
com), 28 (*The Great Escape*/AF archive), 30 (Sophie Marceau/AF
archive), 32 (Fresco Detail, Young Girl Reading, 1st Century BC.
Artist: Unknown/The Print Collector), 43 (anechoic chamber/
ZUMA Press, Inc), 114 (children paying hopscotch, 1970s/
Heritage Image Partnership Ltd), 163 (Indian spear/Valentyna
Chukhlyebova), 164 (tap/Witold Krasowski); Barcroft Media
p.36 (Boris Johnson), 106 (Boris Johnson); Joanna Borysiak
p.17 (beach); Jay Brooks p.106 (Stef and Graham wedding day);
Sophie Calle p.24/5: 'Prenez Soin de Vous ('Take care of yourself'),
2007, © ADAGP, Paris and DACS, London 2015; Diarmuid Carter
p.17 (2); CartoonStock Ltd p.161 (Ikea Interview/Canary Pete);
Companhia das Letras p.40 ('Flores Azuis' by Carola Saavedra/
Kiko Farkas/Máquina Estúdio e Thiago Lacaz/Máquina Estúdio);
Corbis pp.4 (Frida Kahlo/Bettmann), 21 (psychologist Jean Piaget/
Farrell Grehan), 38 (book festival/Andrew Fox), 46 (frustrated
businessman in car/Nick Dolding/cultura); Andrew Crowley
pp.49 (Telegraph Media Group Limited 2009/Jemima Lewis);
Salvador Dali p.6 'Suburbs of a Paranoic Critical Town, Afternoon
on the Outskirts of European History', 1936. Bridgeman Images
© Salvador Dali, Funacio Gala-Salvador Dali, DACS, 2015; Andrea
Dansie p.17 (4); Getty Images pp.21 (boy looking in mirror/
Constance Bannister Corp), 21 (children playing on swings/
David Leahy), 25 (French artists/Alberto Pizzoli), 30 (Adrian
Hodges/Frederick M. Brown), 40 (watercolour background/
Ekely), 46 (clocks/Garry Gay), 49 (Jojo Moyes/J. Quinton),
50 (Mohammad Yunus, Chairman of Grameen Bank/Thomas
Samson), 52 (subway/Don Emmert/AFP), 114 (boy with tablet
computer/Stephen Simpson); Guardian News & Media Ltd
p.35 (Vicky Rhodes/Fabio De Paola © Guardian News & Media Ltd
2014); Daniel Hahn p.40; Mairi Hamilton p.17 (1); David Higham
p.18 (Agents/Jonathan Cape Ltd &Penguin Books/inside Roald
Dahl 'Boy – Tales of Childhood'); Stephanie Hodges pp.26 (blind
date), 105 (blind date); Lisa Imlach/Skyscanner p.11; iStockphoto

pp.37 (portrait blonde woman/Plougmann), 47 (time spiral/
mipan); Beverly Johnson p.41; Proba Kadru p.17 (probakadru.
blogspot.co.uk/Joanna Borysiak/Listening); Frida Kahlo p.4:
Banco de Mexico Diego Riverera Frida Kahlo Museums Trust,
'My Family', 1949–1950, © 2015 Banco de Mexico Diego Rivera
Frida Kahlo Museums Trust.D.D; Kobal Collection pp.19 (*Charlie
and the Chocolate Factory*/Warner Bros.), 28 (*Gladiator*/Dreamwork
Universal), 30/31 (*Braveheart*/Icon/Ladd Co/Paramount),
31 (*Spartacus*/Bryna/Universal), 31 (*Braveheart* poster/Icon/Ladd
Co/Paramount), 32 (*Gladiator* 2000/Dreamworks Universal/Jaap
Buitendijk); Jeremy Lambert p.17 (3); Las Vegas Review Journal
p.101 (Ron Kantowski/Bob Ketelle); The Orion Publishing Group
p.116 (Cover of *GONE GIRL* by Gillian Flynn); Oxford University
Press Video Stills pp.12, 13, 17, 23, 32 (Mary Beard), 33, 43,
50 (Surita Gupta); Penguin Random House LLC p.19 ('*Charlie and
the Chocolate Factory*' by Roald Dahl/illustrated by Quentin Blake
Press Association Images p.36 (animatronic polar bear/David
Parry/PA Wire); Profile Books/*Spell It Out by David Crystal* p.15; The
Random House Group p.18 (*Boy by Roald Dahl*/Boy Cover Artwork
© *Quentin Blake*/Used by arrangement with The Random House
Group Limited); Rex Features pp.29 (*12 Years a Slave*/FoxSearch/
Everett), 36 (Alain Robert climbing the Lloyds building),
36 (Chevrolet Orlando made from Play-Doh/Chevrolet); Lily
Sadeghi-Nejad p.17 (5); Shutterstock pp.35 (sound waves/Mikha
Bakunovich), 37 (people icons/Macrovector), 37 (smiling young
man/Terry Schmidbauer), 38 (surprise/angellodeco), 38 (tablet
computer/rvlsoft), 52 (hammock/Filip Fuxa), 163 (wooden arrow
Andrey Burmakin), 163 (bow and arrows/Christian Weber),
163 (bullet/Ziggylives), 163 (cannon/artkamalov), 163 (ancient
Greek helmet/Vartanov Anatoly), 163 (machine gun/Militarist),
163 (military missile/Orion-v), 163 (ancient bronze shield/Tatian
Popova), 163 (sword/oksana2010), 164 (water droplets/Claudio
Divizia), 164 (water splash/Serg64), 165 (alarm clocks/Chones);
Skyscanner/Mary Porter pp.10, 112; Paul de Villiers p.17 (6);
World Womens Bank/Julie Slama p.51.

*Commissioned Photography by*: Dean Ryan pp.15 (book), 18 (book),
19 (book), 39, 116.

WORKBOOK ACKNOWLEDGEMENTS

*The authors and publisher are grateful to those who have given permission
to reproduce the following extracts and adaptations of copyright material*:
p.6 Extract from "Ang Lee: My family values" by Elaine Lipworth
www.theguardian.com, 26 April 2013. Copyright Guardian New
and Media Ltd 2013. Reproduced by permission. p.9 Adapted
extract from "'Best job in the world' took its toll on tired Briton"
by Bonnie Malkin, *The Telegraph*, 2 January 2010. © Telegraph
Media Group Limited 2010. Reproduced by permission. p.13
Adapted extract from "Does Learning A New Language Give You
A New Personality?" by Cody Delistraty, http://thoughtcatalog.
com, 18 November 2013. © 2015 The Thought & Expression
Co. All rights reserved. Reproduced by permission. p.16 Extract
from "Scientists pinpoint age when childhood memories
fade" by Richard Gray, www.telegraph.co.uk, 10 January
2014. © Telegraph Media Group Limited 2014. Reproduced by
permission. p.19 Adapted extract from "Revenge Is Sweet" by
Lindsay Clydesdale, *Daily Record*, 25 October 2006. Reproduced
by permission of Mirrorpix. p.29 Adapted extract from "How
not to read" by Lionel Shriver, www.theguardian.com, 8
February 2014. Copyright Guardian News and Media Ltd 2014.
Reproduced by permission. p.32 Adapted extract from "Is being
late fashionable or rude?" by Robert Rowland Smith, *The Sunday
Times*, 4 September 2011. Reproduced by permission of News
UK & Ireland Limited. p.35 Extract from "Does money make you
happy?" by Stephen Evans, www.bbc.co.uk, 6 April 2010. © BBC
News Website. Reproduced by permission.

*Sources*: www.pipedown.info

*Illustrations by*: Atsushi Hara c/o Dutch Uncle Agency pp.4, 5, 12,
33, Anna Hymas c/o New Division Ltd p.14, Olivier Latyk c/o
Good Illustration Agency pp.19, Roger Penwill pp.8, 11, 29, Tim
Marrs p.26

*The publisher would like to thank the following for their kind permission
to reproduce photographs*: Alamy Images pp.20 (spear/Valentyna
Chukhlyebova), 23 (Terry Deary/Mark Waugh), 27 (reading/
Images of Birmingham Premium), 28 (The Lord of the Rings/
Ben Molyneux), 28 (The Hunger Games/Cristina Fumi), 35 (bank
card/Paul Fleet), 35 (scratch card/David Lee); Corbis pp.25 (Evely
Glennie/Mike Blake/Reuters), 29 (Lionel Shriver/Jenny Lewis);
Getty Images pp.5 (children/Cultura/Judith Wagner Fotografie),
5 (girl playing/Jodie Griggs), 9 (Ben Southall/Torsten Blackwood/
AFP), 15 (students/Steve Debenport), 31 (siblings/hero Images),
32 (waiting/Stephen Simpson), 34 (coins/JGI/Jamie Grill); Oxford
University Press p.13; Rex Features pp.6 (Ang Lee/), 21 (The Last
Emperor 1987/Columbia/Everett), 21 (Cate Blanchett/Moviestore
25 (Evelyn Glennie/Fabio De Paola), 28 (The Return of the King
2003/New Line/Everett), 28 (The Hunger Games:Mockingjay Part
1); Shutterstock pp.10 (take your daughter to work day/Stacey
Newman), 16 (birthday party/Creativa Images), 20 (arrow/Andre
Burmakin), 20 (bow and arrows/Christian Weber), 20 (bullet/
Ziggylives), 20 (Greek helmet/Vartanov
Anatoly), 20 (rifle/Militarist), 20 (missile/Orion-v), 20 (Bronze
shield/Tatiana Popova), 20 (sword/oksana2010), 23 (Ancient
Egyptian artwork/ksana-gribakina), 35 (banknotes/ppart),
35 (lotto ticket/alexmillos), 36 (woman and dog/Zurijeta).